To Buzz with love from
Mom and Dad
July 18, 197

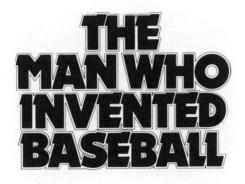

ALSO BY HAROLD PETERSON
The Last of the Mountain Men

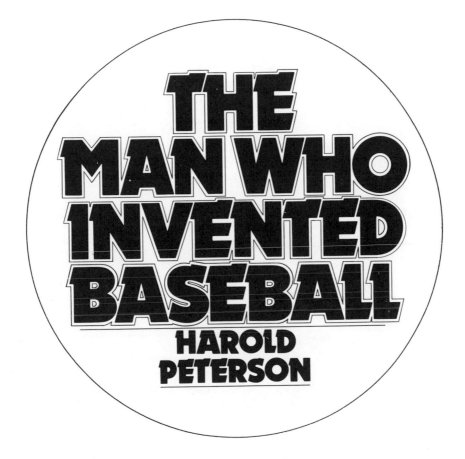

THE MAN WHO INVENTED BASEBALL

HAROLD PETERSON

Charles Scribner's Sons   New York

Printed in the United States of America
Library of Congress Catalog Card Number 72-1183
SBN 684-13185-4

To a certain little
blonde German immigrant girl,
in pigtails,
whose wide grin
somehow survived bombs,
famine, and transplantation
to a hostile New York.

ACKNOWLEDGMENTS

My first thanks must go to those worthy descendants of Alexander Cartwright, Bill Cartwright (and his wife Anne) and Mary Cartwright Check Taylor—not only for permission to use Alick's diary of the journey across the plains and help in establishing other facts of Alexander's life, but also for their friendly letters. Nor can I forget the help offered by the Nantucket Cartwrights, by Jonathan Van Wie and Mrs. Kenneth Van Wie, and by Robert Van Dyke of Honolulu.

Robert Cantwell, that thoroughgoing gentleman, constantly impressed me with his generous aid and kindly inquiries as to my progress. Very important, too, was the encouragement offered by those excellent editors, Andrew Crichton and Bob Creamer—most particularly by Andy. And I do appreciate permission from André Laguerre and *Sports Illustrated* to use excerpts from my SI article on Cartwright. A word of greeting to Jack Tibby, too.

Thanks, also, for permission from Professor Ted Hinckley of San Jose State College and from the *Indiana Magazine of History* to quote from the Joseph Waring Berrien diary, supplementing and supporting Cartwright's journal. I am happy to acknowledge other brief quotes from the pioneer diaries of William Kelly, William Johnston, Peter Decker, and Jacob Stillman.

I am much indebted, as anyone interested in baseball must be, to the heretofore sadly little-known discovery of Stone Age "base ball" by the late Professor Corrado Gini of Rome and to the recognition by Per Maigaard of its close congruence to ancient Scandinavian longball. The Italian demographic magazine *Genus* must be respected for understanding the value of their discovery and giving it what exposure it did get. I suppose I have read most of the scores of early-nineteenth-century American and British books on games and children's diversions, the most significant of which are credited in the body of the text. I have sampled the most important German and French equivalents, with the help of the former Miss Karin Dahncke and others.

Cooperative people at the New York Historical Society, the New York Genealogical Society, and in the specialized reference rooms of the New York Public Library have aided me greatly. I also acknowledge assistance from the Nantucket Historical Association and Edouard Stackpole, curator there and at Mystic Seaport; the Hawaii Archives; the Honolulu public library; the Firefighting Museum in New York; the Nantucket Atheneum; the late Lee Allen and the staff of the Baseball Hall of Fame at Cooperstown; Kansas University; and a number of retired baseball players, whose names are mentioned.

Paul Henderson of Bridgeport, Nebraska, and his wife, Helen, outstanding practical historians of the Oregon and California Trails, were generous and friendly.

A complete bibliography of the old sources exhumed and consulted would be tediously long, running to hundreds of volumes. I hope the mention of many in the text will satisfy most people and serve to express my gratitude for free interchange of the incredible wealth of historical detail which is our inheritance if we will only appreciate it and reclaim it from undeserved obscurity.

HAROLD PETERSON

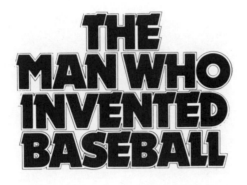

THE MAN WHO INVENTED BASEBALL

ON A QUIET, SUNNY MORNING IN THE SPRING OF 1845, SIX YEARS AFTER Abner Doubleday did not invent baseball in Elihu Phinney's Cooperstown cow pasture (or anywhere else), a black-whiskered twenty-five-year-old volunteer fireman named Alexander Joy Cartwright, Jr., walked off the pleasantly shaded Eastern Post Road, an old maple- and oak-lined New England-bound country lane on Manhattan Island, into a dewy meadow.

The meadow, which was situated under the rocky schisted prominence of Murray Hill called the Inclenberg, lay next to a pastoral little lake, Sunfish Pond. Stagecoaches had but recently stopped here to water their horses on the way to the little villages of Yorkville and Harlem and, eventually, to Bostontown. Through the meadow ran a large, pretty brook, much inhabited by trout and fishermen. Named Old Wreck Kill for a pioneer Dutch ship sunk off its mouth, the brook rose in a large crystal spring among the crags and hills of the interior, rushed in little waterfalls through the boulders and fields and vernal green of mid-Manhattan, and tumbled into turbulent Kipps Bay on the glistening East River.

The steamcars of the Harlaem Rail Road had lately begun running through a cut in the proposed Fourth Avenue on their snorting way to a terminus at City Hall Park, thus bounding the meadow on the west, but the place remained the pleasantest spot in all of the Parade Ground, a large public park once planned to extend from 23rd Street to 34th Street and as far west as Seventh Avenue. The boys and young men of New York were fond of taking their recreation there, where they could watch square-sailed barques and brigantines drift past the community farms on Long Island or look down-island and see the spires of their beautiful city's churches towering above Colonial and Federal houses built in old pegged wood frame or new red brick.

Fresh salt-air breezes laved the playing field every warm afternoon, and land breezes rising from the barley and wheat fields of the farm country to the north warmed it every morning. Deer and raccoons might still venture to the brook in twilight. Blackberries could still be picked along the Middle Road (which led to the hamlet of Bloomingdale at future 86th Street) and eaten with ice cream or cakes purchased at a bright-yellow little farmhouse on Fifth Avenue.

This one cool, warming morning burly Alexander Cartwright joined a group of young men at their usual play, a lighthearted game of ball remembered from their childhood—a game, like most children's games, whose antecedents were mysterious and whose rules were subject to constant change and much laughing dispute. He had often done so before. But this particular day he swung off the brightly lacquered, elaborately decorated omnibus coach which clopped up the Post Road with a carefully drafted diagram in his hand. Stilling the friendly badinage that greeted his arrival (for he was a favorite among his friends, the young businessmen of the city), he beckoned his fellows to gather around. Soberly, he announced that he had a Plan.

Good-natured hoots and cries of derision met this declaration. It was amid considerable cheerful raillery that Cartwright stationed his friends at positions around a perfect ninety-foot square and placed the batter at the fourth "home" base instead of in a special batter's box several feet toward the first base. Even Cartwright smiled at the jibes as he solemnly dictated that there be only three men in the outfield, removed two roving short fielders, put one of them at an entirely new position he called Short Stop, and abolished one of the two catchers behind the batter. But "Alick" was so popular and so persistent that they decided to humor him.

Whoops of delight replaced teasing complaint after a few ground balls had been hit to the basemen, so precisely located by Cartwright that their positions have remained almost exactly the same ever since. Throwing to bases to make outs—as he prescribed— instead of throwing wildly at dodging runners tightened and rationalized the game remarkably; it immediately ceased to be a mere children's amusement. Another sophistication was Alick's new rule of "three hands out, all out." Now, when only three men (instead of the whole team) need be retired to end an inning, scoring runs became difficult enough to require some skill and care.

Moreover, the rapid succession of innings rescued Cartwright's game of Base Ball from the dawdling pace of cricket. Unlike cricket, it encouraged and rewarded good fielding by offering an imminent prospect of getting in out of the sun and getting a chance to hit. Another revolutionary inspiration, the provision of foul lines, accomplished the same laudable purposes by concentrating most of the action within a ninety-degree quadrant of the field.

(The new rules' happy dissociation of the American game from any resemblance to cricket had great partisan appeal to Americans. The burning of the White House thirty-one years before was very fresh in Yankee minds, and fresher yet was the presently threatened war over lands south of 54° 40′ in the Oregon Territory. In New York particularly, Loco Foco Democratic political aspirants daily fanned anti-British hatreds in the new Irish immigrants' breasts.)

Cartwright also prescribed flat bases instead of the casually arranged posts or random rocks, found on the site of the game, which had served in the past. There should be only nine men on a side, instead of the irregular mob usually scattered about. They would bat in a regular order, prescribed before the game.

He thought of some very modern small refinements too. A "balk" by the pitcher allowed a runner to advance. A run scored before a third force-out did not count. Later he originated the idea of the nine-inning game. (Before that innovation, matches ended when one side had scored twenty-one runs or "aces.") But this notion was not immediately accepted.

The game that Cartwright and his friends tried out beneath Murray Hill was phenomenally successful from the start. The standardized shape and dimensions of the playing field meant that teams could meet on equal terms wherever they played, as did the standardized rules. But the best evidence of Alexander's inventive intuition was his setting the distance between bases at ninety feet. He was exactly right, uncannily so. Five feet less would have given base runners an enormous advantage. Five feet more would have given infielders too much time to scoop up a ground ball and get it to the first baseman. But at ninety feet, plays at first base are decided by a step.

Cartwright's innovations meant the beginning of fast team play, the development of the art of the shortstop (who was needed because most balls are hit between second and third bases) and the first baseman (who was the least important baseman in the old games). It necessitated the accurate umpiring of games, suddenly essential because of the closeness of plays. The effect of newly vital umpiring was to bring order to all aspects of the game.

Relatively uncredited by the most diligent archivists of the world's most documented sport, almost unknown to fans who have computer memories for statistics, long vanished and forgotten, Alexander Cartwright is the father of modern baseball.

And baseball, what of that? Of what importance is that?

Baseball is a social phenomenon. It was a social phenomenon in the nineteenth century, when it was the central fact of most American men's leisure, almost the only way they knew how to play. It was a social phenomenon in the early twentieth century, when it became an obsession, the very originator and prototype of a radical change in attitudes: the sea change of Americans from vigorous, un-self-conscious amateur jack-of-all-trades participants into the sedentary, self-conscious, critical spectators they are now. Exactly one full century after Cartwright "invented" it, it was certainly a social phenomenon when soldiers in the biggest and bloodiest war in history said in real, recorded words that they were fighting for Mom's apple pie and for—yes—baseball.

If you don't understand where baseball came from and why it captured Americans so completely, you don't quite understand the United States. (Since nobody but an American understands baseball, a corollary—one supposes—is that only Americans fully understand the United States. Which is correct.)

Not that baseball is like tobacco or the turkey, a native weed or fauna sprung direct from our peculiar soil. The myth that Abner Doubleday invented baseball is one of the most amusingly fraudulent pieces of manufactured history extant. Yet what it lacks in authenticity it amply makes up in obstinate durability, like many myths. Ask who invented baseball at any bar in Brooklyn, Hoboken, St. Louis, or Sacramento. Your average incipient inebriate, who may have trouble remembering the name of the second President, his Senator or his wife's sister, will instantly ejaculate, "Abner Doubleday." Ask any standard, informed, educated quasi-intellectual. Whether he last suffered baseball to cross his mind sometime before the Braves left Boston or whether he just this morning unfavorably compared the style of the 1972 Mets with the 1962 Originals, chances are he will say, "Abner Doubleday, wasn't it?" Better yet, ask any average major leaguer. If he talks at all, he will probably mention Doubleday. Some women have even heard the name. Doubleday, that is.

Apart from the fact that he never had anything to do with baseball, General Doubleday did make a nice figurehead. Handsome, distinguished, he was the holder of a heroic Civil War record that dated from Fort Sumter, where he was credited with firing the first Union shot. At the close of the first day at Gettysburg, he commanded the entire Union Army. He was also an excellent writer and a commanding public speaker. Unfortunately, in all his extensive writings and speeches there is not a solitary reference to baseball. In fact, there is no evidence that he ever played or even saw the game.

Albert Goodwill Spalding, the superb pioneer professional player for the Chicago White Sox and Rockford Forest Citys, founder of the sporting-goods firm, deserves the blame for Doubleday's odd immortalization. Henry Chadwick, the first sportswriter to cover baseball (he saw his first game in 1848), had written numerous, now forgotten, historical sketches, the last in 1903, in which he traced the game's origins to the old English game of rounders. Somewhat unfortunately, the periodical in which these sketches appeared was Spalding's *Baseball Guide*. Spalding so hated the idea that any part of the sport might have started outside the United States that he virtually drafted as inventor the poor general, who would have much preferred to be remembered for his military exploits but who, having died in 1893, was helpless to defend himself.

The bit of fiction that replaced Cartwright with Doubleday was a report made by the Mills Commission, formed by Organized Baseball in 1904 "to determine the origins of the great American pastime." Its chairman was starchy, long-faced old Abraham G. Mills, who had been third president of the National League and was a close friend of Spalding. The mission of the Mills Commission was to purify baseball of any taint of British influence. It was made up of seven men. Among them were Mills himself and two old-time players who had also become involved with the manufacture of baseball equipment, Al Reach and George Wright.

Wright was the most interesting member of the commission, the man who could easily have set the record straight. George had played ball in New York in the 1860's, most notably against the old New York Knickerbockers, a fact whose importance and irony will become apparent later. Unquestionably he was familiar with the older men who had played with Cartwright. But Wright—the only qualified member of the commission—never attended a single meeting.

Whatever historical material the Mills Commission accumulated was conveniently destroyed in a fire that burned the office of the American Sports Publicity Company. Mills issued the report alone in 1907. He was the only person to write it. The report, not surprisingly, concluded that baseball was a purely American sport, not derived from rounders. What was surprising—confabulating, in fact—was the astounding information that the method of playing baseball had been devised by Major General Doubleday at Cooperstown in upstate New York in 1839.

The entire document was a classic example, as it will soon become abundantly clear, of instant improvised history. It depended almost entirely on the uncorroborated ramblings of octogenarian Abner Graves. The one, the only proof that assigned to Doubleday the mysterious paternity of baseball was Graves's vague remark that, sixty-eight years earlier, "Doubleday improved Town Ball to limit the number of players, as many were hurt in collisions" and that "Doubleday called the game 'Base Ball' for there were four bases to it."

Graves said that Doubleday had been a boy, a Green Select School student, playing daily in Cooperstown fields, when he made his momentous limitation in the interest of public safety. In reality, in 1839 Doubleday was a second-year cadet at distant West Point. And he didn't even get a summer vacation.

That merely begins to summarize the cornucopia of reasons why Doubleday couldn't have created baseball. But at the time, no one cared.

Although it already had James Fenimore Cooper, author of *Leatherstocking Tales, The Last of the Mohicans, The Deerslayer* and *The Pathfinder* to vaunt as native son, the beautiful village of Cooperstown gladly suppressed its surprise and clutched another claim to greatness to its breast. Pretty soon its citizens were remembering that the young'uns had indeed customarily played in Mr. Phinney's pasture and deciding that it was there young Abner, bless his heart, had first felt solicitude for the victims of town-ball collisions.

Of course, when organized baseball again cranked up the publicity machines to celebrate the glorious centennial of this event in 1939 and decided that a regulation field should be constructed and a game played between major-league teams on the site, hoary tradition was not allowed to conflict unreasonably with practicality. A field a couple of miles removed from Phinney's farm but more convenient to the center of town and the business district was deemed more suitable as a location for the stadium. Phinney's pasture, a pretty spot between Route 80 and Otsego Lake, remains an unglorified bean field.

That was one of the easier parts of the "centennial" observation. A little further digging in the dirt about the roots of the national institution very rapidly became acutely embarrassing to all concerned. Exactly how embarrassing will be made obvious. Suffice it to say for the moment that Cooperstown nearly lost not only its legend but also the game, the celebration, one of the world's more famous museums, and a steady flood of tourist business that continues to the present day. Cooperstown and baseball reinterred the skeleton almost as quickly as they exhumed it and smoothed over the ground remarkably effectively. But it took some time for the snickering to subside. For quite a while, the truth was out.

Abner Doubleday didn't invent baseball. Baseball invented Abner Doubleday.

CHAPTER TWO

BOOKS—ASIDE, OF COURSE, FROM THE BIBLE (WHICH SERVED AS TEXT FOR all purposes from home remedies to sex education) and possibly *Pilgrim's Progress*—were relatively scarce and little consulted in 1834. Children's allowances ranged from minimal to nonexistent. Had fourteen-year-old Alick Cartwright or fifteen-year-old Abner Doubleday been able and willing, however, to relinquish the sum of about five cents, the price of a pound of steak or lobster, he might possibly have stumbled on the right bookseller's tiny niche and purchased a small volume titled *The Book of Sports*. Written, or rather compiled, by one Robin Carver, it was published by the distinguished old Boston house of Lilly, Wait, Colman and Holden. Thumbing past explications of Dick, Duck and Drake, Puss in the Corner, Blowing Bubbles and Stepping Through your own Fingers, the young chap would have arrived at Games with a Ball. On page 37, the adolescent Cartwright or Doubleday would have found this happy suggestion for a game:

> BASE, or GOAL BALL This game is known under a variety of names. It is sometimes called "round ball," but I believe that "base" or "goal ball" are the names generally adopted in our country. The players divide into two equal parties, and chance decides which shall have first innings. Four stones or stakes are placed from twelve to

twenty yards asunder, as *a, b, c, d,* in the margin; another is put at
e.

One of the party who is out places himself at *e*. He tosses the ball
gently toward *a*, on the right of which one of the *in-party* places
himself, and strikes the ball, if possible, with his bat. If he miss
three times, or if the ball, when struck, be caught by any of the
players of the opposite side who are scattered about the field, he is
out, another takes his place. If none of these accidents take place,
on striking the ball he drops the bat and runs toward *b*, or if he
can, to *c, d* or even to *a* again. If, however, the boy who stands at
e, or any of the outplayers who may happen to have the ball,
strike him with it in his progress from *a* to *b*, *b* to *c*, *c* to *d*, or *d* to
a, he is out. Supposing he can get only to *b*, one of his partners
takes the bat, and strikes at the ball in turn. If the first player can
get only to *c*, or *d*, the second runs to *b* only, or *c*, as the case may
be, and a third player begins; as they get home, that is, to *a*, they
play at the ball by turns, until they all get out. Then, of course, the
out-players take their places.

Extraordinary. Five years before Doubleday "invented" baseball
by drawing, allegedly, a diagram with a stick in the perishable dirt,
it was possible to buy a printed description of something explicitly
named "base ball" in an American book. And little Abner, when
supposedly inspired to improve town ball and thereby create baseball, somehow didn't get it improved as far as this 1834 version in
one respect: the provision for exactly three strikes.

Just to add poison to the wound, an illustration in Carver's book
showed baseball being played in a place indisputably American:
Boston Common, with the great golden dome of the State House
and the townhouses of Beacon Hill in the background. The scene is
almost unchanged in 1972. The illustration ranks as the oldest
known depiction of baseball—identified by that name—in America.

More research of the kind organized baseball might have done
sometime before 1939 inflicts a greater embarrassment to the official
Spalding school of history. Carver's description of baseball is lifted
virtually word for word from an *English* book published in 1829,

William Clarke's *The Boy's Own Book*. There is one significant difference. Clarke calls the game *rounders*.

So much for Spalding's angry denial that baseball might have any relation to that Redcoat game. Vindication for Henry Chadwick, who, though only a sportswriter, knew rounders when he saw it.

But Carver did not invent the name, let alone the game. A nineteenth-century article on Fighting Joe Hooker, the Civil War general who distinguished himself at Lookout Mountain, Antietam, and Williamsburgh but lost ingloriously to Robert E. Lee and Stonewall Jackson at Chancellorsville, said he played baseball as a boy in the very early 1830's: "At baseball, then a very different game from now, he was very expert; catching was his forte. He would take a ball from almost in front of the bat, so eager, active and dexterous were his movements."

Was, maybe, West Point cadet Hooker one of the first "baseball" players? Did the Mills Commission only lucklessly draft the wrong general, putting the museum in Cooperstown instead of Hadley, Massachusetts? Nope. The commission itself actually received and ignored or misread a letter saying that

> J. A. Mendum of 591 Dudley Street, Dorchester, Mass., who is now eighty-three years old, states that . . . in 1830, he, with other pupils of the grammar school in School Street, Portsmouth, N.H., played the genuine game of base ball regularly during the summer. . . . Mr. Stoddard says: "Four Old Cat and Three Old Cat were as well known to Massachusetts boys as was Round Ball. My father played them between 1800 and 1820. The games then bore the same relationship to Rounders that 'scrub' now bears to baseball. If the boys assembled and found there were not enough on hand to make up a team of Round Ball, they would content themselves with Four Old Cat or Three Old Cat."

Astonishingly, despite the direct statement that the O' Cat games were merely watered-down versions of rounders, the Spalding-dominated and -nominated commission used this as well as other letters as evidence of the very opposite: that baseball was derived from Four Old Cat.

Proof that a "base ball" as good as or better than Cooperstown's existed long before 1839 comes from numerous directions.

Festivals, Games and Amusements, written by Horatio Smith and first published in London in 1831, says in passing, "The games and amusements of New England are similar to those of other sections of the United States. The young men are expert in a variety of games at ball—such as cricket, base, cat, football, trap ball. . . ."

In his diary at Brown University from 1823 to 1827, a young man from Bridgewater, Massachusetts, named Williams Latham writes that "base ball" was much played. "We this morning . . . have been playing ball," he complains one day. "But I have never received so much pleasure from it here as I have in Bridgewater. They do not have more than 6 or 7 on a side, so that a great deal of time is spent in running after the ball. Neither do they throw so fair ball. They are afraid the fellow in the middle will hit it with his bat-stick."

The Whig journalist and President-maker Thurlow Weed even recalled the names of some Rochester players of the early 1820's. He wrote in his autobiography:

> A base-ball club, numbering nearly fifty members, met every afternoon during the ball playing season. . . . The ball ground, containing some eight or ten acres, known as Mumford's meadow, by the side of the [Genesee] river, above the falls, is now a compact part of the city. Our best players were Addison Gardiner, Frederick Whittlesey, Samuel L. Selden, Thomas Kempshall, James K. Livingston, Dr. George Marvin, F. F. Backus, Dr. A. G. Smith. . . .

Oliver Wendell Holmes, author of "The One-Hoss Shay" and father of the respected Supreme Court Justice, told a Boston newspaperman that baseball was one of the sports of his college days at Harvard, from which he graduated in 1829.

Right in New York, a kind of baseball was popular at the beginning of the 1800's. A gentleman of the period, Charles Haswell, played it frequently. He reminisced:

> If a base-ball was required, the boy of 1816 founded it with a bit of cork, or if he were singularly fortunate, with some shreds of india rubber. Then it was wound with yarn from a ravelled stocking, and some feminine member of his family covered it with patches from a soiled glove. . . . For a base-ball bat, if anything better than a casual flat or round stick was required, negotiation had to be entered into with some wood-turner. . . . Yet we did play ball, skate, etc. and in the absence of stages or any means of public conveyance, we walked from below Canal Street, the then limit of the city, to Stuyvesant's meadow, the Sunfish Pond, or Cedar Creek. . . .

So something called baseball entertained the young at Cartwright's old playing grounds, the very same place, a quarter century before 1839—and before that, deep into the 1700's, at the Battery. It was an exceedingly disorganized game, however, as the description of football there hints by analogy: "On Saturday afternoons, in the fall of the year, a few students would meet in the 'hollow' on the Battery and play an irregular game of football, generally without teams or sides. . . . This hollow was [also] the locale of base-ball, 'marbles,' etc. . . ."

The "hollow" constituted "very nearly the entire area bounded by Whitehall and State Streets, the sea wall line, and a line about 200 feet to the west."

Baseball absorbed perhaps more of a boy's attention then than it does now. During the spring, only the period of Easter, with its coloring and "cracking" of eggs, "supplanted marbles, kiteflying and base-ball." But baseball goes back that far not only in New York but in many other places. Could Daniel Webster have played the game? Indeed he did, at Dartmouth College in the wilds of northern New Hampshire between 1797 and 1801. Indian students were still common then, and undoubtedly some, clad in Christian homespun, played baseball at Dartmouth with the descendants of Yankees whom their fathers had killed or kidnapped from the burning pioneer villages of Deerfield and Hatfield.

Could it be that, while the Constitutional Convention was fitfully, fretfully meeting in Philadelphia to consider a new, stronger federalism to replace the old Articles of Confederation under which the victorious colonies were drifting into dissolution, baseball was being played in the very imperfectly united states of America? It could.

A diary cited by Princeton historian Varning Lansing Collins contains several allusions to college sports—"hockey on Stony Brook in winter, shinny, quoits, 'baste ball'. . . ." One entry reads, "A fine day, play baste ball in the campus but am beaten for I miss both catching and striking the ball."

The college fathers, however, frowned on baseball as perilous to the limbs and dignity of scholars. In 1787 they warned:

It appearing that a play at present much practised by the smaller boys among the students and by the grammar Scholars with balls and sticks in the back common of the College is in itself low and unbecoming gentlemen Students, and in as much as it is an exercise attended with great danger to the health by sudden and alternate heats and colds and as it tends by accidents almost unavoidable in that play to disfiguring and maiming those who are engaged in it for whose health and safety as well as improvement in Study as far as depends on our exertion we are accountable to their Parents & liable to be severely blamed by them: and in as much as there are many amusements both more honourable and more useful in which they are indulged, Therefore the faculty think it incumbent on them to prohibit both the Students & grammar Scholars from using the play aforesaid.

A game of "bat & ball" is referred to in numerous accounts of New England before the Revolution. William Winterbotham, in *An Historical View of the United States,* published in 1796, says it was common.

Spalding and Mills simply lacked courage and imagination in writing fiction. Why settle for a Civil War figure? Why not have baseball played by Revolutionary soldiers? Between drillings by Von Steuben and Pulaski and horseback visits by that commander-in-chief of the permanently creased brow and worried visage. At Valley Forge, while the first warm days of spring melted the last snow of the terrible winter.

Why not? Because indeed it was. Continental Army bluecoat George Ewing, a volunteer from Connecticut, scratched into his journal—a document to be taken home and exhibited at the town tavern on the four corners in his old age—this notation for April 7, 1778: "Exercised in the afternoon in the intervals playd at base."

One problem, Mr. Spalding. The British soldiers also undoubtedly played at baseball. Jane Austen, of all people, on page 3 of *Northanger Abbey,* of all books, prominently mentioned the game: "Mrs. Morland was a very good woman and wished to see her children everything they ought to be; but her time was so much occupied by lying-in and teaching the little ones, that her elder daughters were inevitably left to shift for themselves; and it was not very wonderful that Catherine should prefer cricket, base-ball, riding on horseback, and running about the country, at the age of fourteen, to books."

Northanger Abbey was written in 1796. Since Miss Austen was the first novelist to traffic in such small and homely trivia as children's games, it might be assumed that baseball was played much earlier in England.

Quite so. In the year 1744 London publisher John Newbery printed the first edition of *A Little Pretty Pocket-Book, Intended*

for the Amusement of Little Master Tommy and Pretty Miss Polly.
In this book, "B" was for

> *Base-ball*
> The *Ball* once struck off,
> Away flies the *Boy*
> To the next destin'd Post,
> And then Home with Joy.

And in the year 1700, when the Puritans had largely won their reformation and were now bringing their purism to extremes, the Reverend Thomas Wilson of Maidstone, in Kent, decried ungodly practices he had witnessed in the 1600's: "I have seen Morris-dancing, cudgel-playing, baseball and cricketts, and many other sports on the Lord's Day."

Who would have thought that baseball, by that name, could have been running afoul of the blue laws as early as 1650? And in England, not Pennsylvania?

Back in the colonies, too, baseball—although not identified as such—may have been getting itself in trouble earlier than anyone might have expected. The late Alexander Hamilton's New York *Evening Post* complained on March 25, 1828, "Let anyone visit Washington Parade, or indeed any of the fields in that neighborhood, and he will find large groups of men and boys playing ball and filling the air with their shouts and yells. At present the annoyance has become absolutely intolerable to those who live in the neighborhood . . ." (which included Hamilton's still-attractive widow). The editorial may have been written, by the way, by the poet William Cullen Bryant, who was one of the *Post's* two editorial writers at the time.

The first American sporting book, *Business and Diversions Inoffensive to God, and necessary for the comfort and support of Human Society*, written by Joseph Secombe in 1739, definitely did not put baseball on the approved list. (Way back in old New Amsterdam, the Dutch were more easygoing. They forbade "Dancing, Card-playing, Tick-tacking, Playing at ball, at bowls, at ninepins" only during church hours.)

But most astonishingly, on Christmas Day of 1621, while other settlers worked to support Plymouth Plantation, Governor William Bradford was shocked to see some colonists "in ye streets at play, openly; some pitching ye barr, & some at stoole ball, and shuch like sports." Bradford quickly put a stop to that. "Ther should be no gameing or reveling in ye streets," he informed the miscreants. Little more than a year after the Puritan dissenters had first landed at Plymouth, less than one year after a fraction of survivors had rejoiced in a spring they had almost despaired of seeing, a game that was at least a predecessor of baseball was being played in their streets.

Predecessor. That is the operative word. The game all the pre-Cartwright people played was only a rudimentary, although highly interesting and considerably evolved, predecessor of baseball. It had two main names besides "base ball": "town ball" and "the Massachusetts game." Town ball became the most common sobriquet because lads from all the Pumpkin Hollows and Hardscrabble Hills and Poverty Flat districts of New England used to play the game on center-village greens on the day of the annual town meetings— or at the few other times the scattered, hard-working townsmen left their little villages and crossroads to gather all together. Along with boiled dinners and speakings and bell ringings, town ball was a staple of such gatherings. Town ball was sometimes also played at barn raisings, husking bees and militia drill days.

Either an India-rubber or a yarn ball might be used and a bat either flattened or round. Players had a wide choice of striking implements. Ax hafts, rake handles and even light wagon tongues were used as bats. Three or four or five bases might be marked by stones or posts at irregular intervals, and as many players as wanted could participate, scattered randomly about the field. Since towns by tradition frequently split into rival halves at town meetings, spontaneous "political parties" based on blood and near settlement as well as on philosophical principle, frugality or the condition of the roads, teams probably followed those lines too. Failing such rivalry, the married men versus the single men was even then a popular division.

Rules varied from town to town. Players (often known as *hands*) did score by making a circuit of the bases and were put out individually when a ball they had hit was caught (or when they were struck between bases with the ball)—at least most often. An inning was frequently called a *hand in*. It was also common, however, for the entire side to be out if one batter's fly ball was caught. This harks back to the simpler forms of rounders. One strange variation, allowing retaliation, will later be shown to have the most extraordinary roots. When the "in" team was caught out, the fielding team, in this version, had to run and dodge into the batting area as fast as possible, because the dispossessed team could retrieve the ball and throw it at any member of the new "in" team. If it succeeded in hitting him, its own inning was resumed as if the ball had never been caught. Whether the batsman (called a *striker*) most commonly stood at a home base or at a point between first and home is a subject of some uncertainty. It seems to this writer that town ball in its pure form stationed the batter at or near home base. The other variation was more properly called the Massachusetts game or "the Boston game."

Alfred Spink, who made the mistake of swallowing all the Spalding fabrications in his book *The National Game*, also described the Massachusetts game while calling it town ball. "The players used a square field, sixty feet on a side, with a base at each corner," Spink said. "The batsman stood in a space four feet square located between the first and fourth base. The pitcher was stationed in a space at the center of the square. . . . [We still speak of "knocking the pitcher out of the box," although many decades have elapsed since he last occupied one.] The number on each side varied from 10 to 20, and the rule was: one out, all out. A base runner was out if hit by the thrown ball . . . and the batter was out if the ball was caught on the fly or first bound." The Massachusetts game's chief difference, otherwise, was that it was more organized and codified than town ball, as befitted a pastime of Bay State Yankees. It did, however, sometimes allow the pitcher to throw a smaller, harder ball fast and overhand. When this refinement came to baseball in the 1850's, it may have been a borrowing from the New England game.

The Athens of the West, the Hub of the Universe, presently known as Boston, may have proper claim to the first organized, recorded, formal ball game of its kind. Two eight-man teams of truck drivers played it on the Common in 1838. Rules were negotiated *ad hoc*. Four stakes, each three feet high, were driven to make bases, which the teamsters called *bounds*. Sixty feet was the distance between first and second bound, forty-five between second and third, and sixty between third and home. The batter actually stood nearer first base than home, being only eighteen feet from first. The pitcher stood forty-five feet away. There were only five fielders (called *scouts*), strangely arranged. One camped close to each base, and the other two played what we would consider short left and right fields. If hitting in any direction was allowed, as it usually

THE MASSACHUSETTS GAME

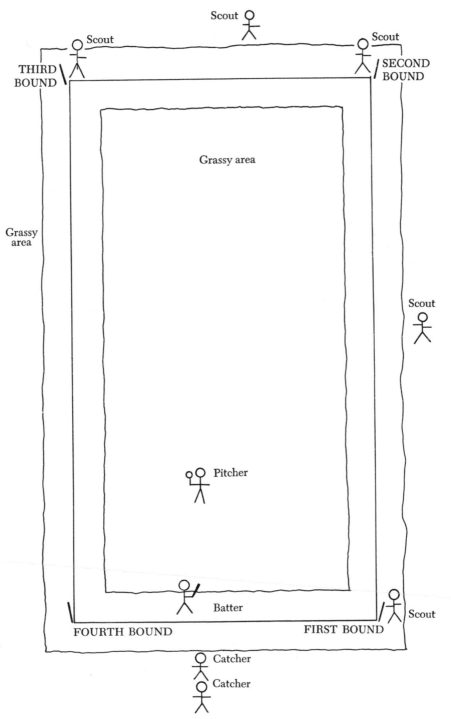

was, the natural tendency of a right-handed hitter to "pull" to left was gratified by the total absence of any fielder in that direction! Very likely the hitters were so maladroit, like little tykes of today, that they clumsily swung late and hit consistently to right. To compensate for the other lack of fielders, there were two catchers, both playing far behind the batter.

The ball, surprisingly modern, was cork or rubber, tightly wrapped in yarn with a calfskin cover, but it measured only six and one half inches in circumference and weighed only two and one fourth ounces. The final score was 22 aces to 19 aces, and the game lasted only two innings because the winners scored 11 aces in each, more than the required 21.

Philadelphia claims the Olympics, formed in 1833 but playing as early as 1831, as the first organized town-ball club, but this becomes mostly a matter of definition. Probably other regular town-ball clubs organized in the 1820's but lacked big-city publicity. Chadwick said of the Philadelphians, "Parties of a dozen or more used to gather of an afternoon once a week on a field adjoining the upper part of Market Street, near where the Episcopal church now stands, to play the old game; and others again would go over to the Camden fields to enjoy the sport. . . . the players were laughed at in those days for playing ball, the prejudice against wasting time in that way being very prevalent in the Quaker City of that period. The Philadelphians have, however, bravely got over it since then." Stubbornly continuing to play town ball until 1860, the Olympics finally yielded to the "New York game" in that year.

There has never been much dispute about this one point: Whether Cartwright, Doubleday or Jeremiah Hepzibiah Wigglesworth were the father of modern baseball, town ball would still be its immediate ancestor on the maternal side.

CHAPTER THREE

"THE OLD APPLE," AS BATTERS FOR UNCOUNTABLE YEARS HAVE INSISTED on calling any baseball, seems to have fallen pretty far from the family tree. Let's hang it back up where it belongs, once and for all.

Modern baseball begins with Cartwright's major improvement on town ball. Town ball, in turn, is—exactly and precisely—nothing other than rounders, a game now played mostly by red-cheeked English schoolgirls. At most, upstate New York countrymen slightly Americanized it. Pre-Cartwright versions of this early "base ball," as rounders was originally called in both the United States and England, tended toward some of the more sophisticated variations. Yet the American games diverged from the basic pattern no more than did many examples in the remoter dukedoms of Britain, which were still called "rounders" and which resembled Yank town ball greatly. Spalding's simple-minded explanation that baseball came directly from Four Old Cat, through a progression from Three Old Cat, Two Old Cat and One Old Cat, is clearly specious. Rural lads, in the nineteenth century as in recent years, played the O' Cat games only when they didn't have enough boys for baseball. The Philadelphia Olympic town-ball club of 1831 also played O' Cat when a quorum of members could not escape the countinghouses and mercantile establishments.

Early baseball and town ball often were also known as *round ball*, another clue that they were rounders. But we need not depend on circumstantial evidence. If he doubted the proof cited earlier, as well as Henry Chadwick's clearly expert opinion, Spalding might have consulted any one of several English books, published around the time of the Mills Commission report, which happened to mention baseball. All innocent of transatlantic chauvinism, the books simply took for granted that everyone knew baseball's genealogy. "Its origin has been, more or less accurately, connected with old-fashioned games of England, France and the early American Colonies, but it may be at once admitted that rounders is the only game which really bears any affinity to it," *Baseball*, by P.G. Knowles and Richard Morton, said casually.

The Sports of the World (1904), written by one Angus Evan Abbott, said generously:

> . . . baseball, *the* game in the United States, although undoubtedly originating in our old game of rounders, has been so built up and improved that the Americans are justified, perhaps, in claiming it as an invention of the New World. . . . Than baseball there is no more exact and scientific game. The Americans have a genius for taking a thing, examining its every part, and developing each part to the utmost. This they have done with our game of rounders, and, from a clumsy, primitive pastime, have so tightened its joints and put such a fine finish on its points that it stands forth a complicated machine of infinite exactitude.

But if rounders be a sort of baseball, rather crude but clearly identifiable, have we really found out where baseball began? Let's do what few of baseball's historians have begun to do. Let's open the next door and usher in the darkness of prehistory, the musky, oddly exciting odor of medievality and primevality, of ribaldly bucolic Old England and of the forgotten fertility rites which cling to this game that is more than a game. Rummaging among the roots of baseball, we encounter the very rarest relics of our civilization's ancient Indo-European origins. From the Ganges to the Yukon, the sober, ritual pursuits of the ancient unified culture have been confused and dispersed in a Babel of diverging tongues and tribes. Each generation of adolescents is educated out of remnant aboriginal myths and rites by increasingly particular, centripetal adult civilizations. But the children, in the secret games and magic they have shared from times out of memory, perpetuate fragments of the

universal rituals and incantations of millennia past. Even the children of the wind-scoured American prairie, as cleansed and steri-
lized of Old World superstition as any, retained mysterious primitive games spiced with incomprehensible language. In new houses
in new towns they played, as medieval children played in the cob-
bled streets of ancient walled cities, long-repressed adult rituals
which have turned into diversions for infants.

In Illinois, we were taught by our elders to believe in a social
philosophy stripped of all feudalism and in a religion purified of an-
imism. Boys as well as girls eschewed the mucky Anglo-Saxon
words and preoccupations. The sweep of the naked land itself con-
tributed. It was no hospitable hiding place for witches, werewolves,
ghosts, or goblins. Or golden castles, storks, or princesses turned
into toads. At times antisepticism went too far: The endless sharp-
cornered squares of sensible straight roads and endless acres of sensible straight rows of corn threatened to suffocate the mild land in
dominant rationalism. Yet we children taught each other the games
of the Medes and Persians. Some of us even dimly sensed the anom-
aly, so jarring was its incongruity. We believed uncritically that all
knowledge was found in books, but many of our games were to be
found in no books at all. We believed in words as conveying all
human communication, yet our games had no names, and their language was often unintelligible in any modern tongue. To cite one
example: In many of our games, there was something called *gool*.
Not *a* gool, not *the* gool, just *gool*. We asked our parents what that
meant. They assured us we must mean *goal*. But *gool* was not really
a goal in the games but more of a magic talisman, and besides we
somehow knew instinctively that gool was something else, something "mysterious" (our favorite word).

That mystery is deeper now, because we have forgotten childish
words and phrases as we learned English and because we cannot
ask the children of 1972. They find their romance and mental stim-
ulation, God help them, in television and *Sesame Street*. (Although,
aha, perhaps there is hope: "Daddy, what's a *sesame*?") Yet we still
do have games relegitimized as adult activity, like baseball. No one
ever examines the *reasons* for them, and that is their salvation from
discard. ("It doesn't have to have a reason," everyone says. "It's a
game.") But we moderns not only examine but dissect everything
else—even sex. Not examining reasons and causes is a mark of primitive societies. ("It doesn't have a reason," they implicitly assume,
"because it's *magic*."

Are our games our magic? The answer is: yes. They certainly started as magic, and they are a dilute kind of magic to us today. The present degree of obsession with sports admits of no rational explanation. Whether pro football or skiing, sports—not religion— are the opiate of the masses. Or, if you prefer, the romantic's release from a religion of rationality long since degenerated into sophistic rationalization.

Examine baseball.

Why run around a square, touching certain stations along the way, to reach "home"? Why hit a spherical object with a cylindrical one? Because it's "fun"? Yes, meeting a ball solidly and cleanly, hearing the dry *tock* of it striking the bat and driving it a country mile, is indeed fun. But *why* is it fun? Why should such an inherently purposeless, meaningless action be satisfying?

What is one "out" into if the ball is caught in an opponent's hands? What are you "safe" from if he does not touch a "base" in time? What in the name of Happy Chandler is a "score"?

There are other mysterious words and actions. The familiarity of still others is misleading, for they are modern substitutions or accretions. To go back only one step or two from baseball is to enter a widening web of mysteries. Take one of the more interesting: Whose Old Cat are we talking about and how long is its tale?

No, take one of the easier first. Why is "rounders" called "rounders"?

Simple explanation: Runners go 'round a circle of bases. Less simply, more correctly, the game in its pure form always had a provision called "hitting one for the rounder." If all the rest of his team were either "out" or on base, the last batter (usually the best) was given three chances to hit a pitch far enough to "make a rounder" —that is, to make a complete circuit of the bases. If he succeeded in doing so before the ball was "grounded" by "crowning" home base with it, his side got a whole new inning. Very discouraging for the other team, who had been grilling out in the hot sun while getting eight or ten or nineteen or more men out.

Most correctly, but most mysteriously, the rounder has a ritual significance, as shall be seen later. But two obvious points jump out. First, the idea of the "force-out" existed a century or two before Cartwright reinvented it. Second, the fact that rounders was named for this peculiarity suggests that the odd idiosyncrasy was considered important. Why this vestigial appendix should be important is not immediately apparent, yet we shall see that it is significant indeed.

This irregularity of the ancestral tree is a mere knot or burl compared with the limbs some of the few serious baseball researchers have gotten out onto while in search of the tap root. Though not in a class with ecology and the population explosion as an insoluble problem, the burning question "Where did rounders come from?" has produced its share of implausible solutions.

Cricket, for one. Americans for generations have felt obliged to simulate some semblance of respect for cricket because of a sniggling suspicion that cricket, in some wildly atypical lapse into indiscreet passion, might have spawned Our National Pastime. Probably at some time every truly devout baseball fanatic has warily attempted to penetrate the recondite obscurities of bowlers and wickets and tea breaks and silly mid-offs. Like Baptists inspecting the Vatican, they have half feared their zeal for the reformed version might be compromised by contact with the traditional. The impressive antiquity of the game's name has burnished cricket's venerable patina. *Creag* or *criece* is an old Saxon word meaning "crooked stick," and it also seems to have been a name of a game played with a ball as early as the 1300's.

Partisans of the American game, relax. It is historically permissible to follow inclination and dissolve in undiluted boredom at the sight of cricket. Baseball is not a cricket expanded from two wickets to four bases. Quite the opposite. Cricket is a Johnny-come-lately narrowing of an antecedent baseball, reverting from the purity of the seminal game by introducing a hockeylike element, the wicket targets. Cricket did not become popular in Britain until the *nineteenth century* and was scarcely mentioned before the middling 1700's. Croquet, another genteel game played with wickets on perfect lawns between teas, also descends from the old game of *criec' et* and probably is more similar to it. (Early, cricket was even spelled *criquet*.) The very fact that the word means "crooked stick" substantiates this and relates cricket more closely to ancient hockey and to primitive golf. Further, early cricket *was* played with hockeylike sticks. Originally, the game was probably played by herdsmen with shepherd's crooks (a word related, obviously, to *criec*). The first wickets were sheep gates.

Intriguing, all the same, are the few early references to cricket. An author of 1685, Edward Phillips, has his lady asking her lover,

"Will you not, when you have me, throw stocks at my head, and cry, 'Would my eyes have been beaten out of my head with a cricket-ball the day before I saw thee'?" An interesting old English book, *The Playground and the Parlour*, by Alfred Elliott, claims that cricket may even derive from a Persian word, *cheegar*. It also declares that it corresponds exactly to the old English game of Hand In, Hand Out and the Scottish game of Cat and Dog. (There's that cat again.) In reality, the games are not the same, but there is a connection.

A rollicking, ribald early playwright of the milkmaid school of humor named Thomas D'Urfey, in a many-volumed, underrated 1719 work called *Pills to Purge Melancholy*, versified:

> Her was the prettiest fellow
> At foot-ball or at cricket,
> At hunting chase, or nimble race,
> How featly her could prick it.

Kent did play All-England in cricket in 1746, and Lord Byron, as a schoolboy, did play on a Harrow eleven against Eton in 1805. Even in the United States, New York merchant James Rivington advertised cricket balls as early as 1766, and cricket was sometimes played at barn-raisings and picnics instead of baseball. Travelers found cricket as far west as Kentucky in 1818 and in Illinois by 1819, one year after statehood. But nine-year-old Abe Lincoln, born in one state and raised in the other, knew only baseball.

D'Urfey's coy milkmaidens also played stoolball, a charmingly bucolic game common in the dusky zone between modern Saxon-Norman civilization, with its overly copious written records, and the misty dawn of that civilization, preserved mostly in oral tradition. Stoolball was played with literal milking stools, placed as bases and targets. Indeed, "cricket" is also a dialect word for stool. It seems clear that cricket comes from stoolball quite directly and that the intermediate wickets were three-legged stools. *The Little Pretty Pocket Book* of 1744, which first described baseball by that name, also illustrated stoolball—stoolball with more than two bases and with the striker holding a baseball-style bat. Our sometimes raunchy, sometimes melodic friend D'Urfey frequently poesized about stoolball:

> Down in the vale on a Summer's day,
> All the lads and lasses went to be merry,

A match for kisses at Stoolball to play,
And for cakes and ale and sider and perry.
    Come all, great, small,
    Short, tall, away to Stoolball.

When King Charles I reversed his predecessors' ban on Sunday sport, a high churchman defended the King's action, saying, ". . . shooting, leaping, pitching the barre, stool-ball, and the like, are rather to be chosen than diceing or carding." (Oddly, when Elizabeth had outlawed all sport on Sunday, in 1572, an opposing writer on religion applauded. His name, as it happened, was Cartwright.)

Nothing definite places stoolball before the fifteenth century. Every kind of clue, however, hints that it was a survival of ancient ritual. As D'Urfey says, "cakes"—in addition to cider and a similar beverage made from fermented pears (perry)—were given as prizes. These were tansy cakes, made with the bitter herb of that name. Tansy cakes were associated with Easter, when they were baked in memory of the Hebrew Passover custom of eating bitter herbs. Stoolball was most commonly played in churchyards, around Easter, and by maidens. By every account, it was closely connected with courting. It was a prominent part of the whole package of springtime pagan customs incorporated by the Church into Easter, all of which were basically fertility rites.

In his first dictionary of the English language, Dr. Samuel Johnson included stoolball. He defined it as "a play in which balls are driven from stool to stool," something of a tautology, especially since he declined to say in what manner or to what purpose. Others are less frustrating. One description is revealing because, although it describes a clearly primitive variety, it presents stoolball as still played in 1831:

> [Stoolball] consists in simply setting a stool upon the ground, and one of the players taking his place before it, while his antagonist, standing at a distance, tosses a ball with the intention of striking the stool. It is the business of the former to prevent this by beating it away with the hand, reckoning one to the game for every stroke of the ball. If, on the contrary, it should be missed on the hand, and touch the stool, the players change places. The conqueror at this game is he who touches the ball most times before it touches the stool.

Not very much like baseball, is it? But this primeval stoolball stands quite close to early cricket, which also had only one wicket.

In isolated rural areas, however, there were peculiar variations. "In some parts of the country, a certain number of stools are set up in a circular form," one account says, ". . . and every one of them is occupied by a single player: when the ball is struck . . . they are every one of them obliged to alter his situation, running in succession from stool to stool, and if he who threw the ball can regain it in time to strike any one of the players before he reaches the stool to which he is running, he takes his place. . . ."

This rendition remarkably resembles Four O' Cat, the multibase American game from which, Spalding maintained, baseball sprang without other ancestors. Most stoolball seems to have been the multibase variety, and since other baseball-like characteristics also appeared occasionally, one might naturally assume that baseball grows out of stoolball. But, to this writer, this seems not the case. Too many elements, such as the concept of teams and fly outs, as well as others which will become strikingly apparent, are missing. He has come across too many even earlier ball games anterior to stoolball. He believes, in short, that there was baseball before there was stoolball—and that stoolball was actually a simplification of earlier baseball.

CHAPTER FOUR

THE DOMESDAY BOOK (DOOMSDAY BOOK) OF 1086, ORDERED BY WIL-
liam the Conqueror as a kind of inventory of what the Normans
had conquered, has become a guidebook to what is "old" in England, and it mentions a game of "bittle battle." *Bittle* happens to
be a Saxon word meaning "stick" or "bat." (*Battle*, for that matter,
is derived from the word *bat*.)

"Run at baris and at the ball," says an old English poem of 1475.
Baris is an early form of the word *base*.

A manuscript illumination of the year 1344 shows a woman
throwing a ball to a man who holds a bat as if to strike at it. Behind
the woman, in the distance, stand several other men and women
watching attentively, as if they were fielders. Another drawing of
roughly the same era, on a genealogical chart of the Kings of England, seems to show a game similar to modern fungo.

A fourteenth-century biography of St. Cuthbert says, ". . . he
pleyde atte balle with the children that his fellowes were." In the
1200's, William Fitzstephen, author of a description of London,
wrote of the schoolboys, apparently describing a long-standing tradition, "Annually upon Shrove Tuesday, they go into the fields after
dinner, and play at the celebrated game of ball."

In *The Sports and Pastimes of the People of England Including the Rural and Domestic Recreations, May Games, Mummeries, Shows, Processions, Pageants and Pompous Spectacles, from the Earliest Period to the Present Time,* a definitive work written in 1801, Joseph Strutt implied that these all might be something he called "club ball," which he meant as a generic term for batting games. But an obscure scholarly article published in the Thirties indicates that they might have been millennia-old games actually more similar to modern baseball than stoolball. These games appear to be convergences of at least two "plays" older yet. The more complicated appears to have been a highly evolved offspring of the simpler but by a fascinating route all across the Indo-European culture, over a period of thousands of years, dating quite literally to the Stone Age.

We shall take that up later. First, let's track down the simpler and more familiar ancestor.

We can now reply with assurance to the question: What was baseball before it was ever called baseball, before it even resembled baseball? The answer is—cat. Sometimes spelled *katt*. Slight variations were called by a welter of other names, the most common being trapball or northern spell.

Trapball, a slight sophistication of basic cat, even made some appearance in the United States. It was played in Colonial Virginia by the boys of Williamsburgh, and a New York paper of 1811 says it was "often practiced at the close of trainings, raisings, shooting matches and on election days." But it survived best in the rural north of England, whence it came. The "trap" of trapball is either a spring device or a lever pivoted in the middle, usually mounted on a wooden shoe-shaped base. The ball is placed on one end, and the other end is struck with a bat. This sends the ball flying up so that it can be hit with the same bat. The batter thus "pitches" his own ball. From that point, trapball varied. Using the name "trap, bat and ball," a typical description begins, significantly, "Two boundaries are equally placed at a great distance from the trap, between which it is necessary for the ball to pass when struck by the batsman; if it falls outside either of them, he loses his innings." So, before Cartwright's modern baseball, we must go all the way back to trapball to find, in England or America, the concept of foul lines and "fair" territory. The account continues:

> Innings are tossed up for, and the player who wins places the ball in the spoon of the trap, touches the trigger with the bat and, as

the ball hops from the trap, strikes it as far as he can. One of the other players (who may be from two to half a dozen) endeavours to catch it. If he do so before it reaches the ground, or hops more than once, or if the striker miss the ball when he aims at it, or hits the trigger more than twice without striking the ball, he loses his innings, and the next in order . . . takes his place. Should the ball be fairly struck and not caught . . . the out-player into whose hands it comes bowls it, from the place where he picks it up, at the trap, which, if he hit, the striker is out. If he miss it, the striker counts one toward the game, which may be any number decided upon.

Although trapball is far more ancient, there are thus other ways in which it much more closely resembles modern baseball than stoolball—for example, the ideas of three strikes and of the batter being "caught out." (Bowling back at the trap, of course, is a precursor of cricket, which descended from both trapball and stoolball.) A 1788 illustration of trapball has been found, and the game has been mentioned at least as early as the 1500's. Trapball is still played, usually by men and particularly in Kent. One modern form there has been badly corrupted by modern soccer or hockey, however. The batter must hit the ball between uprights much like a soccer goal!

Romantically named "northern spell" crops up often enough to bedevil any researcher into English batting games. Played, sure enough, mostly in the northern counties, modern "northern spell" turns out to be a decadent trapball. The only object is to hit the ball as far as possible, a decadence into which present-day baseball sometimes threatens to sink. Yet "northern spell" prefigures two characteristics of modern baseball. First, the ball had to be hit within foul lines not parallel to each other, but diverging at exactly 90 degrees like first- and third-base lines. Second, the game was won by "scores." The distance of hits was measured in scores of yards. The winner was the man who could total the most of these twenty-yard increments in twenty tries. A copper kettle was the traditional prize, one surely not satisfactory to a Johnny Bench. So hard were the ball and bat (of compressed hickory or ash) that a single hit might make ten score. That's 200 yards or 600 feet, a pretty darn good poke.

A wry caricature of any current hot-dog slugger is drawn by an old account of "northern spell," quoted in the sociological journal *Folk Life*, volume one, by Frank Atkinson:

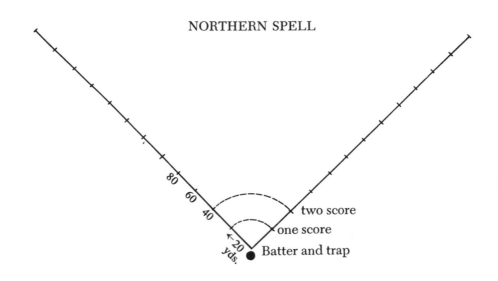

Stripped to his shirt and trousers, the striker toes his peg, and with his pommel [bat] measures the distance from the spell [trap]. . . . He gives a preliminary waggle. . . . The spectators watch him spit on his hands and brace himself for his effort. It is a moment of electric intenseness. . . . the pommel swings through the air with a mighty swish, smiting the "pottie" [ball] with a smart thwack! The next instant, the crowd, with one accord, are pointing and gazing heavenwards; the striker, wildly brandishing his pommel, is prancing down the field after [the ball], fervently urging it to "Get forrard! Get forrard!"

"Northern spell" does not allude to the aurora borealis, or to the charm of fells and moors; it has a revealing linguistic history. The game's real name is *knur and spell*, closer inspection shows. Corruption of the name progressed thus:

> knur and spell
> nur 'n' spell
> nor 'n' spell
> north'n spell

In the accents of north England, "northern" pronounces much like "knur 'n'" anyway. As clues to this, northern spell was also known in Yorkshire as "spell a' knor" and in Newcastle as "spell and ore," both of which are *knur and spell* reversed.

Better clues yet are provided by the words *knur* and *spell* themselves. "Spell" means the game itself and comes from Old Norse *spil*, a play or game. The spell was also called a *trippit*. This was probably its proper name and shows more clearly that northern spell is trapball, particularly since the root word of both English "trap" and "trip" is *tripper*. Further, the game was sometimes explicitly called *trib and knur* in Shropshire, *tribbit* in Yorkshire, and *trippits* in Durham. *Knur* comes from Old Norse, too, and relates to Danish, Dutch, and German words meaning a small knot of wood. That makes knur and cat synonymous, because "cat," in archaic English, means exactly the same thing.

Flatly and definitely, trapball and northern spell are only a slightly mechanized outgrowth of the aboriginal game, cat. Again, a regional name survival confirms. In some Yorkshire villages northern spell is *trippit and coit* (cat), a perfect linking of the three games. Baseball too is a kitten of cat. Or at least a great-great-grandkitten. In one way, Spalding was right when he said baseball derived from cat. But the descent was vastly less direct and more interesting than he said, and cat is scarcely all-American. Cat is indeed Old.

A critical mutation separates cat from its offspring. In original cat the ball often retrogresses to what it once was—a short stick. Usually notched or cut away at one or both ends, or appearing as two cones joined at the tips, the cat tended to be two to six inches long, an inch or so in diameter, and whittled from hardwood. In Sheffield, where the game was called *trip* (another proof of paternity), the cat was a ball with a projecting point. This catches the cat in transition from odd-shaped stick to ball.

A reliable account of cat in the 1700's says, "Tip-cat, or perhaps more properly the game of cat, is a rustic pastime well known in many parts of the kingdom, and is always played with a cudgel or bludgeon resembling that used for trap-ball. Its denomination is derived from a piece of wood called a cat, of about six inches in length and 1½ to 2 inches in diameter, in the shape of a double cone. . . . when the cat is laid upon the ground the player with the cudgel strikes it smartly, and it will rise, with a rotary motion, high enough for him to beat it away as it falls, in the same manner as he would a ball."

Cat was not always so simple, however. Progress toward baseball is very evident in many examples of the developing game. One recipe advised:

. . . four, six or eight holes are made in the ground, at equal dis-
tances, in the form of a circle. At each hole, a player stations himself with a cudgel, and one of the opposite party (who stand out in
the field) throws the cat to the batsman nearest him. When the cat
is struck, the players must change places by running from one hole
to another in succession. Should the cat be driven to a distance,
the players continue running until it is stopped by the out-players.
If the cat, after it is picked up, be thrown between any two of the
holes before the player running from one reach the other, he is out.
But if he do the latter, he claims one toward the game.

Note that the notions of opposing teams, of a circle of holes to be
run, and of throwing the cat between bases already are more like
baseball than stoolball or some rounders. Other improvements of
cat also more closely approximated baseball than some of the intermediate games.

It is pleasing to find old sources that confirm the above reasoning. In *The Sports and Pastimes etc. etc.*, Strutt said of trapball in
1801, ". . . boys and the common herd of rustics who cannot pro-
cure a trap, content themselves with making a round hole in the
ground, and by way of a lever, use the brisket bone of an ox. . . ."
This shows the transition away from a flippable cat toward a primitive trap. Another nineteenth-century authority, Samuel Williams,
says even more explicitly, "The game of CAT, or, as it is generally
called, TIP CAT, takes its name from its being played with a piece of
wood called the cat, shaped like a double cone . . . *supplying the
places of the trap and ball.*"

In *Pilgrim's Progress*, amazingly, John Bunyan has his erring pro-
tagonist, Christian, shamelessly playing cat solitaire in the City of
Destruction:

> The same day as I was in the midst of a game of cat, and having
> struck it one blow from the hole, just as I was about to strike the
> second time a voice did suddenly dart from Heaven into my soul
> which said: "Wilt thou leave thy sins and go to Heaven or have
> thy sins and go to Hell?" At this I was put in an exceeding maze;
> wherefore leaving my cat upon the ground, I looked up to Heaven
> and was as if I had with the eyes of my understanding seen the
> Lord Jesus looking down upon me, as being very hotly displeased
> with me, and as if He did severely threaten me with some grievous
> punishment for these and other ungodly practices.

Evolution from the most primitive forms of cat and trapball toward an antique baseball—which later versions of the two early batting games practically became—followed a course no longer *exactly* discernible. Undoubtedly there were a lot of converging and diverging rivulets. But some additional conclusions are justified.

First, the game's terminology alone identifies it not only as very old but as definitely an import to England from Scandinavia. Second, certain modern features that appeared in cat actually disappeared in successor games until Cartwright and contemporaries rediscovered them. Third, there also seem to have been infusions from foreign games at certain points. The important feature of a pitcher tossing ball or cat to the batter may have been such an introduction. Although it may have been a native stoolball's main influence on baseball, more probably it came from the Continent.

Absolute evidence survives of one transplant, significantly akin to cat native to more northerly England. Three "Catholique" English colleges—Ushaw, Stonyhurst, and St. Edmund's—were impelled by the first, sadly tainted English reformation to relocate in Flanders in 1568. Ironically, after resisting the Protestantization of France and Belgium, the colleges were confiscated in 1793 by a French Revolutionary government made anti-clerical by some of the same excesses that had angered Luther. All returned home to an England now Protestant. The students brought with them a game which had not been known in their part of England, a game called—cat. Ushaw still plays it. A right reverend observer explains:

> The game is played on a wide open space, and the "in" side begins by taking up positions at seven holes in a circular track about 70 to 80 yards in circumference. The striker takes up his position at the hole farthest from the field of play, in which the "out" players arrange themselves so as to gather the ball when it is struck. As soon as the ball has left the striker's stick, the "in" players run as fast as they can around the circle, the object being to make all the progress they can before the ball has been fielded and returned to an "out player whose position is on the track or ring; if he can put the ball into any one of the seven holes before the "in" player has touched that hole, the "in" side is out. . . .

Voilà. Flanders contributes force-outs at any base.

"There are many other ways in which an innings can be terminated, the chief of which is catching the ball either without a bound or on the first bound," the account continues.

Flanders cat did have one highly peculiar quirk. When a team had gotten twice around the ring of bases, plus five holes, the player who was then at the batter's hole tried to score a "cross." After he hit the ball, all the "in" side had to run to the middle of the circle, cross their cat sticks simultaneously, and get back to their respective holes before fielders returned the ball and put it in any hole. The batter was allowed three attempts to score a cross. If he failed, the side was out. The number of crosses decided a game.

"Crosses" are much like the rounders peculiarity of "hitting three for the rounder," but even odder. Present-day base runners wouldn't be at all happy ,about having to carry their bats with them, and pitchers might not entirely enjoy having hastily to relinquish the mound to four bat-wielding runners. Not one Juan Marichal, but four at a time!

A letter written in 1789 to a student at Douay (where Ushaw and St. Edmund's had settled) tells him that a watch is being sent him and cautions, "When you play at ball or katt . . . it will be proper to put it in some safe place. . . ." The writer had been at Douay as student and professor from 1741 to 1769. The way in which he speaks of "katt" shows that the game was an old tradition when he first came to Douay himself.

Instead of the wooden cat, a very hard ball larger than a golf ball but smaller than a tennis ball was employed. Its core was lignum vitae, around which hemp was wrapped. As the ball was wound, it was dipped in hot pitch, and the cover was white sheepskin. Altogether, it was remarkably like baseballs used at various times. In later years white insulating tape sometimes served as the cover, exactly the way American sandlotters recycle an old "league" ball. Like modern baseball bats, the cat sticks were made of supple young ash, which the students worked with hatchet, spokeshave, and rasp.

Cat's traces in French-speaking Europe, once happened upon, are an interesting trail to track. Belgian katt is directly related to four old French games, *balle au camp, balle au chasseur theque* or *tec,* and to *balle empoisonée* (poisoned ball), a variation of *tec.* (No, we will not make anything of the fact that *tec* is nearly cat spelled backward.)

Balle au camp, which may be translated as camp, field or team ball, rather resembles advanced cat. *Theque* seems rarer and is puzzling etymologically. It probably comes from a Frenchified pre- or non-Latin root, Norman or Germanic. *Tec* and *balle empoisonée* have from four to six bases and *batteurs* who strike the ball with *batons*, a "home" base, and a provision for "hitting three for the *ronde*" (rounder!). The batter can twice "refuse" the ball, but if he misses it or refuses a third time, he "goes out." Shades of any after-school pickup game, and to the despair of eighteenth-century French mothers, the rules of *balle empoisonée* also suggest that coats may be used as bases.

Now we have evidence that, just as cat (more properly called *knur and spell*) came from the Nordic countries, the more complicated ancestor of baseball—rounders, *tec* or poisoned ball—came from France. Or rather *through* France, as will be seen. But "poison" ball is not merely a coined neologism for a game so old that its proper name is not French. The notion of a struck runner being "poisoned" rather than merely "out" correctly piques curiosity, not only for a reason that will assume much importance later, but also because of the obvious connection with many simple, ageless children's games. A player who is "out" is often said to be "poison." This is because the games are survivals of ancient fertility rituals in which the opposing sides represent the struggle between dying, decaying "poison" winter and the fresh, renewed life of spring.

There is a quaint twist at the end of all this evidence, gratifying but most ironic.

After this account of the progress of baseball had been diligently worked out, a nineteenth-century statement by Newton Crane, president of the National Base Ball League of Great Britain, an American converted to the English view of the origin of baseball from rounders by confrontation with the evidence during residence there, was found. It confirms several important points and adds an extraordinary footnote. Crane said:

> Baseball, although the American national game, is not only of English origin, but is one of the most ancient of English sports. In a letter of the celebrated Mary Lepel, Lady Hervey, written in 1748, the family of Frederick, Prince of Wales, are described as "diverting themselves with baseball, a play all who are or have been schoolboys are well acquainted with. . . ." The latter was probably what our grandfathers called "bases," and which, by an easy process of development, became rounders, a sport still in-

dulged in by the youth of both sexes in the North and Midlands. The baseball of the last century was one of the numerous games of ball which, descended from the remotest antiquity, furnish a common origin to cricket . . . as well as to baseball.

It has been urged against baseball that it is simply an improved form of rounders. It undoubtedly owes its margin to rounders.°. . .

Here, under the asterisk, Crane inserts this nakedly revealing footnote:

Mr. A. G. Spalding, who has devoted much time to an inquiry into the origins of baseball, inclines to the belief that it is descended from the old French game of *tcheque*, which is still played by French schoolboys. According to Mr. Spalding, *tcheque* was imported into America by the French Huguenots, who settled in the Dutch colony of New Amsterdam. It is certainly true that town-ball, the immediate forerunner of baseball, had its largest following in New York city, and that it had been played there for generations before the Dutch and French customs of New Amsterdam had become lost in the modernized New York.

So Albert Goodwill Spalding knew in 1892 that baseball had come from *tcheque*, a foreign game. He must also have known that *tcheque* was virtually synonymous with rounders. Yet he told almost no one and set up a whole commission to "prove" the opposite!

Although Spalding's anti-English bias, even in what he admitted to Crane, colors his opinion, he could well be right in this titillating idea. Alexander Cartwright's boyhood game may have been *tcheque* in its origins, without the intervening step of rounders.

Der Baseball, die National Begustigung? IT COULD HAVE BEEN.

Ah, the possibilities. Otto von Bismarck throwing out the first ball of the season. Tidy rows of baseballspielers saluting as a brass band plays *"Deutschland uber Alles."* Former Defense Minister Franz Joseph Strauss leaving politics to become Herr Direktor-Kommissioner of the Europischebaseballbund. Nobody boos the umpires, on pain of being barred from the ball parks for life. Georg Herman (Bubi) Rut hits his sixtieth in Amsterdam's Yonker Stadium, *"das Haus das Rut hat gebauern."*

For the second time in two and a half seasons, an infield grounder hits a pebble, and Munich's humiliated head groundskeeper resigns in sloppy disgrace. Rumors that one of Hamburg's teams may move to Nürnberg or Baden-Baden, or perhaps even Stockholm or Zurich, provoke argument in the Bundestag. In the United States, baseball's popularity is restricted mostly to Milwaukee, St. Louis, and Minneapolis.

You vill not laugh. In 1796, one of the earliest writers about German sports, Johann Christoph Friedrich GutsMuths, described in minute detail an extraordinary game that is clearly a "missing link" between baseball and the earliest prehistoric forms of *katt*. While *die Amerikaners* are still chasing *der Indianer* in New England, transitional baseball is so common in Germany that Herr GutsMuths calls it simply *das Deutsche Ballspiel*—the German ball game. In his book *Games for the Exercise and Recreation of Body and Spirit for the Youth and his Educator and all Friends of unguilty Joys of Youth*, GutsMuths says that in the spring "unspoiled" young people forget almost every other amusement.

"The German ball game" was played on a field like the one illustrated, assuming six players on a side.

The rules are interesting, but unless the reader is keen to read GutsMuths's twenty-three pages of instructions in antique 1796 German, he might wish to settle for some excerpts.

Eight, ten, twelve or more could play. Two teams were chosen and a coin tossed to decide who batted first. The pitcher, in a notably odd orientation, stood only two paces from the batter and threw the ball to him very gently in a high arc. It seems almost certain that this represents the original transition away from fungo-style hitting toward modern pitching. The pitcher acted, indeed, as a kind of human "trap."

The batter, after hitting the ball, had to judge whether he could run from the hitting goal to the catching goal. If he could not do so safely, he stayed at the first base and waited for another hitter to move him along. Any number of unsuccessful batters might wait at this base at the same time. Similarly, if the batters hit well enough to run only to the distant second base, they stopped there until another hitter brought them home again.

The "in" side went out whenever the fielding team could do one of these things: (a) catch a fly ball, (b) hit an "in" player while he was running between bases, or (c) bring the ball to the home base before a runner arrived there. Each side tried to keep hitting as long as possible. The number of hits in each inning (*gang*) was added up; the higher total for the game won. However, "little hits, not above the height of an average man, are not counted."

Other quaint rules and advice abounded: "The better the pitcher pitches to suit each individual batter, the better hits will result and consequently the easier it will be for his teammates to catch the ball." "The pitcher must take a good step backward when the ball is hit so that the [bat] does not hit him." "If a disagreement results as to whether a hit was lost, it is played over." "If no hitter is satisfied with a particular pitch, the team can demand that a better pitched

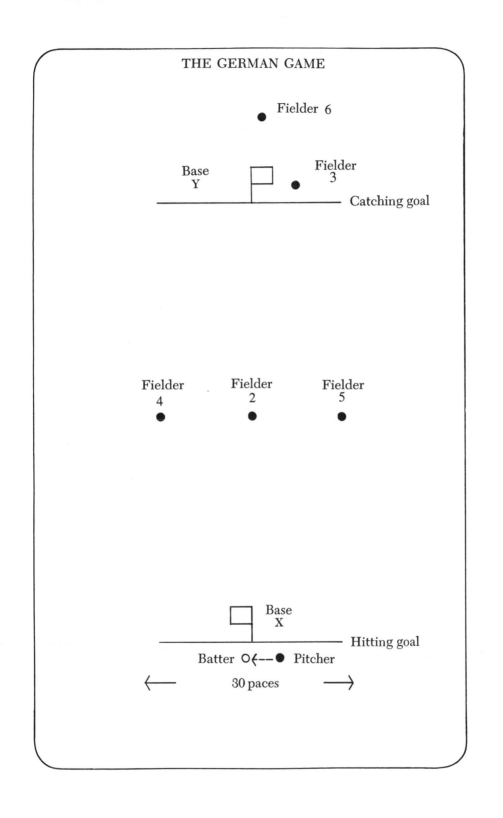

ball be thrown." "If one or the other team wins too often, the rules can be altered so that that team must win double or threefold."

No modern manager would quarrel with some of the rules and admonishment: "The remainder of the serving team must relentlessly watch the ball." "Hitters must have ability to hit the ball full and strong and be able to place the ball where the opposing team is weakest." (Hit it where they ain't, Wilhelm Kuehler.) "The leader of each team must be listened to by his team members."

Some kinks are more significant. Stealing, for one, makes its appearance. Intriguingly, it is connected with a provision again very much like "hitting three for the rounder." Should all other batters be stranded at the bases "due to poor or no hits," the last batter—called the Free-er or Rescuer—is allowed three hits instead of one. If he is a poor hitter, he may simply let the pitched ball fall to the ground while a runner tries to get home "by sneakiness and speed." Since it is essential that this runner arrive safely in order to become the next batter, shrewd old GutsMuths suggests that other runners try to steal second base as a diversion—a double, delayed steal of home— modern baseball strategy!

He concludes dryly, with characteristic German practicality, "Better yet is to make sure the Rescuer is a good hitter." Red Schoendienst couldn't say it better.

The Germanic game apparently spread not only west to Britain but remarkably far east and south, at least in the more primitive form of *barentreiben* or *sauball*. *Barentreiben*, interestingly, combines the German words for "base" and "drive," meaning to hit. *Sau* is a close cognate of sow, our word for the female pig. A relative in Yorkshire was dubbed "piggy." In Poland and Russia, sauball was known as *svinka*, which also means pig. The name probably did describe what the ball was made of. Lest the Russians grow too elated by the potential victory for cultural imperialism in hogging the credit for baseball, let us quickly repeat that *svinka* almost certainly was an import.

An earlier ancestor yet was called *niggelschlagen*, or *triebelspiel*. Of course *triebelspiel* means the "hitting game," and *schlagen* also means "to hit." *Niggel* probably is a dialect form of *negel*, meaning a wooden peg or dowel.

"A rod about 10 centimeters [four inches] in length is laid on a stone so that one end projects," a nineteenth-century German writer describes the game. "When it is struck violently, it flies off and away. In one form, the piece of wood has conical ends," a transition toward the ball.

This, of course, is cat—of a very early whelping. *Niggelschlagen* was a game that women played too; they could catch the wood in their skirts or aprons. Elements of the game are similar to cricket and to the north of England's "northern spell."

In the remotest mountain-locked valleys of Austria there was also played, at least until recently, an ancient game variously called *Titschkerl, Gitschkerl* or *Ritschkerl. Kerl,* as in *churl,* is a dialect word meaning "boy" or "countryman." *Titsch* seems to be merely an onomatopoetic rendition of the sound of the wood bat striking a wood cat. In isolated vales of Switzerland, a quaint variation survives. *Hurmussen,* or *hornigel*—a combination of *niggel* and the German word for hornet—has a wooden cat driven from the top of a slanted block of wood. Instead of catching the hornet, so called for the buzzing sound it makes flying through the air, the fielders must *knock it down* with shovels or wood shingles. Like a sandlotter despairing of catching a long fly, they may knock the hornet down by *throwing* their implements at it.

In a North German version played in the semi-Scandinavian dairy state of Holstein, named *klischspiel* or *klinkholz,* a piece of wood (*holz*) shaped like an old-fashioned hook door latch (*klinke*) was hit from a slanting stick stuck into the ground.

So popular was the game that it crept into such alien territory as Rumania, where it was called *zurka,* Italy (*turca*), and even Asia. This very primitive cat—hitting a small stick with a long one—survived even in England and America after the widespread play of baseball and was called "nipsy."

The wildest geographical leap appears to place this aboriginal cat in the depths of southern India. One dark-skinned Dravidian hill tribe to this day plays *pulat,* "the *pul,* or cat, game," as a religious observance associated with rain and planting. Curiously, two hitting sticks are used—a crooked one and a straight one. Here we may stumble over a living fossil, the transition point from or toward hockeylike games played with crooked sticks. The game is dedicated to two gods, who are brothers sharing a polyandrous wife, an arrangement unlikely to be approved by any American commissioner of baseball. Another game connected with planting is *bombat,* "the stick game." The *bomb* has a niche cut in it to hold a small wooden ball called *mary.* The object is to hit mary with the bomb.

Or at least one object is. Again, if the fielders catch mary in the air, the hitter is dead. If they fail but can roll the ball into a hole in which the bomb bat was originally placed, the hitter is also dead— far too great a similarity to the European games to be mere coincidence. Nor is it coincidence that these surviving games are mostly found in the quietest backwaters and eddies of the Indo-European culture. In mainstream areas, these anachronistic rituals have been swept aside by popular mass sports. But in the crannies of the culture, they are linked to other social archaicisms, evidence suggesting that they date back beyond a millennium.

There the mixed pedigree of baseball might end, with a countryman flipping a short stick out of a hole in the ground with a long stick a thousand or so years ago, only the pagan magic significance remaining to be explained.

But by the strangest sort of chance, some thirty-five years ago, just the right man on just the right kind of mission happened into the one small village on earth that could provide the best clue to baseball's origin and the best evidence of baseball's incredible antiquity. The man was an Italian expert on population problems who happened to be enough of an Americanophile to be familiar with the game of baseball and even its immediate antecedents. The location, bizarrely, was a Berber village in the desert of North Africa. The reason his remarkably correct conclusions, and those of a Danish colleague, are virtually unknown is that they appeared principally in certain small scholarly journals— for example, in Danish-accented English in an Italian demographic journal, *Genus*.

On a 1937 expedition to investigate the disappearing traces of a strange blond strain among the Berber tribes of Libya, Professor Corrado Gini of Rome came upon the lost village of Jadum in the Gebel Nefusa, a hilly high desert plateau in western Tripolitania. To his intense surprise, Professor Gini found the tribesmen playing a game he recognized as rudimentary—or not so rudimentary— baseball. *Ta kurt om el mahag*, the tribesmen called it—"the ball of the mother of the pilgrim."

Jadum was the last stronghold of the blondish tribesmen; Jadum was also the only place in all of North Africa that *om el mahag* was known. What gave Gini chills up the spine was his realization, as an expert in population migrations, that all evidence indicated the game had been introduced by the blonds. But this was spooky, since he knew the light-haired tribesmen to be the remnant of an invasion which took place thousands of years ago—in the Stone Age!

More skin-prickling: He and other scholars believed the blond people to be invaders from northern Europe. The latest invaders had been the Vandals, under King Genseric, who established a Nordic African kingdom in A.D. 429. But Gini considered the Vandals to be too thin a veneer of overlords to leave lasting customs behind. Gini—and other anthropologists—were quite sure that the blond Berbers were northerners who colonized Africa in the *Old* Stone Age—3,000 to 6,000 years before Christ!

"Abundant documentary and other evidence bears witness to their existence and increasing importance as we go back through the centuries up to some thousands of years before our era," Gini says. ". . . this game is now known only to one of the strongholds of their race, where there are good reasons for believing that anthropological and cultural miscegenation has been [minimal]. In this case we would have to admit that the game is a very ancient one, and that in recent times [in America] it has . . . *reacquired* popularity."

Chilling confirmation of Gini's theory comes from a fact the professor did not know. The Stone Age Berber game corresponds almost precisely to GutsMuths' 1796 "German game"—with the eerie qualification that *om el mahag* is almost more modern, more like baseball.

Notice in the diagram on the following page both the similarities to the "German game"—particularly in the relation of the pitcher to the batter—and the progression toward baseball.

A base already explicitly called "home" consists of a rectangle about twelve feet in length, marked by stones or posts reminiscent of early nineteenth-century American baseball. This base combines some features of a "batter's box" and a dugout as well. Some seventy to ninety feet away (observe the exact distance!) is the running base, called *el mahag*.

The players choose two captains, and sides are drawn by chance. Their number varies from three to twenty, but six on a side is usual. (Six is most characteristic of both the "German game" and rounders, as is the range from three to twenty.)

The batting team hits in a regular *batting order*. The batter ("marksman") tries to hit the ball—a leather-covered ball almost ex-

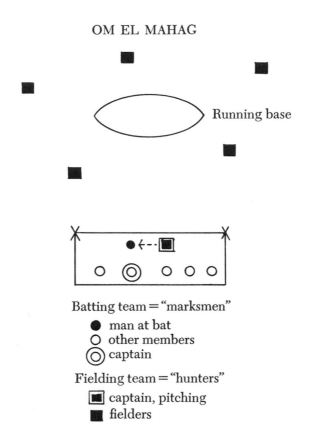

Running base

Batting team = "marksmen"
● man at bat
○ other members
◎ captain

Fielding team = "hunters"
▣ captain, pitching
■ fielders

actly the size of an American baseball—as far as possible, so that other members of his team may have time to run from home to *el mahag* and, if they are able, back home again. The fielding team ("hunters") try to prevent this by catching the ball in the air or by picking it up and throwing it to hit any member of the batting team as he runs between bases. The best hitter, as in the "German game" and rounders, bats last.

The captain gets *three strikes*. His teammates get only two. When a batter misses all his strikes, he hands the bat to the next man and retires to a corner of the home base. He is then said to be "rotten" or to "grow moldy"! (Perhaps better than being "poisoned" or "dead.") If all the batters miss all their strikes, the inning ends and the fielding team goes to bat. "A distinct advantage accrues to the batting team, as the members have much time to stand quiet in the shade, while the men in the field have to stand or run in the sun," Professor Gini says.

The fielders spread themselves and come in or out according to the strengths of the batters, another sophistication. If the ball is caught in the air, of course the inning ends with no ifs or buts. But if a runner is hit, the fielding team must run to the protection of "home" because, just as in the "German game" and one variation of rounders, the batting team may pick up the ball and retaliate by hitting one of the fielders, nullifying the out.

If the ball is hit safely, all members of the batting team who have already batted—including rotten ones—run to the pilgrim's base. And they often *slide* into it, a modernism unmentioned in rounders or the "German game." However, since the tribesmen merely have to avoid being hit by a thrown ball, they may slide sideways or even roll. Each player who has *not* batted who chooses to run to the *mahag* and gets safely back is entitled to an additional strike. The batter must run if this is his last strike, but before that he runs only if he judges his hit to be good enough for a home run. If he miscalculates and can get only to the running base, the next batter hits. But if he is the captain and therefore the last batter, he takes a *three-step lead* from the *mahag* and tries to *steal home*. A fielder tries to hit him by throwing the ball at him. If the captain is not hit, the inning continues, and the batting order begins all over again. As a further sophistication, unknown to rounders, the "German game" and even early baseball, the ball must be hit only within the "fair" rectangular area. Numerous words are used, again, in connection with the game that have no meaning to the tribesmen of today, suggesting that they are very ancient or foreign.

Naked women in other villages play another, shinnylike game called *ta kurt na rrod* among themselves or, clothed, against men. In staid Jadum, this game is played only by men and never naked. But the men do remove their white togalike outer garments to participate in *om el mahag*, almost the only time they take them off. The Berber games do also seem to have a somewhat disguised association with fertility of the crops, with rain and with ritual battles. They are undoubtedly old rites of magic, perhaps those practiced by blond men in faraway Scandinavia thousands of years ago, along the cold *viks* and fjords.

It was from Scandinavia that further confirmation of Gini's hypothesis came. Per Maigaard, a scholar in the history of gymnastics in Copenhagen, became highly excited when Gini happened to deliver his paper on *om el mahag* in that city, for he recognized it as none other than the ancient Nordic game of longball. Longball is so uncannily similar to *om el mahag,* despite the gulf of thousands of years and thousands of miles, that it is simply unnecessary to repeat the description. The few discrepancies tend to be baseball-like— e.g., three strikes for all batters. In the Danish root game, the "out" players were even called "rotten." The "in," "safe" players were explicitly called "fresh," a clue that the game is indeed ritual battle between dying winter and burgeoning spring, particularly since it was definitely associated with Easter and springtime festivals. Some of the variations, in certain rural districts and offshore islands, are fascinating. In one Swedish and Finnish version, and in another from the Danish island of Anholt, there are *two* running goals. This mutation (or ancient survival!) also reached Poland. One Norwegian version even has foul lines at a 90-degree angle, although it has only one running base:

LONGBALL

Basic longball:

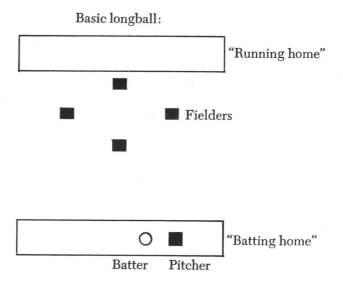

"Running home"

Fielders

"Batting home"

Batter   Pitcher

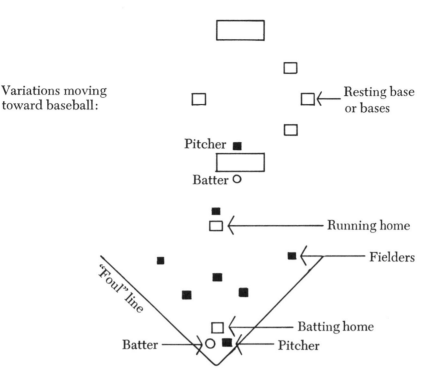

Variations moving toward baseball:

Resting base or bases

Pitcher

Batter

Running home

Fielders

"Foul" line

Batting home

Batter — Pitcher

Perhaps the most remarkable of all the Nordic games is one, of uncertain age, that almost exactly corresponds to the Massachusetts game of baseball, with the exception that the pitcher stands right next to the batter as in longball and *om el mahag*. But there are four running bases, with the batter's base along one side, and the arrangement of fielders is much the same:

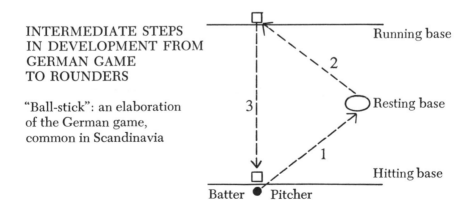

INTERMEDIATE STEPS
IN DEVELOPMENT FROM
GERMAN GAME
TO ROUNDERS

"Ball-stick": an elaboration of the German game, common in Scandinavia

Running base

Resting base

Hitting base

Batter Pitcher

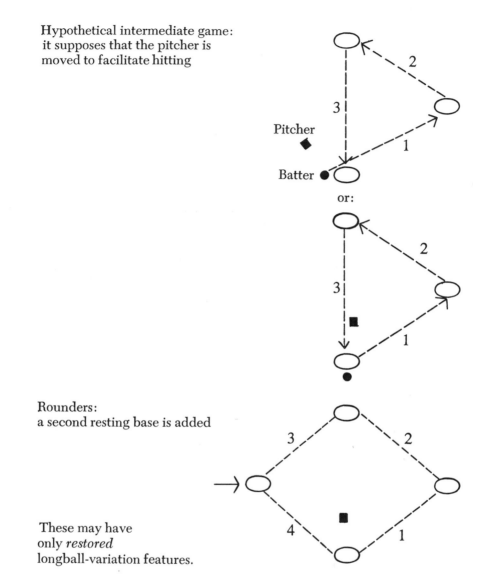

Hypothetical intermediate game:
it supposes that the pitcher is
moved to facilitate hitting

Pitcher

Batter

or:

Rounders:
a second resting base is added

These may have
only *restored*
longball-variation features.

Every bit of anthropological evidence says that these games go
back to the uttermost antiquity, back to the first fertility rites hun-
grily welcoming the late northern spring. Batting games, at least
cat, appear in the old sagas, as Maigaard suggested. In remote out-
posts of Norse invasion, where very old social patterns have been
fossilized in custom, the links are particularly strong. The Berbers

call the runner's base "mother"; some Slavs carried this further and called the captain of the fielding team "mother," even when male. (The game was probably carried to the Slavs by Gothic invasions, just as the Vandals brought it to France and the Angles to England.) Eugen Piasecki, pre-eminent scholar of Slavic games, feels sure that the original contests were between a "father's" side—the batters—and a "mother's" side—the catchers. Certain symbolisms have undoubtedly been apparent throughout, even to the non-Freudian.

Among the Lapps and on the Estonian island of Runo, settled by Swedes, women played a related game, and connections with primitive springtime rites such as egg-carrying were explicit. The ball also undoubtedly represented seed. The way in which it must be placed in holes in the ground in certain primitive games of baseball supports this. To the Berbers, and possibly also the original Vandals, it also represented rain falling from the sky, which must be caught in the fields to support life in a desert country.

The very word *ball* is one of the oldest, strongest and strangest in cultural history. It survives almost unchanged from the old Germanic *ballu*, whose *u* suffix shows to linguists that it is of enormous age. Finnish and Lappish also retain ancient *pallo*, their phonetic equivalent of *ballu*, as the word for "ball." Even in the Romance languages, including Italian itself, *balla* or *palla* supplanted a perfectly good, long-established, and similar Latin word, *pila*. This indicates the great importance the conquering Lombards and other northerners placed on the ball ritual.

Ball is so old and basic that it originally seems to have meant almost any globular clump of anything. It was later refined to mean anything roundish. A *bale* of hay, a *bowl* of porridge or the *bole* of a tree all come from *ball*. *Bullet* and *bubble* are even related. *Ballots* originally were white or black balls. To "blackball" someone survives as an expression.

And have you ever wondered why a dance should be called a "ball" or a "ballet" and a song a "ballad" ? This will drive ballet-omanes mad, but it is true: Ballet derives from some of the same early ball games we have been discussing. A ball would be thrown about, gracefully, in pagan fertility rites. Only thereafter did the ball playing become a dance. Eventually music was added and singing. At last the ball itself disappeared. But even now German girls toss a ball about, to musical accompaniment, as part of an old dance. And you thought calling baseball a "ballet" was a phony affectation?

Some historians are convinced that the first "ball" used in play was the skull of a dead enemy chieftain. (We still say a hairless man is "bald.") That would account for the strange burst of exhilaration one feels from the sharp *tock* of hitting a ball really squarely with a bat (or racquet or golf club). It would account for the oddly passionate eagerness of players to come to bat. The Norse warriors, after all, called their war clubs "battes" and the word is related to "beat."

More likely, the ball at most symbolically represents an enemy. Or it may merely be an ultimately concentrated focus of attention on which the player exerts his will through its extension, the bat. More mystically, the sphere has always exerted a deep hold on the human imagination. The sun and moon are spheres, as are many eggs, fruits, and seeds. Many primitive peoples conceived of the earth and the universe as spheres and sensed that human beings begin from a single spherical cell.

Almost every basic term connected with baseball can likewise be linked to Old Norse (*base* itself arriving through *baers*). But there is one interesting exception, and we might conclude by letting the *cat* out of the bag. Cat, in the sense of tipcat, is *not* one of the many transferences from the animal by the same name, whatever the Oxford English Dictionary may guess to the contrary.

Cat was originally *catapult*, thus coming from the Greek words meaning "away" or "up" and "to beat, strike or knock." *Pult* survived into Old English as a word related to *pelt* (as in pelting rain) but became obsolete around 1400. English children were thus left with a name that meant nothing to them. They shortened it to *cat*, which did mean something, however nonsensical. Children have never been much bothered by whimsical nonsense. They rather enjoy it.

ALEXANDER CARTWRIGHT, YOU MIGHT SAY, VANDALIZED THE SIMPLE, childish game then known as town ball or baseball. He introduced adultness and complexity to a directionless kiddie pastime, all unaware that he was actually reintroducing some refinements originated by crude Norse forefathers in the Stone Age. Cartwright's busy Victorian Gothic mind reproduced certain Gothic details from long before the time of Christ.

But Cartwright's nineteenth-century engineering also, of course, produced more improvements than had ever been known or thought of. They made baseball a game so much different, so much more rational and interesting, that Cartwright may properly be called the *inventor* of baseball, in the sense that the Wright brothers (rather than Leonardo da Vinci) invented the airplane and Thomas Edison (not Benjamin Franklin) invented the electric light.

It was the new sport's cool ratiocination, as well as its physical exhilarations, that won Alick's friends in New York. They loved the way it gave logical reason to stretch and run to the utmost, the way that it justified boyish gamboling over green fields with good nineteenth-century American purposefulness. Most of Cartwright's friends were in businesses such as insurance or banking in Wall Street, but they took real delight in these professions, like small

boys playing Bank or Store or Yankee Trader. Dull, bloodless pe-
destrianism came to these occupations only later, when their "players" became digits in colorless corporations, not friendships in part-
nerships composed of expressive faces and pungent personalities.
Just as they really enjoyed the orderly minuet of formal society, the
measured dignity of their personal relationships, they enjoyed baseball's manly ballet.

At first, Alick and a friend or two would tour the blue flagstoned
sidewalks of Wall Street any particularly pleasant morning, muster-
ing enough players to make a game. Laughing and cajoling, they
would convince the young lawyers and merchants that they were
surely making enough money to satisfy any two men untainted by
avarice and that they were in parlous peril of reaching their matu-
rity wealthy but unhealthy. "Men of sedentary habits require recreation," Cartwright would boom. Very soon the only problem was
deciding who of the throng would get to play. Platoons of young
men were turning out, cheering and gently ragging each other:
"That was a real daisy clipper. . . . I believe he was stroking his
whiskers as that one went by. . . . Oh, my stars, did he compress
the wind that time!"

When the young men ebulliently cavorting on the Parade
Ground meadow beside the old pond became almost excessively
eager and numerous, in the bright, dry September of 1845, orderly
minded Alick characteristically proposed that they establish an organized club. The other ball players readily and happily agreed. On
September 23, they did as Cartwright suggested. The Knickerbocker Base Ball Club, as Alick named it, was the first organized
team playing the modern game. Fortunately, it left no dearth of
mementoes, drawing up a formal constitution and bylaws as well as
writing down Cartwright's rules for posterity. This crowd of young
apprentice capitalists knocking off work early to jolly together on
the Third Avenue stage line to the playing field numbered a good
forty or more. Dozens of them industriously scampered about in
practice. Club officers had arbitrarily to choose several teams to play
in two or more games—perhaps by tossing up a bat in the present
manner, a tradition which is very old.

What was the original Knickerbocker like and how did he live?

All of the Knicks were jovial gentlemen at home in a congenially
genteel setting, the very civilized city of New York. Very civilized.
The unnamed Wall Street lawyer of Herman Melville's short story

"Bartleby the Scrivener" (placed in New York during the period) was so kindhearted and moral, so undone by a clerk who perfectly politely declined to work, that he could not fire the fellow and had to move his offices to escape the ungentlemanly man. He might have been a Knickerbocker.

Alick himself earned a good living as teller in the Corinthian-columned Union Bank, a little dollhouse of a bank by today's standards but an impressive institution in 1845. His superior there, cashier Daniel Ebbets, coincidentally was the father of Charles Hercules Ebbets, who became owner of the Brooklyn Trolleydodgers half a century later and laid out Ebbets Field. (Flatbush, of course, was then a charming, leafy suburban village languid as the motion of its ladies' parasols and billowing yards of skirt.) Lest the wounds of modern Flatbushers be reopened and inflamed, let it be said that there is no record that Charles Ebbets played with the first Manhattan team. However, an E. A. Ebbets, probably his brother, was playing with the Knickerbockers as early as 1846. When Alexander Cartwright left New York three years later this Ebbets vanished at the same time and on the same ship as Alexander's brother, Alfred Cartwright. As some compensation for the fact that the Dodgers, presently known in Brooklyn as the Freeway Fenderbenders, went west to California to dodge Diesel trucks, they were evidently indirectly created by Cartwright himself, for Alick must have given young Ebbets the baseball bug.

By 1845 Alick was prospering. He had already been married for three years to comely Eliza Ann Gerrits Van Wie, of an old Dutch family from Albany (whose population was 2,500 or so). He lived at 76 Eighth Street, a plush address. If mentioned at all in books on baseball (you can read most every one ever written and glean only a few sentences), Cartwright is variously described not as a bank teller but as an engineer, a surveyor, a draftsman, or a New York City fireman. Actually, he was not any of these—except, extracurricularly, a *volunteer* fireman. Cartwright's *father* was a marine surveyor (and former sea captain). Many of Alexander's best friends sold fire insurance, so it was logical for them to be volunteer firemen, besides being good fun and adventure and a civic obligation expected of young gentlemen.

As an English visitor remarked, "The firemen are a body of volunteers, between 300 and 400. They are viewed by their fellow citizens as a class of respectable men and as occupying a station somewhat similar to our local cavalry. I conceive the half-smoked cigars, so plentifully disseminated in every direction by men and boys of all ages, conditions and colours, may be one reason for the many fires." In fact, the great fire of 1845 in mid-July incinerated 214 of the little business buildings in the Wall Street area. (But not while Cartwright and his friends were playing baseball up in rural districts. They may be absolved from blame, for the blaze broke out at 3:00 A.M.) It bankrupted Merchant Marine, the insurance company for which Cartwright's father worked as inspector. And it burned the Union Bank, impelling Alick into the bookselling business.

The City Hall bell signaled smaller conflagrations with great frequency. At night a red lantern suspended from a hole in the cupola would point the direction of the fire, and the firemen would sometimes turn out for an alarm in full evening dress. The volunteers competed extravagantly in plating and paneling their engines with silver and walnut and in furnishing their firehouses with velvet carpeting and chandeliers. So ardent were they in their zeal to arrive at fires ahead of other companies that even the married men would take turns sleeping overnight at the clublike firehouses. Sometimes they would carry their clothes in their hands and dress at the fire. If the fire was disappointingly small, they would retire to a nearby tavern to justify the excursion. Much of Alexander Jr.'s career in New York must remain mysterious, for when he left he was too young a man to have the impression on his native city that he later made elsewhere. But assiduous digging does lend support to the family tradition that Alick was a volunteer fireman. Many of the Knickerbockers were firemen, and their careers as fire-fighting volunteers are among the most documentable facets of their lives in New York.

Benjamin Cartwright, Alick's brother, in 1845 helped reorganize the famed old Oceana Hose Company No. 36. In fact, Benjamin, who was among the most indefatigable of the Oceana fraternity in their typically innumerable Firemen's Balls, award presentations, dinners, parades, and contests, later became one of New York's first Fire Commissioners. A "distinguished merchant," he also became Cashier of the City Bank (a predecessor of the modern First National City)—which meant that he was a high-ranking officer of New York's most prestigious banking institution. One reference even makes him "the late president of the City Bank," but that may be a post-mortem exaggeration. This must be the Benjamin who was

Alick's brother, for when Alfred (Alick's other brother) started out in business, he began in Benjamin Cartwright's profession of accountancy and lived in Benjamin's house at 126 Henry Street.

Careful research shows that several of the Ocean Hose wielders were Knickerbockers. James Whyte Davis, the Wall Street broker, was a member, and William A. Woodhull and Alonzo Slote were particularly zealous fire-fighters in Company No. 36. Woodhull, a "merchant in Front Street," went on to be president of the New York Fire Department from 1850 to 1860. Slote was foreman of the hose company, which is somewhat fitting since he was a partner in the clothing house of Tredwell, Jarman & Slote. Woodhull and Slote were the talk of the New York newspapers after one bad fire on Division Street, when they braved smoke and flames to rescue seven persons from certain asphyxiation. Most of the Oceana members were merchants or clerks. As might be expected of Knickerbockers and Cartwright associates, the company "took, and for many years maintained, a front rank for respectability and efficiency." Its competitions to reach a fire first "were always conducted in good spirit, and the company never had a collision with any other." One night they responded to no fewer than thirteen alarms. The Oceana company fell into just one lapse from perfect taste and decorum. As their first elected secretary they chose William Tweed—the future Boss Tweed of Tammany Hall. Within a few months the members detected their error of discernment and asked Mr. Tweed to resign.

Many other Knickerbockers can be linked to other volunteer fire companies. Walter Avery was a member of Hose No. 1, which, characteristically of these men, also "used to pride itself on its respectability." L. J. Belloni, Jr., a trustee of the Exempt Firemen's Benevolent Fund, served in Engine Company No. 12 with a William Cartwright. Other Knickerbocker names—Curry, Keeler, Lee, Talman, Taylor, Vredenburgh—occur frequently in the fragmentary surviving records. The last, Vredenburgh, besides being scarcely common enough to be coincidence in a small city, has special significance. Johannes Vredenburgh and John Vredenburgh, ancestors of the Alfred Vredenburgh who played baseball with the Knickerbockers, were among the very first thirty-five firemen selected by the Corporation of New York in 1738.

Every company had its pack of "runners," boys and young men who looked upon the exploits of their manly elders with awe, who hung about the firehouse door in hopes that they might be favored

with some errand or chore to perform and who raced after the firemen at each alarm. Alick had been one of them. At fifteen he nearly
caught pneumonia while gawking at the fire of 1835. The original
Oceana firehouse stood at Henry and Catharine streets in 1839, not
far from early Cartwright residences. Most significantly, there was a
Knickerbocker Engine Company No. 12 even handier. Organized
before 1783, the Knickerbocker was located at Pearl and Cherry
streets, in the very center of Franklin Square. In 1832 the Knickerbocker moved three short blocks up Frankfort Street to Rose, where
it abode briefly before settling on William Street near Duane. Cartwright & Grant, the shipping concern in which Alick's father was a
partner, was located at 5 Frankfort Street, only a short distance
away from the firehouse at all these situations and only a few doors
in Alick's younger years. Alick stuck to the glamorous firemen like a
cockleburr.

As good fortune would have it, E. P. Chrystie, an artist who recreated numerous early New York scenes, made an extraordinarily
fine charcoal drawing of this very scene for *As You Pass By*, a history of the city's fire-fighters by Kenneth Dunshee. Although the
firehouse is not identified as the Knickerbocker's, it surely is. Chrystie's drawing catches the exact flavor of this historic area at about
the time. Bonneted little girls operate the long-handled wooden
water pump outside the firehouse while a piglet waits hopefully for
a drink. Two plug-hatted idlers converse leaning on an ornate
street lamp, shouting to be heard as a one-horse, two-wheeled dray
clatters over the paving stones. A group of firemen take their ease
in the shade of the firehouse, leaning comfortably against its clap-
boards. Three doors away is the rather Dutch-style gambrel-roofed
mansion of John Hancock, sunk to the estate of a chair-making shop
run by the father of Boss Tweed. Just beyond is the enormous bal-
ustraded three-story mansion which was George Washington's official residence while President and later the home of DeWitt Clinton.

Apparently Alick Cartwright joined the Knickerbocker Engine
Company and, shortly after it disbanded in 1843, sentimentally
named his new baseball club for it. Possibly young Cartwright first
took note of the Sunfish Pond meadows below Murray Hill as a
suitable playfield when the company used the pond as a water supply in fighting the big House of Refuge fire in 1838, an occasion on
which the "Nicks" playfully sucked up mud and washed rival En-

gine 33 with it. And the Engine Company No. 12 to which the Knickerbocker named Belloni and William Cartwright both belonged may well be the successor company, reorganized in 1847 to fight fires in the vicinity of Lexington and 50th Street, three-fourths of a mile above the playing ground on the old Post Road. Alexander Cartwright may have joined in this reorganization. More likely he accompanied his friends and his brother Benjamin to the Oceana Hose Company.

If the Knickerbocker Base Ball Club was in fact named for, and formed by members of, the old Knickerbocker Engine Company, it was the first precedent for a common practice. The New York Mutuals, for one famous example, were named for the Mutual Hook and Ladder Company and were organized in that company's firehouse. Many another team of Wide-Awakes or Alerts sprang from a fire company of the same cognomen, and logically so. The volunteers were really the first organized teams and their competitions among the first organized team contests. They were so competitive (to the point of fist fights) that the extension of rivalry to the ball field was natural.

The volunteers were considered to cut a dashing figure indeed as they galloped along pulling their fearsomely polished, beribboned, beflagged, streamered, garlanded hand-pumped engine, blowing horns and ringing bells as they ran. Clad in black pantaloons, red shirt and heavy boots, Alick Cartwright was particularly impressive. He was a very big man by 1845 standards. Standing 6′ 2″ and weighing 210 pounds, he possessed handsome large but finely drawn features, intense, quizzical dark eyes and thick dark hair, and was vigorously athletic.

He inhabited an equally handsome, vigorous city, on whose exuberant growth the fires of 1835 and 1845 hardly made an impression. Manhattan Island retained the unique natural beauty of its exuberantly beautiful setting, today so obscured by the grid of colossal corporate crypts and mausoleums that is New York—the ultimate graveyard, the ultimate memorial monument to gruesome taste and misdirected frenetic energy. Where now runs the human sewer of Forty-second Street, just east of Times Square, lay a limpid little pond that fed Old Wreck Kill, at precisely the point now dominated by a pornographic movie house. The pure headwaters of the kill rose in a grottoed spring, now the east edge of Seventh Avenue between 45th and 46th streets, in the middle of Times Square.

New York then, as now, could be smelled miles out to sea (as Robert Boyle points out in his admirable book *The Hudson River*). But instead of the odor of refineries, incinerators and raw sewage, it exuded a heavy incense of blossoming trees. Both Giovanni Verrazano and Henry Hudson were struck by the perfumed air before ever they discovered the harbor. New Amsterdam diarist Jasper Danckaerts tells of sometimes encountering such a sweet smell in walking through Manhattan's glades that he stood transfixed, astonished. "The air in the New-Netherlands is so dry, sweet and healthy, that we could not wish it different," said Adriaen Van der Donck. "In purity, agreeableness and fineness, it would be folly to seek for an example of it in any other country." (In the year 1970, the New York *Times* noted, there was no day on which air quality was as much as "acceptable.") "Our attention is taken prisoner by the beauty of the landscape around us," Van der Donck continued almost disbelievingly. "Here the painter can find rare and beautiful subjects . . . here the huntsman is animated when he views the enchanting prospects presented to the eyes: on the hills, at the brooks and in the valleys, where the game abounds and where the deer are feeding, or gamboling, or resting in the shade in full view." He confessed, "I am incompetent to describe the beauties, the grand and sublime works, wherewith Providence has diversified this land."

Morning stars, bellflowers, sunflowers and red and yellow and mountain lilies overran the fields, turning them riotous in conflicting color. Wild plums and grapes and hazelnuts hung everywhere, pleading to be picked. Wild grasses grew as high as a man's waist and cultivated rye and barley above a man's head. The first settlers never fertilized their land. Even unfertilized, it was too rich for peas, which grew so rank that they fell of their own weight and rotted on the ground. An early settler, Jacob Steendam, was moved to write:

> This is the land with milk and honey flowing
> With healing herbs like thistles freely growing
> The place where buds of Aaron's rod are blowing
> O, this is Eden!

Nicolaes Van Wassenaer found "all sorts of fruits in great profusion" and said, "Birds also fill the woods so that men can scarce go through them for the whistling, the noise and the chattering. Whoever is not lazy can catch them with little difficulty." (Ducks and geese still filled the sky and water in the 1840's. Indeed, there was hunting from the Battery as late as the 1870's.) "The people who reside near the water are frequently disturbed in their rest at night by the noise of the water fowl," complained Van der Donck, "particularly by the swans, which in their season are so plenty that the bays and shores where they resort appear as if dressed in white drapery."

Besides heath hens, grouse, wild turkey and squabs "so numerous that they shut out the sunshine," there were elk, bear, mink, otter, muskrats, raccoons, tens of thousands of beaver, "incredibly numerous deer as fat as any Holland cow," some moose, and "multitudes of wolves." Wolves were still seen in middle Manhattan when Cartwright was a boy. The last mountain lion in the immediate environs of New York was shot in the Palisades (which then rose awesomely straight out of the Hudson instead of from a jumble of industrial corruption on filled land) a good five years after he left the city. Whales, porpoises and seals could still be seen playing in the harbor in Cartwright's time. Lobsters, clams, oysters, and mussels abounded. Gowanus oysters from the East River were up to a foot in diameter. Hundreds of square miles of oyster beds surrounded New York, more than half the world's supply. The beds between Ellis and Bedloe's islands and Communepa and Jersey City were particularly rich. "There are some persons who imagine that the animals of the country will be destroyed in time," Van der Donck said, "but this is an unnecessary anxiety." A British visitor of 1842, although often tart-tongued, rhapsodized about New York:

Here the atmosphere, like that of Italy, is extremely clear. It imparts a lustre to the surrounding landscape and clothes the scenery with an appearance of inconceivable brilliancy. We seemed as if gliding over a sea of fluid gold. In the distance, guarded by unnumbered vessels stood the city, occupying a distinguished station on the banks at the confluence of two of the finest rivers of the world. The whole prospect, enriched by a pleasing variety of wood and water and viewed through the bright medium of this clear atmosphere, combined to form a scene most enchantingly beautiful —too grand, indeed, for the most sanguine imagination to conceive.

Birds, such as for beauty I never saw at large, enliven the scenery with bright plumage. Choice flowers are thick and numberless as autumnal leaves that strew the brooks [and] myriads of butterflies, not the small pale coloured things of northern Europe, but creatures with wings of uncommon size and beauty. . . .

Human handiwork excited scarcely less appreciation:

This city of New York certainly is a noble place. The air of new-ness pervading the whole city never fails to arrest the attention of the stranger. . . . Indeed, the whole of the buildings present so clean an exterior that they seem as if just finished. The number of superb houses is very great. . . . Broadway is the fashionable lounge for all the belles and beaux of the city; its commodious *pave*, completely covered with neat awnings, forms as agreeable a promenade as is to be found, perhaps, in any city in the world. Many a transatlantic poet has endeavored to immortalize this noble walk and its glittering pedestrians.

This visitor, identified solely as "Mrs. Felton," did, however, note that "musquitoes" were common. The lotion prescribed locally was an "ablution in rum."

Even John Adams, quintessential New Englander, exclaimed upon the natural charms of New York each time he saw it, although he was no nature nut, and admitted to his diary, "The Streets of this Town are vastly more regular and elegant than those in Boston, and the Houses are more grand as well as neat." When he took the ferry ride across the river to Jersey City, he wrote simply and elo-quently, "This whole colony of N. Jersey is a Champagne."

The finest, snuggest natural harbor in the world, studded with green islands and castlelike forts, backdropped to the west by cliffs of fluted rock, with opulent mansions and gracious formal grounds to the fore—that was New York. Clipper ships to all the world, hundreds of packets plying the coastal trade, barks, brigantines, schooners, and sloops beyond counting glided in and out of slips, fragile and beautiful. Extravagantly painted and lacquered side-wheeler steamships and ferries, their high reciprocating beams pumping and their wrought-iron-ornamented stacks breathing woodsmoke, coexisted with small skiffs in which flat-hatted men fished for shad with hand-dipped nets. The spars and yards of ship-ping engraved the island like a wintry forest. In a high wind, the rigging sang in aeolian chords, like great rude harps.

A cheerful Dickensian jumble of highly individualistic shops, of little victualers and grog shops, of beer gardens and conversation-rich coffeehouses, of baker's carts selling warm new bread and street-corner oyster stands, of theaters and unabashedly patriotic Fourth-of-July celebrations—that was New York. It had much of the optimistic bustle of the best of London and much of its rich panoply of unhomogenized character in the open, fresh faces of its people, but little of London's poverty and disease. The almost medieval attire of the older Dutch men and women, and the plain severity of the Quaker and Methodist costumes, contrasted piquantly with the courting fineries of the dandies and damsels who promenaded daily at the Park and the Battery.

Very real bluebirds sang in the white blossoms of massive chestnut trees. The offices of the merchants were redolent with spices from India and sugars from the Indies and tea from China and oranges from Spain. Into them tromped bluff down-East sea captains of the Cartwrights' hue with presents of coral and shells, exotic plumed birds and strange-tanged fruit, for their wives and children. A young man might drive his lady up the Post Road to DeVoor's mill to see, three miles below beyond sweet grassy meadows and a wilderness of woodland, the city bask under its spires—crossing on the way no fewer than three Kissing Bridges, "where it is a part of the etiquette to salute the lady who has put herself under your protection."

Sweet air morning and evening swept in from the green meadows and mountains of New Jersey and salt air from the sea. Woodsmoke did not shut out the stars, pressing down large and intense, nor much dilute the sight of the silver moon riding silver clouds across the black sky. Even the poorer residential districts exuded a Currier and Ives look.

If wagon wheels clattered too loudly on paving stones, there was absolute stillness in the farmlands an easy walk from any part of town. If the water from the well or neighborhood wooden-handled pump tasted insufficiently fresh, one could ride the horsecar to drink direct from a tumbling brook, splashing down over leaf-strewn granite boulders. If the wandering pigs which still attended to much of the city's garbage disposal lacked allure, one could walk north and see deer and foxes.

On snowy days, the jungle of sleigh bells filled the cold air. "A Visit from St. Nicholas" may be the best testimonial to old New York's rural tranquility and beauty. The beloved children's poem was inspired by New York's greeting-card perfection on the snowy

Christmas Eve of 1824. Driving back to his farm, "Chelsea," with a sleighful of presents for his children, Clement Moore was a deeply content man. The contagious happiness of New Yorkers joyfully celebrating Jesus' birth, the good-natured greetings of the shopkeepers, the thought of his excited children all combined with the moonlit grandeur of the countryside along the old Bloomingdale Road (now Broadway). Mr. Moore began to compose a little poem for his family: "Twas the night before Christmas, and all through the house . . ."

By the time Alick Cartwright had grown up New York was a city of gaslit fountains, flickering light playing over cascading Croton water. It was a city of open-air markets selling a cornucopia of cheap fresh produce, of public gardens with strolling bands, of handsome polished carriages, of great elms and broad sycamores, of silken ladies strolling with parasols, meeting solid beaver-hatted husbands and sauntering home to blocks of genteel townhouses with sculpted freestone outlining their fronts and handsome lush gardens to their rear. It was a Currier and Ives city of water-color skies, of cleanly carpentered frame houses and warm red brick etched with white lime mortar, of ornate street lanterns and chimney pots, and oaken doors with glass lights and brass knockers. Camphor and tallow lamplight from silk-upholstered drawing rooms and book-lined studies, open to the view of passers-by, threw a pattern of small-paned shuttered windows on clean snow or flowering shrubs. Stars embellished the sky on summer nights.

Life of a summer midday, described by a contemporary European visitor, reveals tranquility cruelly at contrast with the heat- and stench-crazed summer city of today:

> The city is preferable as a place of residence during the summer. Neat awnings shelter the whole of the sidewalks. During the hottest part of the day, little is done by the gentlemen besides loitering about, reading the newspapers and drinking iced punch, and other mysterious compounds; while the ladies, reclining on the sofas, fan themselves, drink lemonade, and doze. Business transactions of all kinds occupy the early hours of the morning, then the ice carts perambulate the city, and provisions for the day are procured. After mid-day the streets are deserted; the shopkeeper closes his doors and slumbers behind the counter; a solemn stillness reigns.

In the Forties, New York urban existence seemed tolerably civilized in other ways:

> In consequence of the high price of labor of every kind, and the comparative ease with which the essentials of life may be obtained, the very lowest of the people are well clad, and take a laudable pride in appearing clean and smart after the toil of the day is over. The theatre is the grand point of attraction for numbers; others assemble in reading rooms, or attend lectures, or religious meetings; taverns and spirit stores have their share of frequenters; while some few congregate to read and hear the wisdom of Thomas Paine. . . . Men converse tirelessly on the Revolutionary war.
>
> None of those ostensible instances of deep moral degradation, the wretched offspring of infamy and want, that force themselves upon our notice in our densely populated cities, are to be met here. In fact, during the whole period of my residence in the United States, I never saw the face of a single beggar. There are no poor's rates, and the few whom misfortune has rendered proper objects for eleemosynary aid, find refuge in alms-houses supported by voluntary contributions.

New Yorkers then were friendly ("The alacrity with which the natives combine to assist a widow, a poor neighbor or a stranger deserves to be recorded. . . .") and honest ("To cheat 'Uncle Sam,' as they term their government, is with them a crime paramount!" the European visitor said in surprise. "And they never fail to treat those foreigners with ineffable contempt, who are so perfidious as to defraud their own governments.") and polite. "We observed, as one woman after another got out," said another European, "that any man sitting near the door would jump down to hand her out, and if it was raining, would hold an umbrella over her, frequently offering to escort her to a shop. . . ."

Nor did farmers in the rural regions of upper Manhattan, Kings and Queens counties and Hudson County in New Jersey go unenvied. "The farmer here spins his own wool and flax and generally weaves his own cloth; he mends his own farming implements, consumes the produce of his own land, and barters the remainder for other necessaries. As he has neither rent, tithes nor taxes to pay, it is no wonder that his industry enables him to live in a *state of absolute profusion.*"

"Dr. Morse's lightning telegraph" had just been strung to Washington, and telegraph wires were appearing on Broadway, but communication with Sandy Hook and the Jersey shore still consisted of a tall semaphore from which were hung coded signals. There were so many oyster houses, oyster saloons and oyster stands that New Yorkers were estimated to gulp down £3,500 worth of fresh mollusks per day. Some 5,000 taverns, 2,000 of them German *bierstuben* (one of them in historic Fraunces Tavern), were operating, and Phineas Barnum's museum was attracting hundreds of curiosity-seekers per day.

Transactions still being made in "York money," fare on the omnipresent omnibuses was half a shilling, 6¼¢—"half a bit." It was paid to the driver through a hole in the roof. Gentlemen often did have to suffer the inconvenience of letting ladies sit upon their laps.

One hundred companies of militia, some nattily uniformed and others in comically unmilitary attire, drilled on parade grounds such as Washington Square (which had been formed by enlargement of an old potters' field, the bones remaining to this hour). They boasted lighthearted names like The Washington Market Chowder Guard, the Bony Fusileers, the Peanut Guard, the Mustache Fusileers, and Sweet's Epicurean Guard from the still existing restaurant of the same name. (The younger Sweet played occasionally with the Knickerbockers.) These units were fiercely democratic, many of their officers being common laborers and many privates substantial businessmen. Many volunteer firemen doubled as militiamen, Cartwright among them.

New York's ladies scorned, from top to bottom and from inside out, any but this year's Paris fashions and were so brightly and prodigiously fitted out with silks and satins and ribbons that European men sometimes mistook them for high-toned *nymphs du pave*, causing great embarrassment all around. "I never saw such luxury and extravagance, such tearing polkas, such stupendous suppers and fine clothes," reported William Makepeace Thackeray. "I watched one young lady at 4 balls in as many dresses, and each dress of the most stunning description." A gown required more than 100 yards of fine fabric. Embroidery brocaded with gold half an inch thick was no rarity.

The flood tide of population and obsessive activity that would eventually drown pretty little old New York was clearly beginning to rise by the late 1840's. In a few years young newspaperman Walt

Whitman would write of "the porpoise-backs of the omnibuses" swimming in huge schools through a "human sea tossing spray of ribbons and plumes." He would tell how "before light, with sharp heavy rattle, as from advanced light artillery, commences the thunderous charge of wheels, rapidly deepening into the steady roll that only dies away again with the last upward stages and late hacks at midnight."

As pleasant as New York was, there were adumbrations of coming decline. It had always been a mercantile city, primarily concerned with economics. John Adams had complained as far back as 1774, "With all the Opulence and Splendor of this City, there is very little good Breeding to be found. We have been treated with an assiduous Respect. But I have not seen one real Gentleman, one well bred Man since I came to Town. At their Entertainments there is no Conversation that is agreable. There is no Modesty—No Attention to one another. They talk very loud, very fast and altogether. If they ask you a Question, before you can utter 3 Words of your Answer, they will break out upon you again—and talk away."

John Quincy Adams said in 1817, "The Mayor complains of poor, that burthen the City, amounting at this Season to fifteen hundred and in winter to near two thousand. Two thirds of them foreigners."

Asa Greene, the father of Cartwright's fellow bookseller and friend Henderson Greene, prematurely (but in honest sadness at the decline of civility) wrote in 1837, ". . . in New York, as well as in all other cities, hospitality, or anything resembling it, is unknown. And this is the result, not of any native churlishness or want of fellow feeling; but simply of the . . . peculiar social condition of the inhabitants of cities. 'What is everybody's business is nobody's.' The citizens live too close together, too crowded, to allow room for hospitality."

The *Merchants' Sketch Book* (of 1844) advised:

Every Western man on his first visit to New-York will be struck with the immensity of the place. It cannot perhaps be better illustrated than by the following tables:

New-York in 1825 contained 166,086 inhabitants
"   "   1830   "   200,859   "
"   "   1835   "   270,099   "
"   "   1840   "   312,710   "

It will therefore contain . . . in 1940, 11,715,720.

Greene projected "the enormous population of *six millions*" by 1900, but doubted that this would actually occur. He called it a "frightful increase."

Had Cartwright continued and flourished in bookselling, he undoubtedly would have published and written as his friends the Greenes did and expressed his similar sentiments. He too sensed some first scent of decay in his beautiful city—the city that attempted so much and failed, in the end, so wretchedly, dying of cancerous growth, dying of trying to incorporate most of the world's warring peoples in one commonwealth.

Alexander Cartwright *(top, center)* stands in an absolutely typical pose with fellow Knickerbockers. The man on his right appears to be his brother, Alfred. Note the raffish, worldly-wise attitude struck by the relaxed cigar-smoking Knickerbocker below. Alick's friends were mugging for the camera. *The Cartwright Family*

South Street docks, New York's most thriving, lay very near the offices of Alexander Cartwright, Sr., Alick's sea captain father. *The Edward W. C. Arnold Collection, Museum of the City of New York*

A characteristic street scene in New York at about the time Alexander Cartwright arrived from Nantucket. *The Edward W. C. Arnold Collection, Museum of the City of New York*

Wall Street, shortly after Cartwright closed his stationery shop and book-store there and went west. *The Edward W. C. Arnold Collection, Museum of the City of New York*

The new Fourth Avenue railroad cut cleaves the pastoral tranquility of Kipp's Village. Progress invades not only the quaint Dutch cottages and little gardens of the burghers, but also the Knickerbockers' playing field, located just to the left of the cut. *Museum of the City of New York*

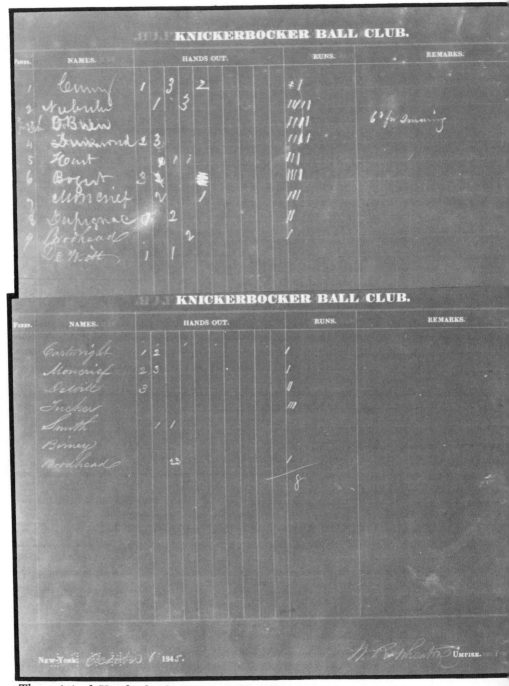

The original Knickerbocker game book, with the first recorded game of baseball. Cartwright's side was retired in order in the first inning. *Manuscript Division, New York Public Library*

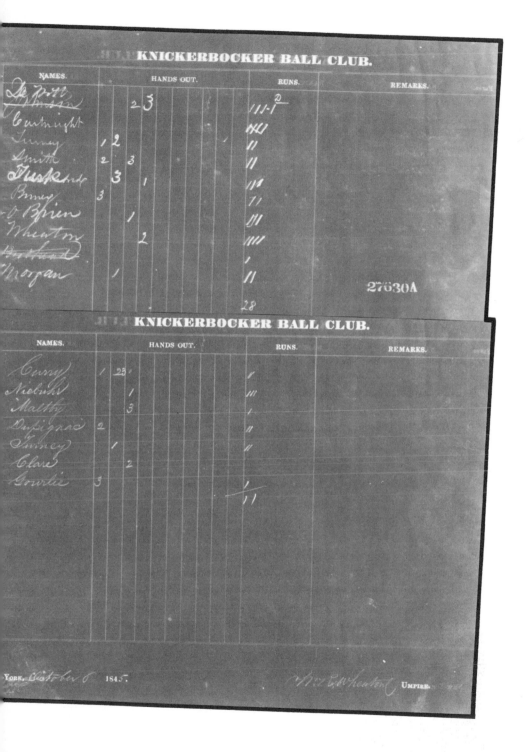

KNICKERBOCKER BALL CLUB.

NAMES.	HANDS OUT.		RUNS.	REMARKS.
De Witt		2 3	/// 1 ²	
Cartright			//////	
Tinney	1 2		//	
Smith	2	3	//	
Tucker	3	1	////	
Birney	3		//	
O Brien		1	///	
Wheaton		2	////	
Dupont			/	
Morgan	1		//	
			28	

27630A

KNICKERBOCKER BALL CLUB.

NAMES.	HANDS OUT.		RUNS.	REMARKS.
Curry	1 2 3		//	
Niebuhr		1	///	
Maltby		3		
Dupignac	2		//	
Tinney	1		//	
Clare		2		
Gourlie	3		/ //	

YORK, October 6 1845.

W. R. Wheaton UMPIRE.

Cartwright and the Knickerbockers often rode by wagon and carriage up the beautiful Post Road to the village of Harlem, where they dined at the Red House, a country inn. In later years baseball supplanted cricket at the adjoining cricket ground, which is shown here. *Museum of the City of New York* ——————————————————————————————→

This remarkable print of New York shows the Elysian Fields in the foreground, with a game of baseball actually in progress in the near lefthand corner. Undoubtedly the Knickerbockers are one of the teams playing. New York has grown since Alexander Cartwright's departure for Hawaii, but the Elysian Fields — with the Colonnade, Stevens Castle, and the busy river shipping all very much in evidence — remain almost unchanged. *Prints Division, The New York Public Library*

"STEALING" THE SECOND BASE.

"THE PURPOSE YOU UNDERTAKE IS DANGEROUS."

The appearance and spirit of early baseball are well represented in this "humorous" print. Note the top-hatted umpire, cane in hand, standing with his left foot comfortably propped on a stool. *Rare Book Division, The New York Public Library*

CHAPTER SEVEN

CONSTRUCTION OF NEW PINK AND BROWN JERSEY FREESTONE HOUSES on the northward edge of the advancing city had already driven Alexander Cartwright and his friends from one earlier rudimentary baseball playing ground not far above the old Peter Stuyvesant estate near what suddenly became 27th Street. That ground, the meadows along Crommessie Vly (Gramercy Brook or Cedar Creek), was now the most sought suburban location in New York.

But what showed on the town maps as the area between 30th and 33rd streets remained rather rural. The quaint little village of Kipsborough or Kips Bay, just the other side of the Eastern Post Road, named for early Dutch settler Jacob Kip, was still intact. Its little gambrel-roofed Dutch houses fronted on streets whose odd directions and homey names—Louisa, Maria, Elbert—ignored the corporation's wire-mesh urban pattern. Its tidy burghers still tended flower gardens and corn and hoed beans in neat little plots behind post-and-split-rail fences. Those gardens bloomed prolific in roses of all kinds, eglantine, tulips, gullyflowers, anemones, baredames and marigolds. The Netherlanders' clove, quince and pear trees blossomed delicately each spring.

The original Jacob Kip mansion—built in 1655 and now the oldest house in Manhattan—was still standing near the mouth of the

Kill t'Oude Wrack. The burned ruins of the mansion of John Murray, the wealthy Quaker merchant whose beautiful widow and daughters entertained George Washington and General Howe in quick succession when the British occupied New York during the late Revolution, still looked down from the Inclenberg.

In this blissful amaranthine setting, the Knickerbockers' numbers and enthusiasm grew and grew. Happy to escape the noise and commercial bustle of the city for some fresh air and exercise, they became a most representative section of the young business gentlemen of New York. Cartwright in later years mentioned a few of the most eager players he found playing below Murray Hill at least as early as 1842. He recorded their names for posterity as "Colonel James Lee, Doctor Ransom, Abraham Tucker, James Fisher and W. Vail."

Lee was colonel of Cartwright's unit of militia and beloved by Alick for bailing him out of some kind of trouble caused when the Mexican War broke out in 1846. Very probably this contretemps was political. Northern Whigs abhorred the war, and Cartwright was almost certainly a Whig. Lee would have understood a stand on conscience, although an ardent patriot—he remembered sneaking out as a four-year-old to see Washington's funeral procession and he was in charge of the procession honoring Lafayette. To avoid arrest and incarceration in the haunted Tower of London for actively supporting the French Revolution, his own father had fled England on a New York-bound ship. (There he had established the business of Lee & Company, which imported almost all the copper tokens used as pennies until the U. S. began coining copper. These cents, stamped "Talbot, Allum & Lee" and bearing the image of a ship under sail, were still in common use in the 1840's, and some Knickerbocker fines were paid in them.) Lee was an exception among the Knickerbockers, being an older man of forty-nine. He often claimed to have played some form of baseball as a boy, not long after the year 1800.

Ransom was Dr. Franklin Ransom, listed as a member of the Medical Society of New York. His name will crop up again later. All that can be found of Abraham Tucker is that he lived at 56 East Broadway, and there were many James Fishers. William Vail was either a cabinetmaker at 180 Franklin Street or, more likely, a clothier at 464 Pearl. Those were the characteristic streets for woodworkers and dry-goods establishments.

The organizers of the original baseball team were W.R. Wheaton, D.F. Curry, E.R. Dupignac, Jr., and W.H. Tucker, besides, of course, Cartwright himself. Wheaton was a young lawyer with offices on Beekman Place who lived fashionably on lower Broadway. William Tucker was doubtless Abraham Tucker's son; they lived together upstairs from the former's tobacco shop on Broadway. Dupignac was the son of Ebenezer Dupignac, a chair maker on Chrystie Street or Cherry Street, down near the waterfront.

By the autumn of 1845, galloping urbanization again had caught up with the young Knickerbockers. A glue factory built by famous inventor Peter Cooper had polluted Sunfish Pond so badly that it was drained and filled in. Old Wreck Kill was obliterated too, a few years later. The beautiful, pure spring and pond at its source, with all the surrounding ravine and hills, were filled and leveled, later becoming the middle of Times Square: symbol sufficient. A depot, the quaint round enginehouse and shops, and a stable for the horse-cars of the New York & Haerlem Rail Road were all planned for the very spot where the Knickerbockers had been accustomed to play. (The railroad thus dispossessed the Knickerbockers for the second time, because its large main depot occupied the club's first informal playing ground at Madison Square.) The Eastern Post Road was discontinued on maps between 23rd and 45th streets and legally reverted to adjoining property owners, although it remained usable until after 1849. Irving Place and Third Avenue were cut ruthlessly straight through the middle of Kipsborough to replace it, leaving only a few diagonal lots as a vestige of the village. Blocks of houses sprang up half a mile north on Third Avenue. It was beginning to look as if the club was going to have to lay out a different field every year.

Like the Dodgers and Giants after them, the Knickerbockers gave up on New York as a place to play baseball and left the city. After drawing up a constitution and bylaws on September 23, 1845, and formally setting down Alick's rules on paper (all of which still exist), they decided on a new and more pleasant location—Hoboken.

The fact that Alick had moved to a new residence certainly had nothing to do with the Knickers' choice. Cartwright was now living at the far eastern end of 4th Street, between Avenues C and D, only a block from the shipbuilding yards and drydocks along the East River. Hoboken was all the way over on the west bank of the Hudson River. To get home Alexander probably sometimes had to walk across the widest part of Manhattan, since cabs and crosstown omnibuses were scarce.

Somehow Cartwright persuaded most—but not all—of the original players to assemble at the ornate old Barclay Street Ferry to seek a new frontier in unspoiled rural New Jersey. (The ferry had been operating in some form or other since the 1780's, when it was hand-rowed. In 1816, when Alexander's father had first seen it, it was pedaled by horsepower.) The players tramped in a troop past the tree-crowded Columbia College campus, dodged barrels and boxes under the awning of the Patterson Stage office, and arrived at the gilt-emblazoned wooden arch of the Hoboken Ferry.

On a particularly fine late-September afternoon, the Knickerbockers steamed across the sparkling blue Hudson and disembarked at the bucolic little lake and resort village. In high spirits, rejoicing in cottony white clouds becalmed in a gentle light-blue sky and the first yellows and russets of autumn beginning to deckle the green leaves, the shouting and joking young men marched up Hudson Street and the River Walk. Past the John Stevens farm they came, past Sybil's Cave (a famous trysting place), past the Pavilion. Birds tested formations for southward flight, and rabbits regarded them curiously.

It was a place of surpassing beauty. The favorite locale of the Hudson River School of painters, whose symphonic sunlight and clouds have been scorned as romantic invention in modern times but were accurate perceptions in the 1840's, was just upriver at Weehawk. There, besides hills and dales and winding paths and a profusion of shaded bowers, in groves of trees, the Knickerbockers found a fine, level, grassy plain.

They strode into a large area known as the Elysian Fields, a popular holiday destination. It was modestly advertised in guidebooks of the time as:

THE MOST DELIGHTFUL OF ALL EXCURSIONS.—A sail across the Hudson River, to Hoboken, and then a walk to the Elysian Fields, along the exceedingly picturesque shores of the place. . . . The grounds now present a charming aspect, the trees being in leaf and the soil covered with a rich turf.

This seemed an ideal spot to play baseball. Besides, it immediately adjoined McCarty's and other hospitable taverns.

The terrible-tempered Mrs. Trollope had found some fault with the Elysian Fields as early as 1831 on this ground: "It is true that at Hoboken, as every where else, there are *reposoires* which, as you pass them, blast the sense for a moment by reeking forth the fumes of whiskey and tobacco. . . ." But then she relented, won over by the sylvan beauties of the place. "The proprietor of the grounds, however, has contrived with great taste to render these abominations not unpleasing to the eye; there is one in particular, which has quite the air of a Grecian temple."

The proprietor was Colonel John Stevens, who ran the Elysian Fields to stimulate his ferryboat business. This same famed engineer built one of the first steamboats and first operated a steamer at sea or in ferry service. He was also the father of the steam railroad in the United States. Stevens proposed the first railroad in America way back in 1811 and built the first locomotive, which operated on a circle of track near the Hoboken Hotel in 1825. He later founded the pioneer Camden & Amboy Railroad, which was to play a part in the virtual vanishing act of Alexander Cartwright. Such an indefatigable inventor was Stevens that he once, when smitten by inspiration while lying in bed without paper at hand, sketched the idea on the back of his wife's nightgown.

The friends merrily marked out a haphazard "diamond"—as Cartwright called his square arrangement of bases—on the level swatch of greensward at what would now be Hudson and 12th streets. A small park at the edge of this area, surrounded by an excessively aromatic coffee plant and other weaker but more noxious industrial smells, is all that remains of the Elysian Fields.

The twenty-eight Knickerbockers who had made the momentous crossing of the Hudson then played a totally non-serious game, too effervescent with youth and a new joy to think of history. Forty-two runs were scored, but there were so many substitutions and side changes that no score or lineup was kept. Cartwright pitched, as usual, since the others seemed to experience some difficulty getting the ball over the plate. Also as usual, he was one of the best hitters.

Besides Cartwright, James Fisher, Ebenezer Dupignac, William Tucker, William Wheaton and Duncan Curry, whom we already know, the pioneer players seem to have been:

Jacob H. Anthony, assistant cashier of the Bank of the State of New York

J.H. Anthony, Jr., his son, a stationer on Pearl Street
Henry T. Anthony, a Wall Street clerk
Walter Avery
Charles Birney, from Brooklyn, secretary of the East River Marine
    Insurance Company
George Broadhead, a Wall Street broker
Edward W. Cone, a Wall Street lawyer
Peter DeWitt, Jr., another Wall Street broker—and possibly a Cart-
    wright in-law
Harry? Hart
F.C. Johnson or Johnston, possibly a physician
Henry T. Morgan, still another Wall Street broker
William D. Maltby, a commission merchant
James Moncrieff, a Wall Street lawyer
Fraley Niebuhr, of the Custom House, a particularly close friend
    of Cartwright and one of the best players
William O'Brien, yet another Wall Street broker
Jonathan O'Brien, his brother, also a broker
David W. Smith
A Mr. Turney
A Mr. Talmadge
Frank H. Turk, a clerk at the post office

There were two others whose names cannot be ascertained.

The explorers had such a good time that they set regular play days, bought a scorebook printed to their specifications, and, on October 6, 1845, played the first recorded game of modern baseball. Only fourteen Knickerbockers were able to absent themselves from business, and they played to eleven runs rather than twenty-one, but otherwise they hewed to the letter of the new rules. Those first lineups are not among the best known, but perhaps they deserve to be. Here they are, in contrast with the Gashouse Gang and Murderer's Row, and with the kind of box score used then and for many years thereafter.

This first official score was, as indicated, 11-8. Cartwright's side lost. As in today's sandlot games among small fry, the players batted more or less in descending order of ability, giving the best the most opportunities to hit. Since Cartwright and Curry were the most experienced and respected players, they batted in the lead-off position. The concept of speedy, banjo-hitting lead-off men and power-hitting clean-up men obviously had not occurred to anyone, for by it the bulky, trundling Cartwright was out of position.

KNICKERBOCKER

LINEUP OF FIRST GAME

October 6, 1845

	Hands Out			Runs
	First inning	Second inning	Third inning	
Cartwright	1	2		I
Moncrief	2	3		I
DeWitt	3			II
Tucker				III
Smith		1	1	
Birney				
Brodhead			2-3	I
				8
Curry	1	2-3		II
Niebuhr			1	III
Maltby			3	I
Dupignac	2			II
Turney			1	II
Clare			2	
Gourlie	3			I
				11

Wm. R. Wheaton, *Umpire*

Despite their places of honor, Cartwright and Curry had rather bad days at bat. Alick was only two for four, and Duncan went two for five. Since no errors were recorded, so as not to hurt the feelings of the gentlemen members, and the batter could look at as many soft, lofted pitches as he wanted, that constituted a slump. In fact, Cartwright's side was retired in order—no runs, no hits, no errors— in the first inning, an almost unheard-of achievement that elicited great huzzahing and cheering from the competition.

The two new players on the winning side were Joseph Clare and Archibald T. Gourlie, both brokers. Archie Gourlie obtained the undying, refulgent glory of drawing baseball's first officially recorded fine. It probably cost him sixpence.

The next session, the Knickerbockers recorded the first game played to twenty-one "aces." Cartwright, demoted to the second position behind Billy Tucker, again had a mediocre day at the plate and again his side lost, 33-26. (The first team to reach 21 would get as many runs as possible, because the other side might exceed them in the bottom of the last inning.) Thomas Thorne, appearing for the first time in Hoboken, acquitted himself creditably.

Poor Alick got himself untangled at the next meeting, having a perfect day at bat. (Contemplate the embarrassment of losing at a game you had invented yourself!) He picked a historic occasion to do it, for enough Knickerbockers showed up to play the first nine-man game of which there is written evidence.

An unknown Mr. Bogart played, and Cartwright's friend Alick Drummond, another insurance agent, made it over the river for the first time. The one extra man, Peter DeWitt, substituted on both sides.

On October 17, 1845, the Knickerbockers gathered for the contest which all other recent sources have mistakenly called their first. Actually, it was their fifth or sixth game in the Elysian Fields, not counting those played below Murray Hill in Manhattan. At least one source also incorrectly implies that only one side's box score is known and, at that, gets only a quarter of the names right, spelling them as Wheatone, Stoncrief, Burke, Gurney, Vanageand and Waldhead. It even cites the two fines as an ambiguous "16," when they were in fact sixpence. To clear up the confusion, this is the correct lineup:

LINEUPS FOR FIFTH GAME
October 17, 1845

Wheaton	Curry
Tucker	Cone
Moncrief	Niebuhr
Morgan	Thorne
Turk	Cartwright
Turney	Birney
Talmadge	DeWitt
Brodhead	O'Brien

Score: 25-23

The Knickerbockers actually played at least fourteen recorded games in the fall of 1845. Undistracted by football, enchanted by their new toy, they persevered until the chilly eighteenth of November. Long-time regulars such as Dr. Daniel L. Adams, William L.

Tallman, and merchant William Van Nortwick entered the lineups within this period, completing the heretofore sadly unrecognized roster of players during the first recorded baseball season at Hoboken.

The winter of 1845–46 qualifies as the first Hot Stove League season ever, and possibly the best. It may well be that those immortal words "Wait till next year!" were first uttered that November, as the speaker warmed his boots on the base of a real parlor stove, perhaps a Charter Oak of gleaming silver and glossy black with a fine brass finial.

On Good Friday of 1846, which was April 10, the Knickerbockers were back at the stand. Four new faces creased into grins at the unprecedented fun; they belonged to Messrs. Langworthy, Fanning, John Paulding, and George Ireland, Jr. Cartwright, who was umpire that day, wrote "Commencement of the *Season*" with a flourish in the game book, and the scoring that day, 40-35, broke the all-time record for Cartwright-style baseball.

Every Tuesday and Friday afternoon the Knickerbockers played, on a schedule as well regulated as the rest of their orderly lives. But the artificial goal of twenty-one "aces" was soon violated. Once they attained the remarkable score of 71-46 in five innings. As one might suppose, most of the hits were long ones, the batters teeing off on the fat pitches. Anything less than a home run was considered somewhat disappointing. This raggedy-andy feature slightly troubled Cartwright's highly organized mind. He suggested that the batter be required to swing at any reasonably good pitch instead of waiting for a perfect one, but for the while the players were not interested. They were having too good a time knocking the ball lopsided.

Two intriguing lagniappes: The umpire for the fourth game of the season was "Alfred D. Forest Cartwright." This hitherto unnoted toe-dabbling remains the only evident participation of Alexander's brother in baseball. Also, George D. Cassio, Alexander's brother-in-law, was a player and umpire in other games.

The most momentous event of Alick's remaining baseball career in Hoboken occurred on June 19, the seventeenth game of the Knickerbockers' second organized season. What may be called, with some propriety, the first match game of baseball took place on that day. The scorer of a later Knick game so considered it, for he wrote in ink over the original penciled scoring, "1st match game."

A shadowy outfit dubbed "New York," whose identity has mysti-
fied researchers, was the opposition. The mystification is mostly
needless, as examination of the lineups will hint:

KNICKERBOCKER BASEBALL CLUB	NEW YORK
Turney	Davis
Adams	Winslow
Tucker	Ransom
Birney	Murphy
Avery	Case
W. Anthony	Johnson
D. Anthony	Austen Thompson,
Daniel Tryon,	proprietor of
commercial merchant	Phoenix Coffeerooms
Paulding	on Pine St.
	Trenchard
	Michael Lalor, "Segar Seller"

Some historians have made much of the fact that the effete gentlemen Knickerbockers, with a year's practice, lost to the supposedly new nine by the embarrassing score of 23-1. Albert Spalding
and John Montgomery Ward lost no opportunity to sneer at them
for this reason. A close observer will see numerous odd things about
these lineups, however. First, as already noted, Dr. Franklin Ransom and Johnson had previously played with the Knickerbockers,
either at Sunfish Pond or at the Elysian Fields. Second, virtually
every one of the New York nine later became prominent Knickerbockers, some of them almost immediately after June 19. Third, not
a single one of the Knickerbockers' best nine hitters appears in the
Knick lineup; indeed, it looks as if they chose very nearly their
worst nine players. Finally, although the "New Yorks" did apparently score twenty-three "aces," the solitary run in the Knickerbocker column does not jibe with the box score.

Conclusions are obvious. First, the Knickerbockers did behave as
gentlemen: Cartwright, Dupignac, Curry, Niebuhr, Moncrieff,
Smith, Broadhead, and the O'Brien brothers—their best and most
enthusiastic nine—all sat out the game in order to give the visitors
a good chance to win. It seems clear to this writer that the "New
Yorks" were also not without experience. Almost certainly they

were the original players who found Hoboken inconvenient and continued playing south of Murray Hill. They did indeed sometimes call themselves the New York Club, but they had little organization. Pointedly, the scorer of the game actually listed *them* as the "K.B.C.," probably because several of the New York nine were older players at Murray Hill. It was only the later scorer, who put in the reference to the first match game, who also scratched this out and identified the Hobokeners as the proper Knickerbockers. His reasoning undoubtedly was that Cartwright had suggested the name and that his group was larger and more active. As construction pre-empted the last of their playing field, the New York nine reunited with the Knickerbockers at the Elysian Fields.

As for the score, careful examination shows that the Knick "muffins"—as the second string was called—put at least eight men on base in the first inning alone, and therefore must have scored at least five runs. They may have scored eleven or more. They did not muff their big chance so badly as first appears. Although Cartwright did not play, he was utilized in the most logical way possible—as umpire. What better arbiter than the inventor of the rules? Umpire Cartwright, who had himself been fined for wandering away somewhere with one of the O'Briens and delaying the June 5 game, got a chance to impose *his* first fine: half a York shilling, levied on James Whyte Davis for swearing.

Games were getting more heated. Despite the gentlemanly code, no fewer than four fines had been assessed in the previous game for improper language and for arguing with the umpire. Cartwright was again fined in October "for disputing the umpire." Since he was charged double the usual amount, his protest must have been vigorous. Later a club gentleman, Mr. Dupignac, was explicitly fined "6ᶜ for saying s--t."

A delightful Currier & Ives lithograph of a Knickerbocker game exists. Allegedly it shows a much later contest, but so many details suggest an earlier period that the caption may be incorrect. (Illustrators' maps and views were frequently a decade or more obsolete.) The general atmosphere of attending ladies under parasols and gentlemen parked in brougham carriages in the outfield is correct. Indeed, as at later matches, the Knickerbockers provided a canvas pavilion to protect the alabaster complexions of the fairer sex from a burning sun unscreened by the clear Hudson County ether. For the gentlemen players and friends, they supplied a brightly striped tent dispensing shade and cooling refreshments, some alcoholic.

The Knickerbockers also revolutionized baseball's sartorial world by taking the field in a natty uniform of blue pantaloons, white flannel shirts and chip (straw) hats—an outfitting later modified to include mohair caps and patent-leather belts. Strangely, although baseball uniforms still preserve the memory of the first team, since the pants are knickerbocker style, the Knickerbockers themselves did not wear knickers!

After the first match, the Knickerbockers played another game, with the two sides thoroughly scrambled, which adds credence to the theory that the teams were not entirely separate clubs. When the pastoral afternoon was over, the ball players banqueted and celebrated in epicurean style with their ladies, perhaps at Partrick's establishment. Crickets and lightning bugs had long since taken possession of the premises, even on this long, light June evening, when the innocently reveling New Yorkers boarded the ferry for home.

For their more usual post-game jollyups, when ladies were not present and more boisterous amusement was permissible, the Knickerbockers commonly returned to Manhattan, where they repaired to one of various caravanseries for a kind of naïvely merry and happy fellowship rare in this suspicious, cramped, crabbed East of the twentieth century. Their favorite was the Fijux Hotel, a little place near the ferry landing at 11 Barclay Street. The little son of owner Fijux was adopted as a sort of club mascot. A later minute book notes, ". . . the young fellow was duly brought forward and received a Kiss from all present. He was then placed in the center of the table and duly christened Charles Knickerbocker Fijux and the Secretary directed to place his name on the Roll." When M. Fijux moved to 42 Murray Street, the Club moved too, although it also held meetings at Schwartz's Hotel at 14 Dey Street and at Smith's on Howard and Broome streets. And thousands of miles away, many years later, a patriarchal Alexander Cartwright with a long white beard wistfully remembered how they would sometimes hire a carriage and ride up the Post Road—the old Weequasics Trail of the Indians—to dine at the exquisite double-colonial Red House Tavern in the white-steepled country village of Haerlem, returning late at night through the slumbering hamlet of Yorkville, laughing and singing in the moonlight flooding the promontories and ravines of the picturesquely wild landscape.

As they reabsorbed the so-called "New York Club," the Knickerbockers more than ever constituted the entirety of organized baseball. They played regularly and acquired many new members, Cartwright taking various offices in the club and concerning himself
with adjustments in the rules. Sporadic groups continued to play in
Manhattan north of New York, but not until 1851 did one—
buttressed by players who had gained experience with the parent
club—feel strong enough to organize and take on the Knickerbockers. In June of that year, "The Washington Club," which had been
practicing at the St. George cricket grounds near the Red House
Tavern, invited the Knicks to play two games in Haerlem. Predicta-
bly, the Washington Club lost both. Undiscouraged, they went on
to become one of the prominent early teams, renamed the Gotham
Club.

Eagle and Empire clubs formed in 1854 and also the Excelsiors in
the town of Brooklyn. Almost immediately they began playing
matches against the Knickerbockers and each other. The Putnam
Club appeared in Williamsburgh in 1855 and the Hoboken and Star
after that, all of them clubs of gentlemen. But simple clerks, me-
chanics and ordinary laborers had discovered Cartwright's exciting
new game too. The next year, 1856, they formed the first two
plebeian workingmen's clubs—the Eckfords of Greenpoint and the
Atlantics of Jamaica.

Suddenly baseball became no less than a mania. Every young
man in the city must play and must belong to a club. Throngs of
them rose at four and five in the morning to practice before work.
They talked and thought of almost nothing else. Employers who
had previously eschewed employees who drank or gambled now
began asking prospective clerks whether they played ball. (But
sometimes the boss too caught the disease and actively sought ball
players.) Such wages-workers eventually formed scores and
hundreds of baseball clubs. Among the earlier organizers, Long Island workmen began the Pastime Club, policemen formed the Man-
hattans, barkeepers the Phantoms, schoolteachers the Metropolitans, and dairymen the Pocahontas Club. Hundreds of spectators
very quickly began lining the foul lines. These early fans (an abbre-
viation of "fanatics," by the way) were called cranks, which is what
losing managers still call them.

It is difficult now to understand what a happy revelation baseball
as an adult game was to the young men of the mid-nineteenth cen-

tury. One must remember that boys almost universally became min-
iature men at age twelve or thirteen, forsaking most outdoor games
as childish, emulating their elders in every possible detail, down to
their amusements. The first baseball sportswriter, Henry Chadwick,
understated in some respects when he wrote:

> Far too many of our American boys jump from the games of their
> early school days . . . into the vicious ways of fast young men. It
> is a sad sight to see boys of from 12 to 15 years of age with ciga-
> rettes in their mouths, canes in their hands, and with precocious
> appetites for stimulants, visiting . . . racecourses, pool-rooms, vari-
> ety-saloons and other vicious places of public amusement, when
> they . . . should be on their regular playgrounds.

Cigars, pipes, vests, and gaiters were the accouterment of many
New York lads not yet adolescent, who swore, drank, played poker
and followed the horse races indistinguishably from grown men.
Their main organized athletic activity was scoring on spittoons with
tobacco juice. Though matters have perhaps changed back in this
direction in the last few years, such behavior has been so unfamiliar
as to be perverse for many decades. Mothers, school marms and
Sunday schools did not alone affect the transformation of Huck
Finn into Frank Merriwell. They had candy-covered help from an
army of coaches and cheerleaders, proffering a dazzling array of
sports and handsome uniforms, beginning with baseball.

Lack of bloody contact, along with baseball's precision and
clear-cut, almost unfudgeable rules, also appealed. American sports
previously had some tendency to run toward eye-gouging, bear-
baiting, cockfighting and brawls with bowie knives. "The boys of a
warlike nation find their chief recreation in sports in which feats of
brutal courage, and of endurance of fatigue and pain, are marked
characteristics," Chadwick said disapprovingly. He approved most
highly of "the American game of base-ball [which] fully illustrates
the nature of fair play" and stresses pure skill and intelligence "un-
aided by such low trickery as . . . cutting up the ball, tripping up
base runners, hiding the ball, wilful collisions with fielders, and
other specially mean tricks of the kind characteristic of corner-lot
loafers in their ball games."

The mushrooming popularity of such basically super-simple (and
often violent) sports as hockey, basketball, soccer, and football and
the decline of interest in baseball and cricket has even been seen by

a number of observers as symptomatic of the decline of today's culture. No less than Professor Corrado Gini subscribes to this. "In a
decadent population, as the Berbers have been for many centuries,
more elaborate achievements decay or disappear," he says. "Even at
Jadum, [soccerlike] *Ta kurt na rrod* is preferred, for the sake of its
simplicity and few rules, to the rigid and complicated *Om el
mahag*. The people I succeeded in collecting for the games had a
distinct propensity to discontinue *Om el mahag* and play *Ta kurt
na rrod*." And did Professor Gini ever try to keep a sandlotful of
kids from playing touch football at World Series time?

But even the initial conversion was not complete. The new low-
er-echelon clubs shocked the Knickerbockers and other original
players by acting as if the only purpose of baseball was to win,
without nice scruples as to exactly how. Chadwick soon had ample
occasion to inveigh against "low trickery." (He never did give up.
To the day of his death, well into the twentieth century, he continued to insist that baseball should be as polite as cricket.)

There is a rather touching contemporary account of the sheer joy
of the Eckfords, first at playing the Gothams, then at making a respectable showing against them, and then at beating them. But another account tells of the Atlantics, who, while playing the
Excelsiors disputed all of the umpire's decisions so rudely and otherwise behaved so crudely that the Excelsiors withdrew from the
game. The particularly belligerent Atlantic captain, Murphy, whose
team was losing, cheekily asked the Excelsior captain, "Will you
call it a draw?" "Have it as you will," the Excelsior said, coldly polite, and walked away. When the Knickerbockers received an invitation from the too zealous Eckfords, they puzzled over how to refuse without giving offense. Propriety was preserved by informing
the Eckfords of a "standing Club rule" of playing only teams that
used the Hoboken field. There was in truth such a standing rule,
but it had stood for only a few minutes, since it was passed at that
meeting.

But the new clubs were the color of the future. By 1858, when
the Knickerbockers, Gothams, Empires, and Eagles were prevailed
upon to call a convention of organized baseball, their leadership
was already largely ceremonial. Nonetheless, the contention by one
anti-Knickerbocker source that the Knicks folded in 1858 is totally
incorrect. The Knicks lasted more than thirty years, by which time
they were a little-known anachronism, and were lively enough as

late as the early 1870's to build a clubhouse on the Elysian Fields.

Conceivably, the story might have been different and the Knickerbockers might have become one of the professional major-league teams of today, just as other amateur clubs did. They did begin to recruit some players primarily for skill, and at a special meeting in 1858 an officer "exhorted the members to rouse themselves to action." He wished them "to understand that he was Young America in his views of Base Ball." President James Whyte Davis, too, "hoped thereafter to see more of the true spirit and vigor of the age developed amongst the members of the club, in short more Young America" because "the Club was in want of new material." They even applied for a field in the new Central Park in New York. At a number of stormy meetings over the years, however, the older Knicks won their battle against professionalism, and the Knickerbockers were bypassed by baseball history.

The Elysian Fields also eventually suffered from democratic and other excesses. "Pity it's haunted by such a gang as frequent it," diarist George Templeton Strong sniffed as early as 1844. "Its groves are sacred to Venus and I saw scarce any one there but snobs and their strumpets. Walked on in momentary expectation of stumbling on some couple engaged in . . . 'the commission of gross vulgarity.'" Sucker-baiter Phineas T. Barnum enticed an enormous crowd of sensation-seekers to the Fields in 1843. "One of those traps to catch the sovereigns of New York was set yesterday at Hoboken," the diarist Phillip Hone wrote. "A buffalo hunt with the lasso was advertised. . . . Thirty thousand men, women and children went over, but the hunt turned tail foremost. . . . One of the herd being caught by the lasso broke through the enclosure, and followed by the rest, dashed into the crowd, overturning everything in their way and occasioning such screaming and scampering among their persecutors as was never before heard of in the peaceful precincts of the Elysian Fields." The end of Hoboken's innocence and the onset of its decay may have been foreshadowed by the ominous discovery, near this time, of the body of murdered Mary Rogers—a sensationally, almost notoriously, beautiful New York shopgirl—in the river at Sybil's Cave. Edgar Allan Poe, a young editor of the New York *Evening Journal,* across the street from Cartwright's place of business, later based "The Mystery of Marie Roget" on it, changing the location to Paris.

From the Knickerbockers' arrival onward, however, the Fields remained Elysian. Only after the immigration flood had pushed aside most other vestiges of old New York were the well-loved pleasure grounds sacrificed at the altar of progress. Grimy coal yards, docks and warehouses replaced it. But Hudson Street south of the Maxwell House Coffee plant, where it begins to rise toward the campus of the Stevens Institute of Technology (located on the site of the Stevens estate), remains attractive. Some trees still line the street, and aesthetic stone townhouses of the type generically called brownstones preserve harmony in style and proportion the length of the avenue. A clock atop the steeple of a pleasant red Lutheran church measures out crude, twentieth-century, hasty hours with nineteenth-century stolid deliberateness and precision. A tiny park survives at this spot, a truncated fragment just above the tracks of the Hoboken Shore Railroad, on which a Diesel mutters along marshaling freight cars. Little more than a city playground, mostly asphalt-paved, it retains the name—Elysian Park.

On the 125th anniversary of the first modern baseball game, on a chilly gray spring day of 1972, it seemed somehow right to find what memories of the Knickerbockers might remain. The little park was empty, its sycamores stiffened to a cold and unhistorical wind. A marker once erected to honor the first game was gone, long since stolen. Only a small plaque mounted on the side of the coffee plant memorialized the event. At length three young fellows did appear. They were taking turns bouncing a basketball along the sidewalk toward the park. Looking blank at questions about the park's history, they were astonished when it was explained that baseball had begun there.

"*Really? Here?* You're kidding me, man," Mario said.

But basically the three saffron-skinned teenagers were not much interested even in this revelation. "I play baseball some, when there's nothing else to do," Mario observed, "but I don't like it. It's boring. You stand around too much. I like something that *moves.*"

"Like soccer," Roman put in. "That has some action."

Another flock of arrivals, almost all of these Cuban, expressed similar sentiments. (A flood of Puerto Ricans and Cubans has almost supplanted the Germans and Irish in these Hudson County towns in the last few years. They number in the millions in the New York area.) "I don't like to play baseball, too slow," Jose Santiago said. "I practice now karate. That's good." Manuel Bottano and Carlos Gonzalez agreed.

However, inspired perhaps by the inquiry about baseball, the boys did later leave off their basketball and play a desultory improvised game in which the batter threw up a rubber ball and hit it with his hand, using bases already marked out on the pavement with spray-paint cans. All the arguments whether runners were safe were conducted in extremely rapid Spanish with occasional words like *fly* and *home* thrown in. "*Dina* a fly," one kid kept yelling. The game did not last very long, degenerating into a mock street fight.

As the onlooker walked away, a small spectator, a lad of about eight with an extraordinarily lush mop of curly black hair who said his name was Jose Crespo, did run after him. "Hey, mister," he called. "Hey, mister, where can I play this Little League baseball? I would like to very much."

A century too late, the visitor continued down to the parking lot which is the last open space on the Knickerbockers' actual playing ground and on down the pathetic remains of the old Shore Road, strewn with junked cars and all manner of garbage. A poster advertising Armour's Star Brand lard, illustrated with two well-fed world-war GIs, hinted at the age of the trash. A lone old man walked a German shepherd dog through the puddles, cobblestones, and trash. An impulsive, unexpectant question paid off.

"Sure, I know baseball started here," the man said in a brogue. "I used to enjoy hearing the old-timers talk about it. There was a fellow of ninety some years who died a few years ago who remembered games here. I wish I remembered his name.

"I came from the old country—me name's Tom Doyle—so I didn't play here. They played rounders there, you know. It's a game something like baseball, but not as up to date. Some people say that's what baseball came from, over there. The children still play it in the commons in County Wicklow, south of Dublin. I was there a couple years ago, and they still play it. They use a piece of wood instead of a ball, and there are six on a side, or as many as they want."

The nearest place full-fledged baseball is played today is the high-school stadium at Columbus Park, drearily surrounded by tenements, garment factories, and one bamboo works. The cold had canceled practice, and it drove the baseball-seeker inside the surprising, encouragingly new Hoboken High School. The school seemed a warm place in more ways than one, a nurturing place.

Notices of a girls' tennis team, a school play, a benefit for the major-ettes adorned the walls, and students in the band practice room in-dulged in innocent horseplay. But a floor-to-ceiling student-painted poster showed a boy shooting heroin, with obvious clear knowledge of all the details of glassine bags, spoons, and matches. And another huge poster, showing a hideous scene of urban pollution taken from nearby life, exhorted, "Don't Let America Die."

"The kids take a pride in the school," a sympathetic counselor, himself a product of Hoboken, said. "Maybe because they have so little else outside it."

At almost that moment, Tony Romano happened to walk in. A city councilman, member of the board of education and former pitcher who might have made the big leagues had he not thrown his arm out, Tony is better known as the brother of John (Honey) Romano, the last Hobokener in the majors. White Sox fans in par-ticular will remember Romano as the man who led the often pallid Hose to their 1965 pennant, a very respectable hitting catcher who batted .299 in 1961 and had twenty-five home runs and eighty-one runs batted in in 1962.

"We played baseball from dawn to dusk, every available mo-ment," Tony began reminiscing. "We played till the cover fell off, then we taped it back on again and kept playing. Half the team had gloves, half didn't. My kid saw the glove I had and said, 'You caught a baseball with *this*?'

"It was block against block, church against church. There were enough empty lots so there was room for anyone to play then, not like now. But you'd still get up as early as you could wake up so that you could get the 'field.' The first kid there would start tossing a ball against a wall, and the first ones that came with the most and biggest people got the lot. The scene at dinnertime was everybody's mother yelling out of windows, *screaming* for you to come home. Of course, you'd yell back that you had another inning, or two, or three. You'd always come home late, and all hell would break loose."

"Our block team was the Wildcats," John Romano recollects. "It was myself, my brother, our cousins. . . . We played the Black-hawks, the Adams Street Gang. . . . Our house was right on the field. I can't tell you how many windows we broke, but our parents never seemed to mind, except for the flying glass. My father was a

great ball player for the Lackawanna Railroad team and the Oxfords. They wanted him to go into professional ball, but he could
make more money working on the docks and playing semi-pro.

"When I went to the minors myself, it was a shock. It was the
first time I had left Hoboken, and it was like going to a foreign
country. Dubuque seemed so spread out. The open country around
it looked like wilderness to me. The first three days I was ready to
pack up, I was so homesick."

Romano amiably answered numerous questions, and one hit pay
dirt when he was asked if Hoboken boys had played "cat."

"Cat? What's that?" Romano asked. "Do you mean a game we
played where you hit a little stick? We used to shave it to a tip, put
it on a curb and hit it to make it jump up in the air."

So John Romano, although he does not remember the name and
rules of the game, played tipcat on the streets of Hoboken. Although he is only thirty-eight years old and left major-league ball
only five years ago, Romano played baseball's 1,000-year-old predecessor.

All of the four Hobokeners who reached the major leagues in recent years have been pitchers or catchers, perhaps because lack of
space, inadequate fields, and the clammy, inhospitable climate prevented the constant play under good conditions necessary to polish
other skills.

"I never did play an awful lot of sandlot ball," says Leo Kiely, a
good Red Sox sinker-ball pitcher from 1951 to 1960 with a useful
3.37 lifetime earned-run average. "I'd just go into the back yard and
throw the ball against a wall, hour after hour. Then I played with
the Build a Better Boy League and the Tammany Club team. We
played where the high school plays now, but then it was all rocks
and everything."

Significantly, Kiely remembered that the Hoboken kids called the
field "The Cricket." There was, indeed, a cricket ground at or near
that site in the Knickerbockers' day. "I don't see how they could
ever have played cricket there," Kiely said. "It was a terrible field."

Son of a Hoboken fire inspector (note the parallel to an earlier
Hoboken player!), Kiely grew up only a few blocks from the Knickerbocker ball field. He worked on the docks as a longshoreman
even during the winters when he was in the majors. He is a typical
son of Hoboken in many ways, not least that he knew nothing of
the town's unique baseball history until he reached the big leagues.

Yet he muses now, "If baseball in Hoboken had kept on the way it started, I suppose Hoboken could have had its own major-league team playing there."

Kiely was asked if he had ever pilgrimaged down to Elysian Park to see where organized baseball began. "Naw," he said. "I seen it all when I was a kid."

Johnny Kucks, the handsome, perpetually smiling sinker-ball pitcher for the Yankees in the Fifties, learned about Hoboken's role in baseball when he was about thirteen, despite the fact that he never played the game in that town. Although Kucks sometimes credited his heavy fast ball to the steaks his father brought home from the Cudahy meat-packing plant in Hoboken, where he was superintendent, the family moved to Jersey City when Johnny was six. His first baseball was played there with the "Cloverdale A.C.," a sandlot team sponsored out of his own pocket by a Negro milkman named Howard Wimpy.

"A fellow in Jersey City asked me if I knew Abner Doubleday started the game in Hoboken," Kucks said recently, all in innocence. He had never even heard Cartwright's name. But he seemed fascinated by Alexander's role and asked numerous questions. And then he said something interesting.

"You know, every guy who ever plays baseball seriously seems to stop and meditate a minute about the precision of the game," Kucks said. "I thought about it often. I decided whoever figured out the measurements so exactly must have been a genius. You always hear guys talking about that. I was always intrigued by how he could just sit down and know how to do everything perfectly. The distance to the bases, for example, is just perfect. Or if they ever made the angle between the foul lines wider than ninety degrees, there would be many, many more home runs. Yogi Berra alone would have hit ten more a year.

"But it's funny how major leaguers never think about *who* invented the game or how it started. I never heard one conversation about that. You just take it for granted that it's been there since Year One."

Kucks was also delighted to hear that Cartwright had worked on Wall Street, since he himself is a stockbroker at 100 Wall.

"I know right where he had his office and store," he said. "I'm going to have to go down to look at that Elysian Park too. I go through Hoboken every day on my way to work."

It was Jerry Molloy, Hoboken's city sports coordinator and probably the town's most rabid baseball fan, who provided the first clues to locating all its big-leaguers. Molloy, a talkative, friendly white-haired former coach at St. Peter's College in Jersey City, also suggested names of the oldest baseball elders in Hoboken, besides himself remembering some baseball reminiscent of Elysian days.

"In 1914, when I was a kid, they still had a field right where the Elysian Field was," Molloy recalled. "The Giants came over with John McGraw on Sunday afternoons to play exhibition games there. New York had a law against playing Sunday games then, I believe. The place, right where the new coffee plant is now, was called the Savannah Oval then. A good semi-pro club named the Savannahs used to play there.

"Nearby, about at Ninth and Jackson, was the Oxford Oval. The Oxfords started in the early 1900's, and they still have a dinner every year, although only a couple of them are left."

"Yes," confirmed Bill Bergen, one of the last Oxfords, "in the early 1900's we had many teams playing on many little fields in town. There was lots of room then. The Oxford Athletic Association originated about 1906. Probably the best was a team called the Hoboken Club that used to play at the old St. George Cricket Ground at Tenth and Clinton. Both minor- and major-league teams would come over and play them.

"I can remember Ty Cobb playing in an exhibition where the Maxwell House plant is now. It was still called the Elysian Field at that time, and most everybody in town still knew about the Knickerbockers. But there was a railroad track that ran right in back of second base. Trains still go in there, but at a different angle, because the field became the coffee company's parking lot before they built the new building there. The second baseman sure had to watch his feet to see he didn't trip on the tracks.

"Later it was called the Savannah Oval. Yes, I think the boats to Savannah landed near there. You just woke me up to that."

Octogenarian Steve Cosmanic, an older Oxford, remembered even more. "I played Ty Cobb's spot one time," he said. "There were two games going on right next to each other on the old Fields, and the outfields overlapped. I was playing right field and Cobb was too. Cobb didn't think much of the Elysian Fields the way they were then. He said to me, 'Where the hell did you get this field?'

"It's true, besides the railroad track, the outfield sloped down toward the river. All the fields were like that. At the Oxford Oval, once a ball passed the left-fielder it went into a bunch of bushes and tin cans. The right-fielder played on the sidewalk.

"The Oxfords started as a bunch of boys all on one block. We were called the Whackers until Dominic Trionolone changed the name. I don't know why he picked 'Oxfords.' [Some of the Knicker-bockers' gentlemanly approach to the game still influenced Ho-boken, apparently.] We built a good field at Marshall and Fourth by filling in a swamp with thousands of loads of ashes and dirt, and we built grandstands. The following spring we came back and it was all ripped down. The people on Jackson Street had used it for firewood.

"Something like that happened to the Hoboken Club. They used to play all the National and American League clubs on Sundays and draw six thousand people or so. But there was a Lieutenant Dristol who claimed it was public land and they had no right to charge admission. I think he wanted his cut. One Sunday he came with a lot of people and knocked the fence down. That was the end of big-time baseball in Hoboken."

CHAPTER EIGHT

On March 1, 1849, at the apex of his interest in the knickerbockers and just as his game was attracting public attention, Alexander Joy Cartwright, Jr., disappeared from New York and from
baseball history. So thoroughly did he vanish from baseball annals
that his death in 1892 passed entirely without notice or comment
on the mainland. His name was by then almost unknown except to
a few friends. Perhaps not one active baseball player was aware
that he had invented the game. Ninety years after his departure
from New York, he was buried in such obscurity that only the enormous inanity of the 1939 perpetration of the Doubleday fiction
could find him again—in the tropical Territory of Hawaii!

Cartwright picked the most romantic possible means of expung-
ing himself from baseball's records, as shall be seen in abundant
measure. But that was natural for Cartwright. Rather a romantic
himself, he certainly sprang from a picturesque background. Un-
mapped and uncharted places were the Cartwrights' milieu, their
home a character-drenched island saturated in intense individual-
ism. For generations back Alexander's forefathers were Yankee sea
captains of the saltiest, fullest-bearded, most daring sort. Cartwrights had commanded whaling vessels, fishing ships, and in-
trepid transatlantic packets since the beginnings of English settle-

ment in America. And the family's roots were in the most rock-solid New England lore imaginable, bound in with all the history of the salt-sprayed, self-sufficient little island nation of Nantucket. The Cartwrights came from a remote, quasi-independent island and returned to a remoter, more independent one. After one brief dabbling in the more urbane pursuits of banking and bookselling, Alexander Cartwright was drawn back to become a sea trader and adventurer. It was precisely this lust for romance that made him be forgotten when credit was being given for the reinvention of baseball.

A remarkable number of inventive and ambitious men came from the tiny population of the offshore islands. One thinks instantly of Henry Luce, who founded the Time Inc. publishing empire, and the Macy who founded the Macy chain of stores. The source of their ambition may be found in the unique nature of the islands and the island dwellers.

Grand chieftain and progenitor of Alick's clan was Cap'n Edward Cartwright. Edward left the little fishing village of Dittisham, Devonshire, where he was born in 1640, to come to America not long after 1660. Here his home port was Hog Island (now Appledore Island) among the foggy and treacherous Isles of Shoals, off His Majesty's province of New Hampshire near the stately old town of Portsmouth. Cartwright became a seafaring man renowned all along the coast, from Block Island to Prince Edward Island, for his courage and his knowledge of channels and harbors.

During interludes in Boston Harbor, the glamorous sea captain met and captivated the fancy of Miss Elizabeth Morris of proper Roxbury. They married and had a son, Nicholas, in 1666. The elder Cartwright removed to Nantucket in the spring of 1676 "to teach fishing." Prudently preparing for his move in 1672, Cartwright had purchased from William Worth the beautiful point named Pocomo Neck. (He bought several additional lots from Indian sachems Wat Noose and Wauwinnet.) This salt-grass-bordered peninsula, separating Head of the Harbor from the lower and Polpis or Quaise harbors, remains one of the loveliest spots on Nantucket or the entire coast. A gentle and delicate littoral landscape in summer, a harshly beautiful windswept but warm land's end in winter, it flames each fall in the orange, red, and rust patchwork of heather. Here the vigorous Master Cartwright settled down to teach the catching and curing of codfish, among other matters of moment.

With occasional lapses into indecorum. Although Edward had been a constable or deputy sheriff on the Isle of Shoals, where his duties included arresting folk for such offenses as drinking, swearing, and Sabbath-breaking, on Nantucket former Constable Cartwright was himself hailed into court and fined for several transgressions, such as "allowing his pigs to run at large on the common." Probably he considered this amusing, for he had a puckered-lip Yankee sense of humor.

Or perhaps that is only the view of the first American Cartwright held by his friends, the sort of history that usually appears in books. If a reader searches far enough, he sometimes can almost re-enter a period and see its inhabitants in the complexity of real life. For Cartwright had enemies too. They have preserved for us the news that Cartwright "was often fined for drunkenness, assault, disturbing the peace, selling rum and for controversies with Indian neighbors." A big, boisterous man, Edward may actually have committed such sins. There was a Dodge City atmosphere about the Isle of Shoals fishing camps which would have required a certain toughness to live there and a rather rough man to survive as constable. But caution is mandatory here. During Nantucket feuds, one faction would rather hilariously rewrite the court records to please themselves and discredit their opponents, and there is evidence tending to show that at least one of Captain Cartwright's "offenses" was manufactured.

Colorful stories surround Edward's marriages, almost unknown stories which would have made scarlet scandals in the 1600's. Cartwright ostensibly died in 1671, you see. A record of the Boston Probate Court says he "was miscarried in a boat at sea and supposed to be drowned." Yet early next year he bought Pocomo Neck and in 1676 appeared on Nantucket with a new wife. When his first wife, Elizabeth Morris, died a little later, she left a large estate of £241 15s. 8d. Perhaps she had money of her own which she did not want to leave to her estranged husband, and therefore invented Edward's death. More likely Edward, wanting nothing more to do with his wife, arranged the only "divorce" possible in those days.

Some of Cartwright's descendants became established in the little village of Ellsworth, in northwestern Connecticut. Although there was no baseball mentioned in early Ellsworth, a remarkable primitive cricket apparently thrived at house- and barn-raisings prior to about 1820. An observer wrote:

These "raisers" were also wicket-ball players of no mean ability from the days of training [or militia] and spring elections to the present day. This "farmer's cricket" as it might be called may puzzle some far-away cousin, so I'll append a slight description. 1. Given a bowling ground fifty to seventy feet long and wide as a rake tail; 2. Given a rake's tail on a couple of bricks at each end of this alley; 3. Given a man in front of each armed with a bat shaped like the figure nine reversed to keep the ball from knocking down the stick; 4. Given a bowler behind each rake's tail armed with a ball five to seven inches in diameter, obliged to make it touch the ground his side of the middle line, fiercely determined to make it twirl over the opposite bit of wood and you have the principal elements. All around are fielders from six to eighty(!), as you may have men enough, of all ages, all trying to put out the batter and to help the bowlers. The rules are cricket rules adapted to the circumstances. Here you have the best rural game there is in its simplicity and comprehensiveness.

Well, it certainly comprehended the maximum number of players.

Meanwhile, back at Nantucket, the Cartwrights were proliferating and carrying on the family's centuries-old seagoing tradition. Young Edward married Ruth West of Martha's Vineyard, who gave birth to sons named Bryant, Abner (Abner *Cartwright?*), Samuel, Gideon, and Judah, plus three more who did not live. Ann Swain, descendant of one of the colony's founders and perhaps a neighbor girl, was wed to Samuel and presented him with a boy, Benjamin. In early spring of 1770, when he was not yet quite twenty years of his age, Benjamin married Rebecca Luce from his grandmother's home, the Vineyard. Becky Luce, incidentally, was of the Luces that produced Henry Luce. Born to Benjamin and Rebecca as the storm clouds of revolution dissipated was a son, whom they named Alexander Joy Cartwright, probably about 1784. Raised to be a ship's master like his father, Alexander had no lack of relatives in that business. Cartwrights abounded on the main.

Alexander's cousin, Captain John Cartwright, was the most famous—or notorious—Cartwright during the Revolutionary period. It was John Cartwright's sorry duty, as master of the sloop *Speedwell*, to sail to the British naval headquarters at Newport in April of 1779 to plead for a status of neutrality for Nantucket.

Actual starvation may have confronted the islanders when they sent Captain Cartwright, who was not a Quaker and therefore doubly unhappy with his mission. He later partly recompensed by commanding the first ship to flaunt the rebellious thirteen stripes in British Canada and Jamaica, even before the war was over.

But even incomplete rolls show that William Cartwright served in the Revolutionary navy, and a Thomas Cartwright was "lost at sea," probably in the navy. In 1780 the Quakers disowned Jonathan Cartwright for "going to sea in an armed vessel" after a long struggle with his conscience. He had already lent a substantial sum of money to the struggling Colonies, with no thought of being repaid, against Quaker teaching.

And it is of no mean significance that Reuben Joy, one of twenty Nantucketers who served with John Paul Jones on the *Ranger* and the *Bon Homme Richard*, led the famous charge that captured the *Serapis* in the most renowned engagement of American naval history. "Joy," Alexander Cartwright's uncommon middle name, invokes a whale of a lot of other associations with sail and seagoing. The surname Joy fairly speckles the maritime history of New England.

David Joy, grandson of the first Joy on Nantucket, took as his second wife Phebe Cartwright Meader, a widow. (When the Nantucketers of oldentime escaped accident, they lived to vigorous elderhood, although the sea swallowed many a husband, and puerperal fever killed many more wives in childbirth. It was common, given the enormous families of the day, for a man to run through two or three wives.) Phebe was the daughter of Samuel Cartwright and therefore Alexander Joy Cartwright's aunt. A famed Nantucket shipmaster, Captain Obed Joy, was born of David and Phebe's union. Uncle Obed survived two shipwrecks within three years in faraway oceans. Knotting the two lines further, Obed married Anna Cartwright, becoming Alexander's brother-in-law as well as his uncle! Since there is good reason to believe that Alexander Joy Cartwright was directly descended from Joys himself, he was probably also a cousin. Obed and Anna compounded confusion by naming their second son Alexander—Alexander Cartwright Joy. This first cousin of Alexander Joy Cartwright later caused further complexity by—no, let that maze suffice for the moment.

Such intertangled relationships were common on the cozy little island. When it was said jokingly to one lady of Nantucket that possibly the entire population was related, she replied very seriously, "Oh, very likely; I have five thousand cousins on Nantucket."

Nowhere, even in New England, has any people reveled in quite so bedrock-deep a sense of identity, relatedness (a basic kind of relevance, after all), and belongingness.

Nantucketers composed doggerels that make up in sharp prickly caricature of the sub-clans' temperaments what they lack in meter and rhyme:

> The Rays and Russells coopers are;
>   The knowing Folgers lazy;
> A learned Coleman very rare,
>   And scarce an honest Hussey.
>
> The Coffins noisy, factious, loud,
>   The silent Gardners plodding,
> The Mitchells good, the Barkers proud,
>   The Macys eat the pudding.

And so on. In a somewhat later version, the Cartwrights and Joys are limned thus:

> Come, Cartwrights, square in thought and act,
>   More sober-hued than gay. . . .
> Come, Joys, 'tis said that you can brag,
>   (And some we know were able)
> We look to you that talk shan't flag,
>   For that's good sauce at table.

Nantucket must have spent its weather-locked winter months contriving these things. The native loved to rhyme. Advertisements, wedding announcements, letters, anything might be put in doggerel. Bartlett Coffin, a blacksmith, sent a note to Hazadiah Cartwright:

> Hazadiah,
> I desire
> That thou an adze would make me;
>   And when 'tis done,
>   Set down the sum—
> The money I'm to stake thee.

Cartwright replied:

> I and my lads
> have made thy adze,

> Though nothing have to boast on;
>   So take it away
>   And the money pay:
> 'Tis cheaper than in Boston.

The tarragon spiciness of these island Yankees can scarcely be exaggerated. And Alexander Cartwright himself had exactly the same kind of sense of humor.

It was that kind of overpowering legend and total enthrallment to the sibilant wash of waves against a wooden hull that Captain Alexander Joy Cartwright left to make his way in the booming seaport of New York.

The Second War of Independence, the War of 1812, had left Nantucket temporarily destitute of its principal livelihood, whaling. More exposed to British naval power than ever, the lonely island had again declared neutrality and had even been obliged to suspend payment of taxes to the Federal Government.

The Cartwrights again had been prominent in trying to alleviate Nantucketers' distress in the War of 1812, in which the islanders had suffered more than during the Revolution. Members of the Federalist party, by then a minority on Nantucket as in Washington, held a meeting on April 30 of 1812 at which it was voted that John Cartwright and six others be formed a committee to "draught a petition to Congress." On a petition signed by many of the island's most prominent citizens, noting that "we shall be destitute of fuel and provisions and our families must be reduced to the extremes of hunger and want," appear the signatures of Alexander Cartwright, George Cartwright, Robert Joy, David Joy, Moses Joy, and Reuben Joy—shipmasters all.

After the peace, conditions became almost worse. Many Nantucketers had to sell property to pay taxes, and the year of 1815 was the coldest in history. Ice cut off communication with the mainland during the winter, and even in June ice formed on ponds and killed vegetation.

Morals too seem to have been affected adversely by the war. John and Charles Cartwright were put on a committee to investigate the worst of the evils. (Somehow, perhaps because of their physical size, the Cartwrights always seemed to get involved in peacekeeping.)

The aftermath of the same war had benefited New York, however. Because New York as usual had been less than extreme in its defense of the United States cause, the British chose it as the dumping ground for their excess goods bottled up by the war, hoping also to injure infant American manufacturing. This, together with its central location on the seaboard, access to the Hudson River and later the Erie Canal and a magnificent harbor, enabled New York to drain shipping away from all other ports. Alexander Cartwright, like many a young man before and since, was almost required to come to the city to earn a living. Besides all that, Alexander had been one of the Nantucket men captured by the British navy, and he had not enjoyed the British prison ship.

Cartwright settled permanently in New York in 1816, but he had scouted the city thoroughly before that on previous voyages. He appears in New York records as early as 1812, when he was fined for berthing improperly. The city Common Council seems to have rescinded the fine, however, for its minutes state, "Petitions from Alexander J. Cartwright & from Vose & Lightbaum praying remission of penalties inquirred under the law regulating the lying of Vessels in the Public Slips, were read and referred to the Council of the Board with authority to remit the penalties. . . ."

Captain Cartwright was also fined in 1816, perhaps upon the very occasion of his arrival to live in New York, for "landing passengers illegally." Contrary to the flavor of aliens and ship-jumping this conjures up, his offense seems to have been mere failure to register with the incipient bureaucracy, for on September 23, "Upon the Report of the attorney penalties were remitted to Captn Barber, Cartwright [and many others] incurred by not reporting passengers agreably to law."

The young bachelor soon concluded to like his new home, despite these annoyances. When Alexander Cartwright first arrived in 1816, New York was a fine place to make money. Captain Cartwright's first voyages earned him healthy profits. And, not least, New York abounded in attractive girls, of a far fancier variety than those on Nantucket. Handsomest of all, Captain Cartwright thought, was Miss Ester Rebecca Burlock. And, indeed, for at least a generation, many New Yorkers had considered the Burlock women the greatest beauties on the island. Blithe young ladies they were, too, tomboyish brilliant horsewomen, able to ride the wildest animals without saddle or bridle.

Captain Cartwright fell in love instantly, proposed almost immediately, and married Miss Burlock as soon as decorum permitted. After the proper intervals, the couple had three sons and four daughters. The oldest, Alexander Jr., acquired his own fame, of course, as the man who invented baseball, but his younger brother, Alfred DeForest, is also interesting because he "vanished" from New York at the same time and, even more, because of his name.

As the fact that she gave her son the name Alfred DeForest indicates, Ester Burlock was descended from the almost unknown *real* founder of New Amsterdam (way back in 1624), who wasn't Dutch at all! While the Cartwrights and the Joys could boast only of having been among the earlier settlers of the Massachusetts Bay Colony and of Nantucket, the DeForests had been the leaders of the original party colonizing New York.

The DeForests were Walloon Huguenots—stocky, relatively dark-skinned, mercurial Celtic Protestants who fled Belgium to escape persecution, torture, and death in the Inquisition. During that forcible re-Catholicization of their homeland, at least 100,000 Walloons were killed, and some half a million left. The DeForests went to Leyden in Holland, where they were neighbors and friends of the English Puritan pilgrims who had also sought refuge there. They were great admirers of William Bradford, the English leader, and they constantly talked with the English pilgrims, often discussing settling together somewhere in America.

DeForest first thought of moving to Guiana—that "fertill place" in a "hott climat," as Bradford called it—but was also influenced by Bradford's eventual choice of Virginia, where English colonists had recently become established at James Towne. When the *Mayflower* company, inadvertently landing in the northern "Cape Cod" region instead of Virginia, survived their first harsh winter of 1620, DeForest was much encouraged. He applied to the English king for permission to plant his colony in Virginia. The request was granted, but under the conditions that they all must take an oath to "bee conformable to the Churche of England" and that, since "it is not expedient that the sayd families should bee sett downe in one gross bodie," they be scattered among "the naturall Englishe." Naturally, DeForest refused, even when the English king's ministers reminded him that it was "so Royall a favour in his Ma'tie and so singular a benefitt to the said Walloons and ffrenchmen to be admitted to live in that fruitfull land under so mighty and pious a Monarch as his Ma'tie is." Instead, in the ships and under the sponsorship of the

Dutch West Indies Company, the Walloons set sail in two separate parties, saying regretful farewells at Madeira.

One party sailed to Guiana, where they settled on the Wyapoko River, admiring the strange tropical fruits and vegetables. There they were stranded by the company, contrary to its promise to send more supplies and colonists. They endured much suffering. Jesse DeForest himself died of sunstroke in the equatorial heat. By 1625 they were obliged to give up the struggle.

The *Maeckereel* (the good ship *Mackerel*) meanwhile arrived at what the colonists named Nieuw Nederlandt late in December of 1624. There they found a French captain just preparing to claim the land for hated Catholic Louis. They drove France off with one well-placed cannon and landed to found a Dutch colony. Wallabout Bay, opposite Manhattan on the Brooklyn side, obscurely and redundantly preserves their memory to this day, for it is really "Waalbogt"—Walloons' Bay.

The surviving DeForests moved to the north part of Manhattan in 1637, son Henri resettling on a hundred morgens of land "between the hills and the kill that runs round the island"—that is, between Morningside Heights and Harlem Creek and between what are now 124th and 109th streets, in the toils of present-day Harlem. Isaac, his brother, settled on a mile-long 100-acre strip of land starting opposite Henri on Harlem Creek and extending to Hellegat opposite Bronck's Kill, where he had built an 18' × 30' house for $160. When Indian attacks necessitated that the settlers gather in a village in 1658, a part of this became the site of Nieuw Haerlem, where Alexander Cartwright and his Knickerbockers were to repair for moonlit joy rides after baseball games 190 years later. Isaac's wagon-track farm lane became Haerlem's first street.

Isaac, tired of Indian raids, moved to the Marckveldt (Market Square) and then to Brouwer Straet. He had Brewer Street paved at his own expense, and this first paved lane thus became known as Stone Street, on which little street the Alexander Cartwright family lived for one year in 1846 and 1847, probably quite unaware of its history.

DeForests remained prominent in city affairs and prosperous in business for years. While Alexander Cartwright, Jr., lived in New York, a DeForest was an alderman (who married another Burlock girl) and DeForest & Company was a leading shipping agent.

When he first arrived in New York and was not yet a cousin of the

DeForests by marriage, Alexander Sr. lived at the corner of Grand and Roosevelt streets, now in the lowest lower East Side but then well uptown. This bucolic neighborhood of little gardens, neat picket fences and quaint, modest, gabled and gambreled wooden houses along cobblestoned streets probably somewhat reminded Captain Cartwright of home as he stepped briskly along its brick sidewalks. Do not visit the warrens of the present-day lower East Side if you wish to reconstruct the look and feeling of Cartwright's first dwelling. Visit Nantucket instead, or the more modest houses of the restored Colonial capital of Virginia, Williamsburg. So far has New York progressed in 156 years.

The tricornered hats and knee breeches of recent Colonial and early Federal days had not entirely yielded to beaver hats and stove-pipe trousers. Most of the buildings and street scenes remained. Captain Cartwright undoubtedly frequented the famed old Tontine Coffee House at the corner of Wall and Water streets, at the head of Coffee House Slip, where the leading sea traders gathered daily to share merry jest, earnest political conversation, and endless gossip of business. Attractive Federal townhouses with tiny dormers and ornate doorways, converted to business establishments, still lined the streets of the mercantile section. Whale-oil lamps still lit the lanes and houses, and the forests of masts and rigging at the streets' ends increased monthly.

Grand Street proved too far inland from his beloved ships, and in 1817 Cartwright moved to the east end of Water Street, at No. 364, where he could look out across the wharves to the comings and goings of the square riggers. Perhaps because he or his wife Ester regarded the waterfront as a bit too gamey for raising a family—an early nineteenth-century respectable one, at any account—Cartwright moved back to the genteel locale of Lombardy Street, a block and a half from the water, in 1818. (Lombardy became Monroe Street after that Democratic-Republican President had been retired from office long enough to seem less objectionable to the largely Federalist shippingmen. This was west of the monumental Hendrick Rutgers mansion, built of bricks imported from Holland in 1754, and its manicured grounds.) On this street Cartwright maintained his shipping-business premises for four years. In the little house on Lombardy Street, in this New York that was so beautiful in springtime, Alexander Joy Cartwright, Jr., was born on a fine baseball opening day, April 17, 1820.

Little Alick entered a New York City whose doors were seldom locked and where "it was not considered at all necessary that counters of banks should be shut in by iron gratings, since sneak-thieves and the like were seldom heard of." Its entertainments were quilting parties, candy-pullings and conversation refreshed by hickory nuts, apples, new cider, and doughnuts. Street lamps went unlit when the moon was as much as a quarter full. Vendors of clams, oysters, buns, yeast, hot spiced gingerbread, tea rusk, hot corn, and baked pears sang their wares everywhere, tantalizing little boys and grown men. Little boys were also tantalized by visions of ice cream (in vanilla, lemon, or strawberry) at the shops of Mrs. Usher or John Contoit, where pound cake, lemonade (and claret and cognac) were also to be had. Their fathers, although whiskey was unknown and champagne rare, could obtain rum at three cents the glass and ale at two cents, paying for all these purchases with Spanish coins extracted from the lining of their beaver hats, which also held segars, handkerchief, and gloves.

Five stages ran daily to Greenwich Village, but only one to Harlem. Excellent fishing for striped bass, weakfish, drum, and porgies was available from the Battery. Cows wandered the streets, and children played in haylofts and beside brooks. Women wore leghorn bonnets, ribbons hanging to the ground, tortoise-shell combs, and fur muffs large enough to serve as shopping bags. There were fewer than 4,000 Catholics in all of New York. Young Alexander could ride a horse from the Cartwrights' own stable or walk to see the shipyards, sailmakers, and rope walks. He could press his nose against the window of a bakery making delectable cream puffs or a chocolate store grinding chocolate into paste between white stone rollers. He might buy iceland moss drops or molasses candy or roll his hoop or simply lie down on the grass and listen to the bees buzz. At night the low rumble of the stages over the cobblestones would put him to sleep. In winter he and his friends would get sleigh rides, with the harness bells sounding cheerful, straw and blankets to keep their feet warm, and all the grownups along the sidewalks smiling at their delight. And he would play the primitive baseball of the time, for Alexander was said to have enjoyed the game above all else from his earliest childhood.

Before that, when Alexander was about a year old, he was bundled up and moved to 13 Rivington Street, within a perambulator stroll of open country and only a few houses east of pretty Bowery

Road, the beginning of the Boston Post Road. On Rivington, the Cartwrights lived until 1827, when Alick was seven.

A few years later they were on Cherry Street, way out near Corlaer's Hook, in a house that provided the best view yet of the harbor and shipping on the East River, as well as the picturesque village of Brooklyn (Breuckelen, the older Dutch persisted in calling it) on the green heights opposite, reached by a ferry docking nearby. Cherry Street supplied this view by rising on the lower edge of the hill called Crown Point, a natural vantage point at Manhattan's southeast corner which the British and Hessians had occupied and fortified in the first war for independence and which had once been the site of a massacre of local Indians whom the Dutch had mistakenly believed to be gathering for an assault. A lovely sandy beach was a place for the Cartwrights to swim and fish and for ten-year-old Alexander to dig for the treasure his father told him the pirate captains Kidd and Teach had buried there.

For some reason, possibly because it was new and fashionable and Mrs. Cartwright therefore liked it, the family later moved to 271 Mott Street in 1832, way up near Bleecker Street and Washington Square. Although Mott Street has become nearly synonymous with Chinatown, the first Chinaman was not to make his appearance in the area for several decades. Cows were as common as people, which appropriately illustrates the radical change of the neighborhood, since the appearance of a spotted Holstein now would create about the same sensation that the appearance of a pigtailed Chinese would have in 1832. There the Cartwrights could walk three blocks west to Niblo's Gardens, the most popular spot for theatricals, music, and refreshment in the city.

In 1836, the Cartwrights' urbane and carefree life in the pleasantest parts of the city ended. "Captain Cartwright lost most of his fortune in unfortunate investments," according to an old family tradition. His losses may have been in the early stages of the economic downturn causing the panic of 1837. The panic was, until 1929, the most severe in 324 years of American enterprise. Within three weeks, 250 businesses in New York failed, with liabilities over the gargantuan sum of $100 million. (The mysterious firm of "Cartwright & Grant" may have been involved. Perhaps Mr. Grant's business advice was none too sound.) Sixteen-year-old Alexander, in the best tradition of plucky nineteenth-century youth, demanded to leave school and begin to contribute to the family's support. He entered the Wall Street offices of Coit & Cochrane, Stock Brokers, as the lowliest clerk. Levi Coit, a merchant in New York seemingly from the beginning of time (he appears in the very earliest business directories) apparently had some acquaintance with the elder Cartwright and therefore gave his son a job.

Back down to more modest quarters on Rivington Street moved the Cartwrights. The cap'n struggled for a time to continue his investments in shipping until convinced by the panic that it would be wisdom to withdraw from speculation. He sadly took a much duller job as an inspector for the Marine Insurance Company in 1838, consoled by the fact that his duties still took him out on the wharves rather than confining him to the sterile stone of the huge Merchants Exchange, which stretched a whole block long and several stories high on Wall Street. And it was certainly a good respectable connection, for the president was related to Nathan Hale and the vice-president descended from the same Governor John Winthrop who had known a previous Joy in the Bay Colony. That year the captain was able to move back to an excellent neighborhood, at 305 Broome Street near Forsythe, a fashionable area near the Bowery and St. Stephen's Church. There he stayed for the unusually lengthy period of nine years, until he retired to the suburbs of 24th Street in 1847. Interestingly, by that time—since December of 1843—he was working for Philip Hone, a highly respected former mayor of the city whose diary ranks among the most incisive accounts of New York in the nineteenth century. As Marine Inspector for Hone's American Mutual Insurance Company, its fourth-ranking officer, he drew a comfortable salary of $1,000 per year. The company's regard for him may be seen in that the Fire Inspector received only $300 per year and Philip Hone, Jr., working as a clerk, $450.

Young Alexander, by dint of hard work and application, had meanwhile earned the approbation of his elders in the countinghouses of Wall Street. His cheerful diligence enabled him to land the job of teller—then still a responsible and respected position—at the reputable Union Bank. Armed with the promise of this evidence of his station as a rising young man of the community, although only twenty-two, he proposed to Eliza Ann Gerrits Van Wie, the daughter of an old and prominent Albany family.

"Her father was Pieter Gerrit Van Wie," grandson Bruce Cartwright, Jr., told the Boston *Transcript*'s Yankee readers in 1915. "There is a tradition that . . . her father disappeared shortly after her birth, when she was taken to New York to live with her uncle Robinson. Her mother's name was Walsh, from Ireland, according to a memorandum left by my grandfather. Her aunt Robinson was also a Walsh. Eliza was very proud of her Walsh blood, claiming that her immediate ancestor had much to do with the Jacobite cause and Bonnie Prince Charles."

Dutch patroons with a large estate overlooking the Hudson River below Albany, the early Van Wies leased to New York in perpetuity the land on which the state capitol—and infamous modern $3 billion mall—is built. (As long as the state pays its annual peppercorn or nutmeg or whatever, their descendants have no power to keep Nelson Rockefeller from building whatever he likes on it.) A Van Wie Creek to the south preserves the name, which was Van der Weringen in the Netherlands. "Yet the first Van Wie was a pirate," said Jonathan Van Wie, a member of the family still living in New York City in 1972. "From the Frisian Islands, off the coast of Holland. He was ready to be executed in 1659, but they gave him the choice of deportation to America." Either buccaneer Van Wie was framed in the first place, or else he reformed suitable for framing. He and his family became the most respected of citizens in the new world.

When Eliza and Alexander married on the first Saturday of June in 1842, they were wed at the Third Free Presbyterian Church. At the corner of Thompson and Houston streets until 1858, the Free Church was so called because of its insistence that pews be neither rented nor sold. Its members were known for an evangelistic spirit, a strong anti-slavery stance, and maintenance of Christian standards in their personal lives.

A fine new uptown address at 76 Eighth Street, then in an elegant section known as Clinton Place but still reputable in the New York of today, was the newlyweds' first home. Alick and Eliza soon had four children as handsome as they. Like most of the children of parents who have weakened their roots and the continuity of family traditions by moving to a large and polyglot city, the young couple partially cut the skein of Christian names which extended back earlier than the Cartwrights' first history in Devonshire. They named their first son DeWitt, for Alick's friend, Knickerbocker Peter DeWitt; their second Bruce; their third child Kathleen Lee, for the colonel who befriended Alexander during the Mexican War. But the fourth and last child, born in 1848, received the name of Alexander Joy Cartwright III.

With their new responsibilities and dignity as family men, Alick and his brother Alfred went into business for themselves in 1845, opening a bookstore and stationer's shop on Wall Street. The store's location fluctuated only between numbers 67 and 17 on the end of Wall Street where the new Trinity Church was abuilding, but Alexander lived all over town—way east at 558 Fourth Street, far downtown at 4 Stone Street, far uptown at 341 Sixth Avenue, from 1847 to 1849.

Most of Alick's and Alf's stores were on the ground floor, a step or two below street level. Outdoor shelves and counters were laden with books and pamphlets to attract the passing bibliophile. A feature of New York street life in those days was a whole class of literary loungers who would wander from bookstore to bookstore as a hummingbird or bee drifts from flower to flower, sipping knowledge like nectar.

Of an occasional evening, the brothers would visit the entertaining book-auction house of Cooley, Keese & Company. Cooley and Keese's dry-witted auctioneers were creditable comedians, and people flocked to the sales. The informal "Bread and Cheese Club" at Wiley's bookshop—patronized by James Fenimore Cooper, Fitz-Greene Halleck, J. K. Paulding, Verplanck, Percival, and William Cullen Bryant—had disbanded, but Cooper and Poe and his sweet wife Annabel Lee were often to be seen.

The Cartwright brothers thought of their lovely, optimistic city much as did another early bookseller who wrote of "a vast city. . . sending forth the hum of more than 200,000 inhabitants. Freedom, peace and plenty are in their dwellings, and their destiny is as unclouded as the glorious vault of Heaven which stretches with all its stars above their heads." Even much later, un-Micawberish, waspish Charles Dickens remarked on "the immaculate blue sky which ever smiles on New York."

The patent Russ pavements of the city itself exuded a comfortable and reassuring spirit. Wide-spreading sycamores and old elms dignified Battery Park, and the nearly complete tower of Trinity Church soared far above Wall Street, easily overshadowing the strivings of commerce.

Linen and woolen drapers, and all the other merchants, left

quantities of goods on boxes and tables in the street, with no thought of precaution against theft. New York felt no great need of a regular police force before the 1850's. Complaining, however, of an increase in crime, the manual of the city corporation for 1846 listed a total of one case of murder and four cases of rape.

Stating the nearest commonplace piece of fact, Philip Hone could offhandedly call New York "a churchgoing community which boasts of its Sunday Schools and temperance societies." In 1849 a small New York confined to the tip of Manhattan possessed forty-one Episcopal churches, forty Presbyterian, thirty-one Methodist, twenty-three Baptist, seventeen Dutch Reformed, sixteen Roman Catholic, and many others of smaller denominations.

The older merchants, pompous in their swallow-tailed coats of glossy broadcloth and high choker collars and ruffled shirts, flattered by due respect of their worth, were a satisfied, dignified, unrestless body of men. When they met "on change" at the foot of Wall Street to hear announcements of the arrivals of a sea of ships, or retired to their counting-rooms, from whose small-paned and narrow-mutined windows they could survey their secure domain, they were content. But the brothers Cartwright were young men. When they visited their father on the same Coffee House Slip, they saw with different eyes the lifting topsails of the ships faring forth around the world and back again, venturing every bay of every ocean. When the serried masting of ships knotted Manhattan in a corded web of rigging, when the cleft of every street was barred at dockside by the yards and top hamper of vessels unloading the yield of seven seas, when the slanting shadows of rows of bowsprits and figureheads fell on the cobblestones of narrow South Street, the young men may have felt bound and overshadowed. They certainly felt restless, however much they liked bookselling and baseball and bustling Wall Street and their many friends.

Established as they were in one of the most enjoyable cities of the world, the Cartwrights had a promising business of their own, devoted wives, attractive children, and a warm circle of friends. And Alexander's hobby of his own inventing was already showing signs of becoming much more than a mere pastime.

Yet when they accompanied Captain Cartwright to the Astor House, where shipbuilders, captains and traders talked till late at night of ships and ports, they felt more unrest.

CHAPTER NINE

ALEXANDER JOY CARTWRIGHT, JR., VANISHED FROM NEW YORK FOR A simple but highly romantic reason: He went west in the gold rush.

To rediscover the inventor who was lost so long, one must leap backward in time to the third winter following his founding of modern baseball. The year was 1848. The place, a gravelly willow-grown gravel bar along the winding Rio Americano (near what was to become the mining town of Coloma, California). On a chill, misty January day, a deathly quiet place in a lonesome wilderness became one of the world's focal points. Within the time it took August Sutter's millwheel to make one turn, the placid post-Revolutionary society of nineteenth-century America was launched into a great lunge westward, driven by the triple engines of greed, gold, and glory.

For mill foreman Jim Marshall happened to notice, scattered atop the dirt heap dug from the mill race, flakes of some dully shining metallic substance. "This day some kind of mettle was found in the tail race that looks like goald, first discovered by James Martial, the Boss of the Mill," a Mormon worker wrote. Crazy Jim Marshall, strange agent of predestination. The mill race should never have been dug. It was needed only because wheelwright Marshall had built the mill in the wrong place, where water would have had to run uphill to turn its wheel. The mill itself should never have been built. The plan to raft logs down the wild American River was impractical.

Sutter did not believe Marshall until he had pounded the metal, bitten it, put it in acid. Then, oppressed by deep foreboding, he swore his workmen to secrecy. More interested in steady jobs than a few bits of metal, they agreed. It was Sutter himself who, goaded by his dangerous knowledge, could not resist telling. Even then, the news slowly spread around San Francisco without waking the sleepy frontier outpost. Gold dust was seen, but no one thought much about it. Until one day Mormon elder Sam Brannan ran down the main street waving a bottle of it and shouting, "Gold! Gold from the American River!" The pueblo's torpor evaporated in an instant. By the next day, picks and shovels and supplies were selling for fifty times what they had before.

Had that soft yellow metal never been found, the great interior spaces of the mountain and desert West might, a hundred years later, still have been a semi-autonomous Indian nation, the slow flood of the teeming outside world lapping at its foothills only as late as the 1950's and '60's, held back by a depression and two wars and by indifference to a region apparently barren of all but beauty. But gold was found, perhaps unfortunately, and as inexorably as the rotation of the mill wheel, America stopped being a land in which prosperity was mostly a slow accretion of small goods created by unremitting work, a reward earned slowly but certainly. Wealth before was a hand-adzed beam, hewn by hours of labor, to be mortised into a house which might stand half a millennium. Wealth afterward was a mining-stock certificate which might be worth thousands one day and pennies the next.

Brannan's cry of "Gold on the American River!" spread and fevered the brains of all who heard it. But it did not race eastward like prairie fire, as is commonly believed. Although attempts at secrecy were little hindrance, the depth of the wilderness and the length of the passage around Cape Horn certainly were. Rumors did not reach New York until July.

Five months after leaving San Francisco, a ship owned by the father of William Vail, a Knickerbocker, docked at South Street with a cargo of hides from California. The captain brought to his owner the first printed confirmation of the discovery, the March 15 copy of the new territory's pioneer paper, *The Californian*. An obscure little notice at the bottom of page two said, "Gold mine found. In the newly made raceway of the Saw Mill recently erected by Captain Sutter, on the American Fork, gold has been found in considerable quantities. One person brought $30 worth to New Helvetia, gathered there in a short time."

Half buried in the middle of a dense column of type, the next day's New York *Herald* reported, "The gold discovered in December [sic] last on the south branch of the American Fork . . . is only three feet below the surface. . . . Without allowing any golden hopes to puzzle my prophetic vision of the future, I would predict for California a Peruvian harvest of the precious metals. . . ." Yet enthusiasm languished. Everyone knew that there was no gold in California. Encyclopedias published as late as 1852 in New York continued to say so. It was widely suspected that the rumors were a device to lure immigrants to the howling wilds. Finally Governor Mason and William Tecumseh Sherman sent 230 ounces in a tea caddy to Washington. The gold arrived at the end of November. On December 7, lame-duck President Polk confirmed the news in his State of the Union message. "The supply is very large," he said.

Then the fever outsped telegraph and truth. Nuggets that had been the size of acorns became the size of hen's eggs and of apples, and they lay strewn about atop the ground besides. Excited men talked long dark evenings away in every chimney corner of every hill farm in New England. Lantern light shone out in wavering lines through the chinks of Southern cabins long after choretime, and whale-oil lamps burned late in the Federal houses of New York as families tried the foreign word *Cal-ee-for-nee-ay* on their tongues. On Sixth Avenue near 21st Street, in one of those Greek Revival houses, Alexander Joy Cartwright, Jr., contracted to buy *his* Conestoga wagon, wrote his outfitter to arrange supplies. But twenty-nine-year-old Cartwright was not so mesmerized by fever to see gold as some of his friends. Big, genial, outgoing Alick planned to go west with the 49ers for fun and adventure. Along the way, characteristically, he became a Johnny Appleseed of baseball, proselytizing recruits to the game from Hoboken to Hangtown and eventually to Honolulu.

Ironically, we would never have known this or much else about Alexander Cartwright had organized baseball not decided to invent Abner Doubleday. While the game's moguls were planning and publicizing the "centennial" of 1939 at Cooperstown, a letter arrived from the remote territory of Hawaii. The hoopla had been loud enough to reach the mid-Pacific. Bruce Cartwright, Jr., happened to know enough and take enough pride in his late grandfather's achievement to write a modest demurrer which set off the chain of investigation which eventually toppled the whole Doubleday fabrication.

Even the few facts that Bruce Cartwright mentioned in his letter were truer and more complete than the Mills Commission fictions. When the centennial organizers made the merest beginnings at researching Cartwright's claim, its validity immediately became apparent. That some concession must be made was soon obvious. Organized baseball put up a small plaque honoring Cartwright in its Hall of Fame (and also in Hoboken). To this day, no commemoration of Doubleday appears in the museum that was erected in his home town, the ostensible site of his inauguration of the game!

Bruce Cartwright Jr. died a few weeks after writing his historic letter. Had he died earlier, the true story would very possibly never have been known. As it was, his abrupt death largely cut off further recognition of his grandfather's contribution and enabled organized baseball to settle back into an embarrassed silence about the true origins of the sport. Many, many details are undoubtedly permanently lost. In the Hall of Fame itself, virtually the only evidences of Cartwright are the plaque and a few letters deep in the files, including the letter from Bruce. But Bruce's letter provided just enough clues to begin this revival of the search for baseball's gestation, which started in 1968, another thirty years after Bruce Jr.'s hesitant correction.

Besides the basic story of Cartwright's invention and of his disappearance, and the establishment of the fact that he and his descendants had resurfaced in Hawaii, the letter revealed that somewhere in Honolulu there apparently existed not only the diary kept by Cartwright on his journey across the plains but also the original ball used by the Knickerbockers, made of parchment covered with catgut and brought west by Alexander as a memento! (When Lee Allen, the dedicated and encyclopedic late baseball historian at Cooperstown, was first told of these in the course of preparation of this book, he practically started salivating. You could see him mentally designing the display case. The recovery of two such relics would be purely astonishing.)

Cooperstown had been sent a copy of the diary, as Bruce's letter had promised, but the diary itself was nowhere to be found by 1968. All that was left was Bruce's tantalizing description. "It took him 156 days to travel from Newark, N.J., to San Francisco," he wrote. "He walked the whole distance. Whenever they rested and had enough people to form two baseball nines, they played 'base ball,' according to letters to old Knickerbockers. I can work out his 'Log' day by day from March 1, 1849, when he left Newark, to August 10, 1849, when he arrived in San Francisco, if it is desired."

In my possession there was also a 1939 letter from a Honolulu businessman and Cartwright acquaintance. He wrote:

> The centennial has a more particular significance to Honolulu than any other city in the United States, for it was on August 28, 1849, that Alexander Joy Cartwright Jr., the father of modern base-ball, landed in Honolulu to make the then little hamlet of the Sandwich Islands his home.
>
> As a consequence, Honolulu is one of the oldest baseball cities in the United States and has never, at any time, relinquished its special love of the national pastime. It is hard to conceive of a more rabid baseball city than Honolulu when we take into consideration the fact that Honolulu has more baseball clubs and leagues than any other city of like size [215,000 population, approximately].
>
> In 1845, [Cartwright] laid out the first baseball diamond, as it is now used, and planned a new game. He also organized the Knickerbocker Baseball Club, which is the rightful ancestor of the big-league teams of today. A ceremony fitting the occasion will attend the unveiling on June 12, 1939, of a duplicate plaque of the one . . . in the Hall of Fame. It will be placed in Honolulu "Hale" —City Hall.

Dishearteningly, by 1968 all Cartwright descendants had died or left Hawaii. There was just one mention that one Cartwright had moved to Santa Rosa, California. Not very hopefully, a call was put in to the Santa Rosa information operator. Did she have a listing for a William Edward Cartwright? She *did*? Eureka!

William turned out to be not only alive and real in Santa Rosa but friendly and helpful too. Bill did indeed have the last remaining copy of his great-grandfather's log and would send it along "as soon as my wife, Anne, can type a copy." Shades of his ancestor, he also turned out to be a zealot in behalf of popularizing a brand-new sport—skibobbing, a kind of bicycling on skis that allows almost anyone to get out on the slopes and perform expertly. Ironically, the effort is handicapped by William Cartwright's own obscurity in the sports world.

After a fervent pitch for skibobbing, William added quite casually, "By the way, my son is following in his great-great-grandfather's footsteps as a member of the 'Indians' team of the Rincon Valley Little League. He's quite a good ball player, too."

Alexander Joy Cartwright IV—a Little Leaguer!

The log, when it arrived, was a remarkable document—one of the most interesting accounts of life on the Oregon Trail during the gold rush as well as a revealing depiction of the man who invented baseball. But the original Knickerbocker ball had somehow been lost; Bill did not know how. And Bruce Cartwright, Sr., Alexander's son, being an unnecessarily stuffy sort of man, had burned the original diary because it contained information "potentially damaging to prominent people in California and Hawaii." Bruce saved only what he considered of proper historical interest, omitting all of the scandal and, because he was not interested in the game himself, most of the baseball. Too bad, for what remains in the bowlderized version is fascinating. Reading even the incomplete diary is to see the past as present, to live the life of the 1840's and the westward hegira as its experiencers did.

Happily, letters and scattered other old sources also give a picture of Cartwright's sowing of baseball in the wilderness. One says that Alexander taught the game to "enthusiastic saloonkeepers and miners, to Indians and white settlers along the way" and "at nearly every frontier town and Army post where his wagon train visited." A secondary source describes the New Yorkers who accompanied Cartwright "laughing as they watched the converts to the game attempt to imitate their own grace and skill with the bat and ball, such as catching the ball with the hands cupped and allowing the hands to 'give' with the catch." Another source says, perhaps apocryphally, that one such match was interrupted by Indian attack.

"In 1848 gold was discovered in California and the news was published in all the newspapers of the country," William Cartwright paraphrases the introduction of his father's journal. "Alexander Joy Cartwright and his brother, Alfred DeForest Cartwright, finally decided to go to California in search of a fortune. Alfred, after providing for his wife and family, sailed for San Francisco, California, from Newport, R.I., by way of Cape Horn. Soon after this A.J.C. Jr. had an opportunity to join an expedition 'across the plains.'

"On March 1, 1849, Alexander, in company with Captain Thomas W. Seely and Captain Benjamin Franklin Woolsey, joined a party heading west. [It was a democratic company. It included besides Alick, a varnish dealer, a low-paid newspaper reporter, and a common laborer. Oddly, one of Seely's ancestors was magistrate at the Isle of Shoals when Edward Cartwright, Alick's ancestor, was constable there.]

"They proceeded to Pittsburg, Pa.," the narrative continues, "where they purchased their outfits, which were shipped to Independence, Missouri. They followed and arrived in St. Louis, Missouri, one month and 11 days (about April 11, 1849) from the time they left Newark, N.J."

When Alick walked down to the Hudson River landings this last time, he boarded not the Hoboken ferry at Barclay Street but the ferry for Jersey City and Newark, leaving from the foot of Cortlandt Street. At Newark station, the party embarked on the New Jersey Rail Road's 7:30 A.M. morning express "line" of steam cars, which showed that they had good heads on their shoulders as well as a few extra York shillings in their pockets. They might have taken the *Independence* or another one of the C & A's steamers to Amboy and ridden the Camden & Amboy for a dollar less than the four dollars they were paying to journey first class to Philadelphia, but the C & A was notorious to seasoned travelers. Its ferries were dirty and crowded, its trains usually late, frequently off the track and often dangerous. To make up lost time, C & A engineers often ran at excessive speeds, over twenty-five or even thirty miles per hour, and had a bad habit of leaving meeting points in vain attempts to reach the next siding before encountering an opposing train. One crash had nearly killed Congressman John Quincy Adams, the former President, and had critically injured Cornelius Vanderbilt. The faster New Jersey R.R., contrarily, could truthfully advertise that "no passenger within the cars had suffered in life or limb." Its sperm candles did, however, occasionally blow out when the cars were in motion. The New Jersey R.R. kept a passenger complaint book in its depots, provided free ferries and instead of inspecting tickets merely accepted a nod from the honorable gentleman as assurance that he had paid his fare.

At New Brunswick, the pioneers had to change to the cars of the

New Brunswick & Trenton Railroad, a part of the Camden & Amboy, and at Trenton to the Philadelphia & Trenton, an associated company. Arriving at Walnut Street Wharf shortly before noon, they undoubtedly stayed overnight in Philadelphia before proceeding to the Pennsylvania Central Railway depot, where they paid eleven dollars apiece for the privilege of riding over the mountains to Pittsburgh in little more than twenty-four hours traveling time.

(The latter-day Penn Central, which long ago absorbed the Camden & Amboy and partakes of its immoderately seedy character, hastens a modern traveler to Pittsburgh in seven hours and forty-three minutes for $20.25. But its lumpish executives exorcised romance from its pedestrian peregrinations years ago. Its sole surviving day train, the drearily named *Keystone*, offers only indifferent day coaches in lieu of parlor cars and unbuttered sandwiches in place of dinner in the dining car.)

Philadelphia was to occupy a unique position in the history of Cartwright's game. The city's first baseball team, the Minerva Club, organized in June of 1857 and thus became one of the very first outside New York. The Winona, United, and Benedict clubs were all formed before the Civil War, and the first match game was played on June 11, 1860, between the Equity and Winona clubs. Perhaps the greatest continuity anywhere between the earliest Cartwright-style baseball and the contemporary game is and was provided by a group of Philadelphia lawyers and merchants who, in 1859, began playing baseball under the name of the Athletics. They called themselves that because they were all members of the prestigious Philadelphia Athletic Club, a social organization for gentlemen. On April 7, 1860, they formally founded the Athletic Base Ball Club as a separate entity. By July 24 they were skilled enough to participate in the first inter-city match, a game at the Camac's Woods cricket grounds between the New York Excelsiors and an all-star team selected from the Athletics, Olympics, Benedicts, Winonas, Equities, and Uniteds. The Philadelphia upstarts won, 15–4.

An ungentlemanly lust for winning set in. In 1864, the Athletics became the first club to hire a star player away from another city, luring the Eckfords' crack second baseman by offering him the large sum of $1,000. The name of the player who jumped? None other than Al Reach. By 1864, a game with the Actives on their grounds at 25th and Jefferson drew an incredible crowd of 18,000, so rowdy that 125 policemen were needed to control it. The "first national championship," so called by the press, also involved the Reach-captained Athletics and an enormous crowd. Fully 40,000 sensation-seekers were attracted by the "Grand Match" of October 1, 1866. They pressed so tightly in upon the playing field that barely enough room could be cleared to begin the game. Eight thousand tickets were sold in advance for 25 cents apiece. As much as five dollars was paid for elevated views of the field. Housetops, trees, and fences around the 15th and Columbia playing ground were covered with spectators. "The trees bore human fruit," one newspaper put it. And the game had to be called "on account of crowd" in the bottom of the first inning when the baseball-mad mob surged in on the already foreshortened field.

For ninety-six years, from 1859 to 1955, when the A's fled to Kansas City, there was always a club called the Athletics playing baseball in Philadelphia. A charter member of the National Association of Professional Base Ball Players (the direct predecessor of the National League), they won its first championship in 1871 with a 22-7 record.

Philadelphia later also harbored an extraordinary personal continuity, a one-man link between early baseball and the contemporary game. In 1886 the three-year-old Phillies, a club bought by Al Reach and moved to Philadelphia from Worcester, Mass., played a game against Washington in which a stringy rookie named Cornelius McGillicuddy caught for the Nationals. Fifteen years later the same Connie Mack (as he was known for the convenience of sportswriters) received a quarter interest in the Athletics to become manager when the American League went big-time in 1901. It was a position he occupied for no less than half a century. By 1950 the gentlemanly eighty-eight-year-old Mack was a living anachronism, a man who had been in the major leagues for sixty-six years and who had been playing or managing baseball for eighty-three.

Mack, who was still "honorary leader" of the Athletics until he died in 1956, fifteen months after the A's moved to Missouri, began playing the game so early that Cartwright's version was not yet known by the younger boys in his mill town of East Brookfield, Massachusetts.

"It wasn't exactly baseball, but a sort of rounders or town ball," Connie remembered midway through the twentieth century. "With our bare toes we drew two rings thirty feet apart, with a batter in each ring. The pitcher stood outside the ring and tossed the ball to the batter. When the batter hit it, he ran for the opposite ring. He had to hit the ball out of the ring to be safe and keep his time at bat, and I can still recall the thrill of knocking the ball over the heads of the boys on that Brookfield field. It was not until I was older and bigger that I was permitted to graduate into the 'big boys' game,' where we had a big bat and a leather-covered ball, three bases and a home plate."

At that, Brookfield was not so unsophisticated. As late as 1898, when Ty Cobb was eleven years old, the only game boys in deepest Georgia played was town ball. The reason he became baseball's best base stealer, Cobb once said, was that he had learned to dodge balls thrown at him by town-ball players. And he was so adept at placing his hits because town ball allowed an unlimited number of fielders.

In 1849 Cartwright and his friends continued west from a Philadelphia still ignorant of baseball. Yet they preceded by only sixteen years a triumphal baseball tour of Pennsylvania by the Athletics. By 1865 Cartwright's game had become so much the mass madness that there were forty-eight clubs in the state and even the smallest towns clamored to see baseball games. The Athletics helped popularize baseball further by playing even infant clubs in remote places. Besides appearing at larger places like Lancaster and Harrisburg, they did not disdain Williamsport (which they beat 101-8) and Danville (which they beat 162-14). The Athletics got as far west as Pittsburgh in June of 1868, when they humiliated the native Olympics and Alleghenies nearly as badly.

Pittsburgh, where Cartwright stepped down from the modernity of a railway train and prepared to enter the West, seems an appropriate place to start retracing his trail of 1849 in more detail. To this point he traveled comparatively rapidly, having little contact with the land and inhabitants. Afterward he would walk or ride slowly, through demi-frontier. Following Cartwright's route, one might perhaps discover whether baseball remained a national preoccupation or if it had given way to more serious or violent concerns. Question: Was baseball flourishing or dying? Was it victim of a terminally diseased and conflicted latter-day American society that prefers the mirror of professional football, that no longer has patience or empathy for the orderly tranquillity of baseball?

To compare the beginnings of baseball with the America that has, perhaps, grown too old to play it, the author spent weeks on the road. The search for Alick's game told something about the present state of baseball, but more about the states, seen in a clear cross-section from a different perspective. Out of the reassuringly long continuum of pleasant places and people emerged a transcontinental series of intensely local vignettes.

PITTSBURGH, PENNSYLVANIA. At the starting point, on Memorial Day, the Pittsburgh Pirates were at home to—appropriately—the Metropolitans of New York, a team named for (but not descended from) a club contemporary with the old Knickerbockers. There was a kind of justice in the fact that the Metropolitans won both games, particularly since the hosts had elected to start a double-header at the bizarre hour of 10:30 A.M. on a field the approximate consistency of cold porridge. But it was reassuring and proper that the Pittsburgh management still be piratical.

A returned Union soldier, Al Pratt, had started Pittsburgh's first organized club, the Enterprise, in 1866. Formed soon after were the Xanthas and the Olympics. Undiscouraged by their trouncing at the hands of the Athletics, apparently, the latter took on the newly all-professional Cincinnati Red Stockings in 1869. Sadly for the locals, their beloved Olympics lost again, 54-2.

Even that didn't convince Pittsburgh immediately. It wasn't until 1876 that the Alleghenies paid all their players. But in 1882, when Pittsburgh became the founder of the American Association, first major rival of the National League, its representative was an all-pro Allegheny team. Its club retained that name for more than twenty years until—as a result of a freebooting career that saw them buy up most of the Columbus team in 1884, jump the American Association to take over the National League's Kansas City franchise in 1886, and raid the Philadelphia Athletics in 1891—they began being called "the Pirates" around the league.

Connie Mack, coincidentally, also came to the Pirates (sometimes known as "the Stogies," probably because their city was so smoky) in 1891, after the collapse of the ill-fated, athlete-owned Players Association. (Practically the only good player the Pirates had not lost to the Players Association in 1890, interestingly, was the famed center fielder and evangelist, Billy Sunday.) Although a jumper in 1890, Mack was converted into enough of an organization man to become manager of the Pirates in 1894.

CADIZ, OHIO. The tardiness of the Cartwright party's arrival in St.

Louis indicates that they probably continued west by land over the old National Road. The present U.S. 40 follows this route through Zanesville, Columbus, London and Springfield, Ohio; Richmond, Greenfield, Indianapolis, Brazil and Terre Haute, Indiana; and Marshall, Effingham and the old state capital of Vandalia in Illinois.

Near the recreated museum village of Gnadenhutten, a German frontier settlement, lies the only somewhat more modern village of Cadiz, among fresh green New England-style hills scarred in places by strip mines. Business blocks built in the Federal style surround the ornate green-copper-domed courthouse; mist blows through the great elms and around sleepy Victorian houses. Among notices of ice-cream socials and portraits of high-school seniors, store-window placards advertise a Decoration Day with all the traditional appurtenances: band music, a march to the cemetery, orations, a chicken fry, to be followed by . . . Well, almost traditional: The baseball feature is a Little League game. Alas, Alick, grown men no longer play baseball here.

But ten years after you passed by, the baseball fever was just beginning to rage here. After the Civil War it obsessed the boys and men. The Franklin Club, first in the old Northwest Territory, was organized as early as 1857. The North-Western Association of Base Ball Players, the first league in this half-settled country, was organized by 1865.

COLUMBUS, OHIO. Columbus was a major-league town in 1883, 1884, 1889, 1890, and 1891, when the American Association was major league. Since then it has been a bastion of minor-league Triple A ball. But the latter-day Columbus Redbirds are no more. In baseball, as in most other matters, Ohio State University is the only thing left in Columbus.

On this particular day, the Ohio State baseball field north of the university poultry sheds was hosting the finals of the Ohio high-school state tournament. Bumper-stickered cars crowded the parking lots and spectators crowded the grandstand as Old Fort played Seaman and Anna entertained Hannibal River Local. Ron Rau, a lanky blond right-hander soon to be typecast as the Rookie in a major-league training camp, beat Seaman with a six-hitter. After one day's rest he beat Anna in the finals, 6-0, allowing one hit and walking no one.

More remarkable was the Class AA performance of a southpaw from Shaw High in East Cleveland, a reedy young man named

Buddy Schultz. In the semifinals Shultz beat Columbus' Marion-Franklin 6-0, striking out thirteen without a walk. Twenty minutes later, Schultz was cranking up again. This time he beat Rogers of Toledo 1-0 on a two-hitter and struck out fourteen men.

Cartwright, accustomed to the free-hitting baseball of Knicker-bocker times, would have been astonished by both feats. So much has the level of baseball improved that the Nationals of Washington, the first team to make a Western trip (they appeared at Columbus, Cincinnati, Louisville, Indianapolis, St. Louis, and Chicago in 1867), would undoubtedly have lost even more ignominiously to either high-school pitcher, although they beat St. Louis 113-26.

LONDON, OHIO. London is twenty miles beyond Columbus, a distance it must have taken Cartwright almost exactly a day to travel. He probably stopped at the Colonial Red Brick Tavern, built in 1836, which is still operating (and serving an excellent mock turtle soup). More than just the Tavern recalls baseball's earliest days. In the waning light of afternoon Babe Ruth Leaguers are working out on one of the country's most picturesquely located diamonds—directly in the middle of a county fairgrounds race track. The 1850's atmosphere spills down out of the cavernous old grandstand onto the field. The left fielder stands in what is both an infield and an outfield, and he plays with his back to an ornate white judge's stand.

SPRINGFIELD, OHIO. At Wittenberg College pretty girls, flourishing fraternities, and an uncommonly tranquil elm-shaded campus update Cartwright's game—to the Twenties. Some major-league teams put names on uniforms; Wittenberg has pioneered nicknames. When II K A plays ΦMA, the Pekes' neatly sewed shirt lettering reads Boobie, New York, or Hunch.

INDIANAPOLIS. There were still Indians in the wilds of Indiana when Cartwright passed through, but now the only Indians are a Class AAA baseball team. Indiana's capital had a team in the National League for four seasons—1878, 1887, 1888, and 1889. As winner of the first Federal League pennant and as an original member of the American League, Indianapolis had a respectable major-league record, even if it did once lose a game 24-0 because the entire team was drunk. The present Indians maintain the antic tradition in the American Association. For one thing, they have an infuriating Indian mascot who dances around a wigwam in center field whenever the team scores. One game, Tulsa players took out after the mascot. They caught him about halfway to the fence, tied him to the flagpole, and didn't untie him until the half inning was over.

And finally, Indianapolis has the only minor-league ball park named Bush Stadium. Rube Marquard was once an Indian stalwart. Somehow it fits.

BRAZIL, INDIANA. Hoosier hysteria may not be solely a winter phenomenon. In early June, sectionals and regionals are still top-of-page news. But the Brazil Sectional semifinal between the Brazil Red Devils and the Rosedale Hot Shots was doused by the spring monsoons when the writer went through, and the field was fit to catch catfish in. "I hope you didn't come all this way just to watch a baseball game," a garageman said.

THE NATIONAL ROAD THROUGH ILLINOIS TO ST. LOUIS. Beyond Terre Haute, where Mordecai (Three-Finger) Brown sojourned during his minor-league apprenticeship, lies the Lincoln country. Illinoisans still speak of Lincoln as if he were alive, and he is still a standard against which little boys are expected to measure themselves. In the profound and beautiful stillness of the Lincoln log-cabin homestead in Coles County, it is easy to imagine that the wandering Lincolns have but recently moved on and that their son may soon appear in Vandalia or Springfield, a country lawyer seeking his first political office.

Cartwright, while journeying this way, may possibly have realized that his ancestor, Thomas Joy, had lived in Salem and Hingham in the Bay Colony at the same times as Samuel Lincoln in the 1630's and '40's. In those small and cohesive settlements the two men must have known each other. As a good fellow Whig and future Republican, Cartwright knew that Congressman Abraham Lincoln also opposed the Mexican War. He presumably knew that Lincoln had obtained his seat by defeating a fabled frontier preacher, the Methodist circuit rider Peter Cartwright. He must have been interested in the wayside-tavern speculations as to whether Representative Lincoln would accept appointment as governor of Oregon Territory. But he could not have known that in 1860, when Lincoln was interrupted while at bat in a game of baseball by news that a delegation had come to tell him he had been nominated for the Presidency, the gaunt Illinoisan would reply, "Tell them to wait until I make another hit."

Six score and more years after 1860, dedication has died down somewhat. The weather turned hot as well as humid, and baseball

Spires and sidewheel steamboats make St. Louis look metropolitan at the time of the gold rush when Cartwright passed through; but the covered wagon reminds us that it was a city at the edge of wilderness. *Prints Division, The New York Public Library*

The perfect rural grandstand and the tree-shaded sidelines at Rossville, Nebraska, conjure images of cold lemonade, watermelon, and home-cranked ice cream as derbied spectators cheer turn-of-the century baseball. *H. Peterson*

At Jefferson City, Missouri, an American Legion tournament dominates nightlife where Cartwright's steamboat put in on its way to Independence and Westport. *H. Peterson*

Outfield lights barely illumine a cloudy Missouri night as somnolent spectators watch an amateur game in a little grandstand behind a chickenwire backstop. *H. Peterson*

A stage coach station still standing on the Oregon Trail in Central Nebraska. *H. Peterson*

Directly behind homeplate, at the McGrew, Nebraska, municipal stadium, rises that quintessential landmark of the Oregon Trail, Chimney Rock. *H. Peterson*

In the vicinity of Great South Pass, wagon ruts still cross the Wyoming sagelands. *H. Peterson*

Desert lies all about the Nevada railroad town of Carlin, still only a dot on the Old California Trail. Seen through a knothole in a weathered board fence, a tyke plays a desultory first base. *H. Peterson*

This latticed South Seas bungalow was Cartwright's home in Honolulu in the 1850's. The man standing in front may be intended to represent Alexander himself. In the larger panoramic scene, the house is the one in the immediate foreground. *Prints Division, The New York Public Library*

evaporated. Only in the gentle climate of early evening did children venture forth to play mixed games on pastures smelling of new-mown hay and shared with ponies. But on half a dozen stations, a typically cheerleading St. Louis announcer did convey ill-suppressed excitement to the Cardinal Baseball Network. In several hundred small towns, conversation paused around the Sunday dinner table and porch swing springs ceased squeaking to hear the three-and-two pitch to Little Lou Brock. As customary, St. Louis, one of the strongest baseball towns ever since its first organized game in 1860, was winning.

ST. LOUIS. The French castles are gone from the bluffs of Carondolet. The exciting wooden frontier city is a dreary burg of brick. Long ago the days when every post and pillar was labeled with California placards, every store seemed to contain nothing but mining and outfitting supplies, and the constantly recurring question was "Are you for California?"

Here abolitionist Cartwright encountered his first slaves and his first slave state. Perhaps he was as perplexed by the reality as another westering abolitionist, William Kelly, who wrote in vexation, "[The slaves] seem a jolly, contented lot, generally on the broad grin, poking fun and jokes at one another; rendering it the next thing to impossible to pity their deplorable state, while they themselves are so provokingly happy." The slaves' state was indeed deplorable, but in the vigor of youth it was not intolerable, and like the white men around them they believed—justifiably—in a future that could only get better. There are ways in which it was better to be a slave in 1849 than it is to be a free man in 1973.

Bruce Cartwright's rendition of Alexander's log says:

St. Louis was then the center of the fur trade. Here they obtained their first impressions of the Great West. A.J.C. Jr. often told friends in Honolulu of his experiences crossing the plains and some of them have told them to the writer. He saw in St. Louis "Mountain-men in their buck-skin suits with fringes and fur caps, most of whom carried powder horns and long Kentucky rifles." There were also Indians in buck-skin and feathers and ladies in the latest Paris gowns. There were many gambling halls and saloons. Fights were of frequent occurrence. Signs of great business activity were everywhere. Ware-houses were stacked with the produce of the West; huge steam-boats were at the docks loading and unloading cargoes.

He spoke of the Rocky Mountain House, which seemed to be

the most popular tavern there. It was running "wide open." Men of all classes were spending their money like water. The "din was terrific." A banjo and violin furnished music to which fandangoes were danced, the ladies being most part French women from Carondolet [*a suburban district of St. Louis*]. [*This is a highly genteel description. Carondolet might better be called a red-light district.*]

Cartwright said later that he played baseball at St. Louis. That possibly gave early impetus to baseball interest in the city, which was evident surprisingly soon for a town so far west. The St. Louis Unions were a charter member of the first North-Western Association in 1865 and, as we have seen, they were able to attract the Nationals that far in 1866. They played the Philadelphia Athletics in 1868, losing 54-12.

A St. Louis newspaper was unhappy over this result. "The unhooded falcon, cast off from the fair hand of Philadelphia," it began floridly, "has swooped from the Schuylkill to the Missouri . . . and along the route, over which the fleet wings of the Athletics swept, there are quarries stricken hard and heavily."

The St. Louis Browns, captained by John Lucas, entered the old National Association in 1875 and became a charter member of the National League in 1876. Their first outfield is still remembered: Eddie Cuthbert, who was the first man to steal a base as a Philadelphia Keystone in 1865, played left field; Lipman Pike played center; and good ol' Joe Blong was in right.

These Browns finished second to the Chicago White Stockings. A real oddity is that both the Browns and the White Stockings later abandoned their venerable names; in each case, an upstart American League team salvaged the old appellation. The White Stockings are, instead, the National League ancestors of the Cubs, the Browns the National League predecessors of the present Cardinals. But not directly. The Browns' glory years in the 1880's under Charles Comiskey and Chris Von Der Ahe were spent in the American Association. Oddly, too, for two years there was a Union Association and National League club called the St. Louis Maroons, owned by a nephew of John Lucas. Probably the Maroons, who later moved to Indianapolis, gave a St. Louis newspaper writer the idea, in 1899, of brightening up the Browns' drab image with a more colorful nickname. Actually, color was always a baseball commodity in plentiful supply in St. Louis: the Spider gang of Cy Young in the late '90's,

the Gas House Gang, the Polish gang of the 1950's with Stan Mu-
sial, Ray Jablonski and Rip Repulski, not to mention Enos (Country) Slaughter and Marty Marion.

In recent times, no more hilarious heroes have appeared than
those two Italian kids who lived across the street from each other
on St. Louis's "Dago Hill"—Joe Garagiola and Lawrence (Yogi)
Berra. Together they remember scraping clean the top of "the Clay
Mine" (the neighborhood dump) for a baseball field and using two
wrecked cars as dugouts. They remember finding and nailing together broken bats and painting bases on the streets. For his tryout
with the Cardinals, Garagiola had to search all over the Hill to
come up with one glove (from Walgreen's) and one pair of baseball
shoes, reduced from size 10 to size 5 by the simple expedient of
stuffing rags in the toes. By the end of the tryout, the ends stuck
straight up like the toes of a court jester. Garagiola still tells of the
day after Cardinal fans had sponsored a Joe Garagiola Night, when
a street vendor he had known all his life came up to him and said
proudly, "Gioi, you the firsta boy what comes from the Hill witha
name witha ends a, e, i, o, getta name in the paper and no killa
somebody."

ALONG THE MISSOURI RIVER. At St. Louis Cartwright boarded a
steamboat and proceeded up the Missouri to Independence, which
he reached five days later. The month and a half that they had
spent with the group they had been traveling with convinced Cartwright and several of his companions that they would be better
served by separating, so Alick and his friends joined a party led by
a "Colonel Russel, an ex-army officer and frontier character; wild,
woolley and very dissipated as they afterwards found out."

No need to wonder why Cartwright separated from his group if
they were the New Yorkers one traveler, Joseph Berrien, encountered in the St. Louis-to-Independence steamboat at the same time.
Remarking on the number of turkeys and geese along the Missouri,
Berrien said:

> Talking of Geese reminds me that we have a large quantity of
> them on board . . . and those of the greenest kind. There is a
> party of New Yorkers on board dressed in uniforms of Blue Cassi-
> mere, armed with Government Rifles Bowie Knives and Colts Re-
> volvers who are the most lackadaisycal Milk and Waterish fellows
> I ever saw. They are . . . as green as a pumpkin vine. From their
> appearance one would suppose they had never seen more of the

world than can be seen from behind the counter of a paltry Dry
Goods or Thread and Needle Store and their ridiculous affectation
of Military Style and Etiquette joined to their egregrious vanity,
Hoggishness of Manners and evident high estimation of themselves
to the exclusion of others exposes them to the ridicule of all. . . .

Happily the timing barely prevents Cartwright and his friends
being aboard this vessel, the *Alice*. Perhaps, however, they enjoyed
a group of fellow travelers like the ones Berrien saw, "4 or 5 violin-
ists, a French Horn player, a flute & Clarionet" who took advantage
of a stop at Camden, Missouri, "to give us a concert and such scraping of violins, braying of Horns, breathing of flutes, mixed up with
the voices of some ½ dozen vocalists of most discordant tone, together with the braying of mules, Barking of Dogs and the swearing of our Mate who is a most ferocious fellow, was perhaps never
heard before."

Or maybe they rejoiced in company such as described by fellow
traveler, William Kelly, aboard the *Sacramento* at the same time:
"We had every variety of character—Whig, Democrat, Locofoco,
Loafer, Owner and Abolitionist—in continual disputation, wrangling
about politics . . . and only coinciding in their mode of manufacturing tobacco-juice." Then more than now, Americans enjoyed
arguing politics, each one convinced he ably represented the most
efficacious plan of government ever imagined.

JEFFERSON CITY, ON THE MISSOURI. Today the purest baseball ambi-
ence in the length of this land-faring is to be found in Missouri, a
state of archaic charm. Come evening, the staticky crowd noises
bouncing off the ionosphere amid the somnolence come from
KLIK, Jefferson City, courtesy of the Ku-Ku Drive-In. Nobody is
tuning in St. Louis. The reassuring sounds are all there: the tock of
the bat, the pauses, the pitcher penalized for going to his mouth,
the comforting cadences of announcers speaking their liturgy of
clichés. The names are the familiar Saxon names of major-league
batsmen, but not in familiar major-league order. Could this be
Tulsa? Quincy? No, this is Republic playing Jefferson City, and the
league is American Legion.

Save for a baseball double-header lasting to the small hours, this
little capital city where Cartwright's steamboat once landed is
closed down tight at sunset. But late at night the stands out at the
ball park are full of fans shielded by windbreakers from the soggy
air and the clammy breezes that bend dark, heavy trees out of the

surrounding blackness into the light. They say old-timey fan things like "You ever seen those old catcher's mitts? Kid gloves give more protection."

The game—a taut, engrossing final of an invitation tournament—is won by Republic 4-3. Jeff City runs off the field yelling colorful ball-player sayings like #X$%. The Republicans jump into each other's arms, saying, "Wow."

At early breakfast the Republican team is celebratory, but Manager Doug Greene is solemn as a judge, which he is. "We have a lot of boys with active bodies and strong minds who might go sour if they didn't have something to occupy them," he says. "We scout for these boys all over southwest Missouri. Most come from real small towns without high-school teams. The result is that some have gotten scholarships: our third baseman to Arkansas, the shortstop to Arizona State, the center fielder to Kansas State. Jerry Carroll will be drafted this year, and my son Terry may be next year."

Players cheerfully agree that their home towns are little. "My town is so small all the street signs are on one post," an infielder says. "And mine," says a pitcher, "is so little it's only there three days a week."

FORT OSAGE, MISSOURI. Cartwright's party came through here, not that there is anything to commemorate the visit. A plaque marks the beginning of the Federal Government's survey of the Santa Fe Trail, a westernmost U.S. fort constructed by William Clark (of Lewis and Clark) and the place where eighty-two-year-old Daniel Boone rested on his last long hunting trip. Within home-run distance of the plaque, Little Leaguers play ball. They have all heard of Boone and the Trail; not one has heard of Alexander Cartwright.

INDEPENDENCE, MISSOURI; KANSAS CITY. At Independence, in Colonel William Henry (Owl) Russell, Cartwright obtained a guide who was no phony or pantywaist. He was an authentic frontiersman and scout, almost too authentic. Famed historian Francis Parkman found at Fort Bernard, on the Oregon Trail, "Russel's or Boggs' comp'y, engaged in drinking . . . and refitting. . . . Russel drunk as a pigeon." At Fort Laramie, Parkman found "a part of Russel's comp'y, which becoming dissatisfied with their pragmatic, stump-orator leader, has split itself into half a dozen pieces."

One of them, also Oregon-bound, George McKinstry, noted, "Mr. Ewing moved a committee of 5 be appointed to punish officers which was passed by a respectable majority the Capt Russell then resigned and the greatest confusion arose flameing speeches were made which became quite personal."

A friend and former secretary of Henry Clay, a former lawyer, Kentucky state representative and U.S. marshal, "Owl" Russell was called even by an admirer "a large man, expansive in manner, boastful and bombastic in speech." He received his nickname when he once mistook the chorus of "whoos" from a flock of owls as a sentry's challenge and thundered back, "Colonel William H. Russell of Kentucky—a bosom friend of Henry Clay!" However, he was also a man of many substantial abilities and endearing qualities. He had helped win California under Frémont and had served as its first Secretary of State.

"My duties as commandant are troublesome beyond anything I can conceive of," he himself wrote of his trials as wagonmaster. "I am annoyed with all manner of complaints, one will not do this, and another has done something that must be atoned for, and occasionally, through variety, we have a fight among ourselves *only* to *show* what they can *do*, should the Indians attack us."

Under Russell's advice, at any rate, Cartwright and friends moved to a place they called "Boundary" for a week to rest and get things in shape for the journey. Even experts were puzzled by this mysterious contemporary name. The author first believed Boundary to be an early name for Westport, Missouri. This history-steeped jumping-off point of Westport is now swallowed up in Kansas City, with only one heavily disguised original log-cabin building still standing. It is marked today by a new Westport Shopping Center built in mock-frontier false-front style, laundromat and all. My deeper investigation proved that "Russell's Encampment," as it was also called, actually lay twelve miles west of Independence on the Santa Fe Trace, thereby confirming Westport as the location of Boundary. Add a new name to the lore of the trail.

Any Russell camp reveled in a reputation as the fun place to visit. Even a very sober diarist, William Johnston of Pittsburgh, said in April of 1849, "We visited the camp of Col. Russell [at Independence], composed of a large party, among whom we had numerous acquaintances, with whom we spent some pleasant hours"; and again two weeks later, "at the camp of Colonel Russell [we] were most hospitably entertained by that gentleman and others."

On April 17, Johnston wrote, "Col. Russell's large train began its march today. . . . Our proposed guide, Jim Stewart (the even more famous mountain man) tells us to be in no haste. He says that the parties starting early are making woeful mistakes. . . . He will engage to pass 'every mother's son of them.' "

But Russell (and Cartwright) marched only to Boundary. Johnston's notation of another visit with his company on April 19 confirms this, as does Kelly's note that he "took up quarters near Colonel Russell's rendezvous."

There, as at many other rest stops, Cartwright and his party spent their leisure playing baseball, the first time the new game had been seen in that country. Undoubtedly Colonel Russell, and perhaps even Jim Stewart, took part. Alick told friends in Honolulu later that he "taught people to play Base-ball at nearly every stop on his journey across the plains" and that "it was comical to see mountain-men and indians playing the game."

At Kansas City the most prominent visible evidence of Alexander Cartwright's game, on the recreated trip, was a gaunt steel-and-concrete structure set close by the slums that were put to the torch in the season of rioting that attended the Johnson Administration. This was Municipal Stadium. Looking at the whole milieu, one felt stirrings of an unexpected emotion: sympathy for Charles O. Finley, the much-disliked present Athletics owner, who moved the onetime Philadelphia team from Kansas City on to Oakland. But the new Royals' owner, Ewing Kauffman, did start with one big advantage: convenient new rubble-paved parking lots.

Symbolically, Kauffman, who had to sell off 19,000 shares of stock in his pharmaceutical company to buy the Royals and who is still losing money on the venture, attended Westport High School within a couple of hundred yards of the place where Cartwright played with trappers and Indians.

"I had the normal youth's interest in baseball," Kauffman says. "I played in grade school and high school. Since I was small and underweight, I had to pick a position others didn't want, so I claimed to be a right-fielder. My parents couldn't give me a lot of material possessions—I played with a cheap dime-store glove—and I never dreamed I'd ever be able to own a team. No, I never had a desire to be a major-leaguer, and at fifty-four I don't think I want to get in condition to work out with the team like Gussie Busch. Anyway, I'd rather play golf."

ST. JOSEPH, MISSOURI. St. Joe, another former outfitting point for the trails west, is north of Independence and Westport. Berrien, who outfitted here, found it a "very pretty place" containing "some very beautiful and substantial houses built of Brick," 1,500 inhabitants, eighteen stores, two steam sawmills, three churches, two newspapers, and a triweekly stage. The Pony Express also began here. By the time of this trip, however, one of St. Joseph's main claims to national attention is the NAIA (National Association of Intercollegiate Athletics) annual baseball tournament. It is a good tournament, offering good baseball.

The showmanship is all first rate from warm-ups on. Helium lights come on. An iridescent cloud of insecticide drifts in from right field. A good organist plays. William Jewell College of Liberty, Missouri, executes well-choreographed pepper and fungo in left field, Eastern Michigan in right. The lower minors are dead. But at this small-college championship the lights are brighter and the infield smoother than they ever were in the bush leagues. The outfield walls are green and devoid of advertisement; clumps of juniper grow on a grassy bank outside the third-base line.

Baseball may be too slow for the man who has driven to a big-city game, risking his life and fenders in twenty miles of heavy traffic, fought his way into a remote parking lot, and shouldered through a hot, beery, pushing crowd. It may be perishing tedious when the season is 162 games and the seats are $3.50 and the league is twelve teams of often-shuffled faces and owners move franchises with the alacrity of boom-town madams. Or it may be baseball is dead—as paying business—in all but the biggest cities with television markets and mass audiences, the partly captive audiences trapped in the ghettos of urban congestions. But in the small cities and country towns, as an amateur sport as Cartwright knew it, baseball survives—and has class the majors could imitate.

"The college game may be beginning to replace the old minor leagues," says Fred Flook after his Jewell team has won 4-3. "The coaching is better, and so is the play."

But Flook, the picture of a manager, handsome with his cap on and balding with it off, is frank to admit that the game is not what it once was. He has seen too much of the old kind for that. "I was the third of four boys and we played since we could pick up a glove," he says. "We were born on a farm near Olathe, Kansas, and would milk fifteen cows and play ball afterward. Our dad always had time to play with us. Back when Father played, it was all local ball. Just like a Sunday social, home-made ice cream and all. When

I was coaching at Coldwater High School in Kansas, I drove to Buffalo, Oklahoma, to play on a town team, but mostly it was semi-pro, sometimes against men who made the big leagues. Now, the neighborhood I live in, there'll be sandlot games once a week. There are organized kids' leagues, but by the time a boy is fifteen or sixteen, he's been drilling eight or nine years and he's bored. I try to keep our practices a relaxation period. We choose up teams and just play, or play Indian baseball.

"I knew of Liberty years before I went here, because they used to have mule sales and my grandparents would come over. It's near the original home of Jesse James, you know, and the site of his first bank holdup, in which a Jewell student was killed. I guess James still holds the local stealing record."

FROM BOUNDARY WESTWARD ON THE TRAILS. From this point on, Cartwright's diary was preserved in direct transcription by his descendants. It has major historical importance as a hitherto almost unknown narration of one of the very first wagon trains west in 1849. For its accuracy concerning persons and places, the log ranks among the best. Paul Henderson, the congenial "caboose historian" of Bridgeport, Nebraska—a long-time railroader turned leading expert on the Oregon Trail—considers its language uniquely good and regards the diary as a significant furthering of the history of the early West. Its main flaw, aside from the deletions by Cartwright's son, is a left-handed one: Cartwright started so much earlier than most parties and traveled so rapidly that not many other diarists had an opportunity to chronicle meetings with him.

The author has humbly, and with some reluctance, added notations and observations on the present-day scene and present-day baseball. The log is so fresh and valuable a document, however, that for the most part I have let Alick simply tell his enviable experience in his own words, in the authentic voice of 1849 frontier America.

The setting is pristine prairie carpeted with spring flowers, hop vines, gooseberries, wild plums, and raspberries. A spring breeze blows a thousand unblemished miles east, west, north, and south. Alexander Joy Cartwright, Jr., a determined young adventurer with a clear-eyed look of optimism, begins to speak in his cheery, rumbling way.

A.J.C.'S NOTES

April 23, 1849—Monday

. . . *During the past week we have passed the time in fixing the wagon-covers, stowing away property etc. varied by hunting and fishing, swimming and playing "Base-ball". I have the ball and book of rules with me that we used back home.*

Tonight we held a council and decided to strike out for California along the Santa Fe Trail until we reach the Oregon Trail, then follow that to the South Pass and then North of the Great Salt Lake in the land of the Utes, through the Sierra Nevada Mountains to California. . . .

April 24, 1849—Tuesday

. . . *The weather being clear and warm and all nature smiling propitiously, at 7 o'clock* A.M. *we started under the guidance of Colonel Russel. The company consists of 32 waggons and 119 men. We were off for the "Gold Diggins" of California. Our trail lay over the Prairie on the Santa Fe Route.*

A cover of luxuriant grass covers the Prairie, dotted here and there with clumps of gaudy wild-flowers. At 12 o'clock we arrived at "Lone Elm", a poor solitary tree in a wide expanse of prairie, miserable and weathered. Here we watered our animals and refreshed the "inner man". After resting half an hour we started for "Bull Creek" where we intended to camp for the night. At 3:30 o'clock we came to a frog-pond where we decided to make our first camp. We formed our waggons in a "Corral" which did not present a very showy appearance, it being the "maiden essay" of most of the Company however we shall do better after a few trials. We supped on coffee and cold ham. Our appetites are excellent and our health good. The night is warm and clear with a new moon riding through the sky. We travelled 28 miles all of which I walked.

April 25, 1849—Wednesday

. . . *Turned out at 4 o'clock, the weather being clear and very warm. We got breakfast, "catched-up" and "rolled". At 7 o'clock still followed the Sante Fe Trail over a most beautiful country. At 11 o'clock we arrived at "Bull Creek" where we lowered our waggons down the steep banks. After crossing the creek we called a halt and took a hearty lunch with "extras", under the shade of a beautiful grove of trees that filled the creek bottom. [Near Bull*

*Creek a solitary, crudely lettered sign directed, "Road to Oregon."
Thus began the longest wagon road in the world.]*

*At 2 o'clock we started again and "rolled" through the same beauti-
ful park-like country though which we have passed all day. Well-
wooded hills rise from the prairie here and there. We have passed
through dells through which flow streams of clear sparkling water
over pebbly beds. About 5 o'clock we came to camp on the "Wakaroosa", a well-timbered stream, the banks of which are very steep.
We had to lower our waggons down one bank and hoist them up
the other. This was done with ropes, the waggons being first un-
loaded and then loaded again, which was accomplished with considerable labour. Here we saw "Indian signs". After taking care of
our stock we had supper on cocoa and bread. After supper several
of the Company joined us around our fire. We passed the time in
singing and chatting about our probable adventures. It was decided
to put out guards from now on as we are coming into the hunting-
grounds of the Indians.*

*Ned Townsend stood watch from 11 o'clock to 2:30 o'clock, but was
not relieved until 3:30 which caused a little grumbling. We had a
little "flare-up" on the road today between Tom and a "sucker"
from Illinoise. Things looked serious but the "sucker" apologized.
Our train travelled 15 miles today, all of which I walked.*

April 26, 1849—Thursday
*. . .We were up bright and early at 4:30 o'clock, got breakfast and
"rolled" from camp at 6 o'clock. Everyone in fine spirits. The trail
lay over the same fine prairie country with its crystal streams and
wild-flowers everywhere. At 9:30 o'clock we ascended the dividing
ridge from the top of which and standing on a heap of stones that
marks the grave of some poor traveller, we had the finest view that
I have ever beheld. In the distance on one side the "Wakaroosa
Mountains" of a hundred shapes covered with green forests and
meadows, on the other side the Caw River stretched away until hid
from view by clumps of trees which diversified this most beautiful
scenery. Here we left a memo for any friend that may come after
us. About 1 o'clock we called a halt at a branch of Coon Creek
where we lunched under grand old trees on a beautiful country
until we came to camp at "Springs" about 4 p.m.*

*There was a great deal of dissatisfaction today in consequence of
the great number of waggons in our train, as an accident to one de-*

lays the whole train. I do not think we will be able to continue much longer without division of the party. We travelled 23 miles today.

Pottowattomie Indians

April 27, 1849—Friday
. . . This morning the weather was clear and fine. Ned Townsend and I started in advance of the teams across country for the "Kansas" by a route said to be shorter than that taken by the train. Acting upon the advice of Colonel Russel I shouldered a double-barrelled gun. After a four hour walk through a beautiful country, diversified by a variety of scenery, in many places so quiet and exquisitely homely that we asked ourselves many times over where were the snug farm-houses and lowing heads, and the waving fields of grain that should be here? A quiet solitude the most profound reigned supreme. No signs of life but the countless flocks of plover and an indefinite variety of small birds. At length we came to the conclusions that we had missed the trail, but kept on until we met 2 Indians who were friendly and directed us to the Baptist Mission, which we reached after 2 miles further travel.

Here we found 2 excellent farms under cultivation. On introducing ourselves to Mr. Dilly, the missionary, we were informed that we were in the country of the Pottowattomie and a long distance from the Kansas Ferry. We accepted his hospitable invitation to dine and with appetites sharpened by a 20 mile walk, did ample justice to his solid fare. After dinner we visited the other farm where we found the Chief of the tribe his squaw and many warriors.

They are a fine manly looking tribe and appear very fond of showy dress. One young fellow on horse-back I shall never forget; he was a perfect Apollo in shape and sat his horse—a beautiful spirited animal—as if he were apart of him. He was dressed in a blue "breech-cloth", a bandana kerchief in turban form around his head; his feet shod with neat, close-fitting mocassins, while for upper dress he had about a dozen kerchiefs of different gay colors, the end knotted together on one shoulder while the flag-ends passed under the opposite arm and streamed in the wind. He was armed with a very fine flint-lock rifle of which he appeared very proud. I gained his heart by the gift of a red silk-kerchief.

After looking over the farm, visiting the blacksmith shop, etc., we returned to the house of Mr. Dilly who gave us considerable information regarding the character and habits of "his people".

We found here 2 young ladies, one a teacher, the other Miss Lackin, the daughter of a Government physician.

The Pottowattomies are the wealthiest tribe under the protection of the United States.

After receiving directions as to our route we left this habitable home in the wild and after travelling 2 miles we met a gentleman on horse-back who volunteered to put us on our trail.

We found him to be a man of great information concerning the different tribes that inhabit this section of the country, having married an Indian woman and traded among them for 17 years. He was originally from New York, his name was Cleghorn. He accompanied us to our camp where we arrived about 5 o'clock having walked 30 miles.

We paid him the civilities of the camp and listened with wonder to the tales he told of vast herds of buffalo that at times covered the country. On his taking his leave we went after plover, many thousand of which were flying about. In a short while we bagged a mess and soon had them strung on a stick and broiled in the primitive Indian style. The train travelled 19 miles today.

This old mountain man modified his history slightly for Cartwright's benefit. A letter from Willow Creek (the Pawnee mission) in 1844 more accurately said of "James Cleghorn, government interpreter," "He is a Frenchman who has lived with the Pawnees for 38 years; and the only objection to Cleghorn as a man is that he lives with two squaws, to either of which he is not legally married, but treats them and his children as respectfully as a married man would his family."

A MILE WEST OF WESTPORT. The first sign of baseball on the old trail in 1973 is at a grade school 1.1 miles west of Westport, where a little grass-lot diamond lies singularly silent on a smiling spring Sunday midafternoon, reflecting the decline of the pickup game everywhere. The only small boy in sight is too busy to play baseball; his older sister is teaching him how to ride a bike.

Innumerable motor bikes, cycles, swimming pools, and tennis

courts later, a gaggle of little girls is found practicing at a church on Santa Fe Drive in Mission, Kansas. Shouts a woman, throwing out the moppet equivalent of fungoes, "Play in right field, Tricia." Tricia: "I forgot where it is." Woman (undaunted): "All right, Trish. Catch this on the fly." The ball falls in front of Trish, who waits, immobilized by terror, for it to bounce toward her. The ball hits her calf. "Ow," she protests. She hops up and down in pain. End of a right fielder's career.

JOHNSON COUNTY, KANSAS. Baseball has come to resemble the lightning bug: dormant during the day, alive and lit up at night. As darkness falls, the game is marked by light standards towering above the horizon. The biggest such moth attractor in Kansas is the remarkable Johnson County 3 & 2 League facility, which looms up on the old trail itself. On eight fully equipped well-lighted diamonds, eighteen boys' leagues, composed of 154 teams and some 2,800 players, run off a summer schedule of more than 1,400 games. Scores of cars crowd the parking lot and hundreds of paying spectators watch teams in five categories of talent or throng the carnival-like midway connecting the fields. Hundreds of players in all sizes and colors of uniforms clatter along the walks and warm up among the refreshment stands. The whole enterprise requires a sixty-five-page bound book of rules, instructions, and schedules.

"We think this is the biggest youth sports complex in the country," cheerleads 3 & 2 Secretary Helen Hudson, a bright-eyed chatterbox of a baseball fan. "We have two hundred and forty thousand dollars invested in the grounds and an annual budget of eighty thousand dollars. There are three hundred and sixty more boys in the morning baseball school, too.

"Three boys from the program have been drafted by the Royals. By the way, did you know Ewing Kauffman has a team out here? It's called 'The Sociables' after the breath tablets his company makes. He called it his interim team."

DE SOTO, KANSAS. In a tropically soft evening, the State Bank of Spring Hill is playing. Or rather, the teenage proxies of State Bank pose and play before a full complement of those pretty Kansas girls on a field freshly limed with on-deck circles and coaches' boxes. Beyond the left-field fence couples gather on the tennis courts for square dancing—music playing, huge gallon pitchers of refreshments, the women in bright wide-skirted dresses and the men in string ties. Drifting sounds collide. "Hand over hand around the floor, promenade back—he's out—like you did before."

LAWRENCE, KANSAS. A few Kansas University grad students desultorily toss a ball around, but over at Haskell Indian Institute (near where Cartwright saw his first "Indian signs") the ball field is dead. It was here that Cartwright wrote, "It was decided to put out guards from now on as we are coming into the hunting grounds of the Indians."

BIG SPRINGS, KANSAS. Near here, at the Baptist mission, Cartwright saw his first Pottawattomies. If Cartwright played baseball at that campground, it must have been near the ball field which is now close by the mission—small, but lighted for night games.

April 28, 1849—Saturday
4:30 saw us up and dressed. We breakfasted "on board" after which all hands "turned to" to lower the waggons down to the ferry. This job kept us until 5 P.M. when we found ourselves on the opposite side of the "Kansas" having crossed our first large stream without accident. We "rolled" about a mile from the river and came to camp in the broad timber belting it. There was much quarreling today and this evening we held a council and decided to "split up."

Most emigrant groups started with impractically large wagon trains, making travel tedious and dusty. Campsites and supplies of firewood and water soon dictated that they split into much smaller parties, which divided again, in many cases, as the travelers came to fear the road less. Kindred spirits gathered together, as did those of different persuasions as to a prudent day's travel.

Crossing the Kansas, Cartwright used the Pappan Ferry, within the present limits of Topeka. The English diarist William Kelly, who crossed here at about this time, said of the place, "The trading post is a small hamlet, composed of some half dozen shops, and a little straggling suburb of wigwams."

Kelly also noted that the wolves were so unafraid of human beings that they would creep into camp and tear up the softer portions of harness unless driven off. He commented on a tavern at the Indian Territory line called the "House of Refuge," which was built exactly on the border. It was a resort of desperate men, who would simply cross from part of the tavern to another when the law approached.

Cartwright made no further notes until May 17 (or Bruce retained none), by which time he and his smaller train had reached the South Fork of the Platte River about twenty miles upstream from the Forks of Platte. Bruce Cartwright, Jr., did estimate dates for the intervening stretch, and to confirm them and to discover whether other emigrants might have recorded Alexander's train the author has read the few other diaries that exist, written by other emigrants during the same period.

Joseph Waring Berrien preceded Cartwright through this section of trail by barely one full day. His diary matches perfectly with Cartwright's, from the junction of the road from St. Joe. Indeed, if Cartwright or some other of Colonel Russell's party struck the St. Joe road farther east than usual, they may have been the occasion of Berrien's notation, "Caught by 7 waggons from Pittsburgh, driving energetic fellows. The Captain is said to have accompanied Bryant in his journey . . . in 1846." William Henry (Owl) Russell did lead the famed Oregon party of which Edwin Bryant was chronicler, and the Cartwright group did obtain their wagons and supplies in Pittsburgh.

Berrien found the weather very cold, rainy and windy until May 4, when it turned hot, but he wrote happily of the wild roses growing in the beautiful, gentle valley of the Blue River. "Wild garlic or Chives" grew there too, and he made several salads of the fresh greens "which were very excellent." Several elk and herds of antelope were seen every day.

He reached Fort Kearney on May 9, still one day ahead of Cartwright. "The fort is principally built of sods cut from the floor of the valley [of the Platte]," he noted, and added, "We met 2 Dragoons who had just left with the mail. This furnished an opportunity of sending letters home. . . ." Cartwright undoubtedly took the same chance to write home to his parents and friends.

Near the fort Berrien came upon a lone skeleton, its skull fractured. Other travelers found a desolate army of skeletons here, apparently the victims of a large Indian battle.

Two days west of Fort Kearney, the first buffalo appeared. "I had always discredited the stories I had heard of their great numbers but I do so no longer," Berrien said in awe. "I am certain I saw during the day at least 20,000. They covered the vast plain for miles, the surface of the earth being black with them." Near Fort Laramie, Cartwright was to see a herd numbering some 300,000 by conservative and systematic estimate.

Mormons traveling east from Salt Lake crossed their path May 14. They gave great accounts of the gold region, mentioning one miner who had collected $750 worth in one day.

From the supporting diaries and dates, Cartwright's progress can be determined quite exactly:

April 29, 1849	Proceeded along the Kaw River in Kansas
April 30	Crossed Red Vermillion Creek
May 1	Crossed the Black Vermillion near present Bigelow, Kansas
May 2	Crossed the Big Blue at Schroyer, near Marysville, Kansas, still a very pretty town
May 3 and 4	Spent two long days crossing the high divide to the Little Blue River, with beautiful sweeping views of eastern Kansas. Grass was "scarce and backward."
May 5	Struck the Little Blue near Fairbury, Nebraska
May 6 to 9	Proceeded up the Little Blue to a point near Hastings, Nebraska, and then struck out for the Platte River, passing near the site of Juniata
May 10	Up the Platte to Fort Kearney
May 12	Camped at Plum Creek
May 13 to 16	Continued up the Platte past the Junction and proceeded about twenty miles along the South Fork

TOPEKA, KANSAS. An Atchison, Topeka & Santa Fe softball team has recently defeated Dustin Optical 6-1 to remain unbeaten. Texaco, Hallmark Cards, the Kansas Reception and Diagnostic Center, and Indian Dry Wall have also felt the wrath of the Santa Fe. The Santa Fe coach says that his highballers have attracted as many as 2,500 spectators to tournament games and invites the inquirer to tonight's game against Dry Wall. Unfortunately, the railroad is washed out by one of those melodramatic Kansas thunderstorms which splatter the whole sky with oil-paint colors and lightning. Rain gushes, hailstones tattoo and Santa Fe Park, down by the levee near where Cartwright crossed the Kansas River at Papans Ferry, is wetter than Noah's raincoat. As a result the game is called.

ROSSVILLE, KANSAS. Up the storied valley of the Big Blue, in this typical prairie town, the archetypical Sunday semipro stadium survives. Great oaks march down to the foul lines, ring the outfield and shade the little grandstand, neat in white paint. In big, precise, dark-green block capitals the backstop wall is lettered ROSSVILLE. It is pure cool green nostalgia. You can almost see the watermelons, the boaters and derby hats of spectators, and the ballooning knickers and flat-topped caps of the players.

HANOVER AND HOLLENBERG, KANSAS; FAIRBURY AND HEBRON, NEBRASKA. In all the little towns along the Little Blue, the big sports news was the College World Series at Omaha, in which Harvard and Southern Illinois had just lost their first games. Alexander Cartwright, who conceived of baseball as a game for gentry, would have been greatly gratified by Harvard's participation and downcast by its defeat, on the assumption that it was still a school for gentlemen. Here, however, it was Southern Illinois' loss that was resented, largely because the uniquely nicknamed Salukis had introduced four bat girls.

Alcove Spring, Hollenberg Pony Express Station and lizard-inhabited old burying grounds with small blank rocks as anonymous headstones bring back the frontier. One can roll with Cartwright over the blue-green hills and swells along the Little Blue, cresting rise after rise with awesome views of an ocean of rippling, chesthigh, flowering grasses, each time dipping back into hollows redolent with mint and fragrant herbs crushed under wagon tires, hoofs, and boots. A theatrical *Götterdämmerung* sunset lights the river blue and gold, and then there is cricket song and dark.

MINDEN, NEBRASKA. Somewhere in the long twilight of the night before the rolling country has changed to Platte flatlands, the lush high grass has begun to give way to short dry buffalo grass and wild wheat, and the once muddy rivers meander through low sand hills. They are now so clear that big fish seem to walk through the shallow water on their ventral fins. Signs are planted in the center of Minden's Main Street, across from the white-domed courthouse in its leafy square. They announce, "Legion Baseball Today."

FORT KEARNEY, NEBRASKA. This section of the diary is lost. But Fort Kearney was a major supply post for emigrants, and Cartwright surely stopped here, as almost all pioneers did. During the summer of 1849 there were as many as 500 wagons clustered around Fort Kearney and at the nearby trading post of Dobetown, and 175 soldiers stationed at the fort itself.

Westward from Fort Kearney, the still unspoiled natural grassland presses in upon the irrigated cropland along the Platte. The grassland turns, on the south edge of the flood plain, into low sunwashed, buff-colored hills familiar as the backdrops for Remington paintings of pony soldiers in pursuit of aborigines. One range of higher hills, from which silent Sioux watched the wagon trains, swells up for some height, but subsides again. Not until the ascent of the divide between the North Fork and the South Fork of the Platte did the wagoneers get a taste of the mountains to come. A trail of precious possessions, discarded, would later mark the long upgrades, but at first the prospect of those weirdly configured hills was exhilarating after the weeks of flatness.

Cartwright's complete notes resume on May 17. On that day also Joseph Berrien of Belleville, Illinois, said, "The evening previous 5 mule teams hove in sight on the opposite bank [of the South Platte] and as they appeared anxious to cross, some of our party went to direct them to the ford. They proved to be acquaintances of Col Jarrot from Illinois and are anxious to join our company. left our camp about 7 and moved to a higher spot. it rained so hard that we gave up all idea of travelling any more that day. At 10 the 5 waggons joined us at our camp and remained with us until next morning. . . . An alarm of Indians during the night. Camp aroused and Mules picketed in the corral."

There can be no doubt that this party of five mule teams and wagons that shared the Jarrot-Berrien camp's Indian excitement was Cartwright's. In his wagon that evening, with the hard rain pelting on the canvas and the mules braying at the scent of approaching Sioux or Pawnee, Cartwright scrawled his own account of the meeting.

May 17, 1849—Wednesday
. . . This morning we crossed the South Fork of the Platte about 20 miles above the Junction. It having rained heavily for the past few days, and still continuing, the River was quite high. We are now 5 waggons in company. We were the last to attempt the crossing but the first to succeed. The superiority of our animals was here very apparent. After a few moments rest on the other side we returned

to the middle of the stream to the assistance of those who were un-able to advance further because of the weight of their waggons or the weakness of their animals. With a great deal of labour, and by doubling the teams, we at last succeeded in landing all safely on the opposite shore.

I am still suffering from dysentery caused by eating too freely of buffalo.

After a short delay sufficient to arrange our disordered waggons etc., . . . we came upon the camp of Colonel Jarrott of Illinoise. The mules in this train appear to be in very bad condition, so much so that we altered our previous determination of travelling with them for a while and decided to continue our journey tomorrow in advance of them. I have found in this company a gentleman of the name of Green, formerly of New York, a brother of Henderson Green. He had met with a severe accident having been run over by his waggon, injuring both his legs. He was doing well. Today I have suffered a great deal of pain, but hope by strict diet to be alright in a few days. The grass being good we concluded to camp for the rest of the day and refresh ourselves and wearied beasts. It has rained nearly the whole day and is preparing for it again. Atmosphere cold and disagreeable. Distance travelled—including one mile crossing —4 miles.

Henderson Greene, a friend of Cartwright, was also a bookseller, having a store at 463 Broadway in New York. He may have gone west too, for his name is missing from city directories after 1849. His brother was a member of Berrien's own Belleville Company and was a friend of Berrien's. Colonel Jarrot was the organizer and leader of the Illinoisans' wagon train.

The next morning Berrien wrote, "left camp at 6 and travelled slowly up the valley crossing some deep sandy gullies and water courses on our way. 4 out of the 5 waggons finding they could out-travell us left us and went on before and I was very much tempted to join them, the one remained with us and will probably continue to do so." He had previously thought, "The drive very slow and I am very much dissatisfied with our progress," but observed soberly, "Grass very poor. . . . perhaps it is best to be cautious."

Cartwright thought differently and once again whipped up his lightning mule express to the Pacific.

May 18, 1849—Thursday

Started today at 7 o'clock in company with the Jarrots. Our route lay along the South side of the South Fork, now over the low bottom land, anon over the bluffs. The grass appears better than any we have seen for several days past. Called a halt at 11 o'clock, got up a "sort of meal", good enough for such appetites as ours however. While lying down here Tom [Captain Thomas Seely] was severely bitten on the hand by some sort of insect.

1¼ o'clock, rolled on our winding way with three other waggons in company, Jarrott's train being too "slow coaches" for us.

The country along our route still presents the same appearance, low irregular bottom and high bluffs. Saw several buffalo and plenty of antelope, none near enough to shoot. Came to camp on the bottom near the river just as it commenced a heavy thunder-storm. Jarrott encamped about ½ mile in our rear. On the opposite bank 2 ox-teams are encamped.

The river has risen so much since we crossed that 'tis probable they will be delayed several days, before they can cross. The Platte, like all mountain streams, rises at this season of the year very rapidly and when at its height runs with a swift current so strong as to take away any animals that may attempt to cross, off its legs. Ignorance of this force has caused great loss at this end and other crossings.

After the shower I walked up on the bluffs, saw 2 beautiful varieties of mosses with small purple and blue flowers. Tom has suffered severe pain from the bite on his hand. There being no wood we cooked our supper with "chips". Camp good for grass, water and fish. Distance 16 miles.

May 19, 1849—Friday

. . . We rolled from our camp at 7 o'clock. Weather half and half. Our trail lay along the North bank of the South Fork, until about 10 o'clock when we struck the trail that leads across to the North Fork.

. . . Here we were met by several Sioux, well mounted and armed. They were accompanied by two white men who had lived among them for several years. Their camp was just off to the left of the trail and was very large though containing at this time but few inhabitants, most of the warriors having started on a "war party"

against the Pawnees. The Sioux are a magnificent race of Indians. The men are tall and finely formed with classic features and nobel carriage. Frank and open in manner of address. The women many of them the most beautiful I have ever beheld. They were principally clothed in beautifully dressed skins, some of them richly ornamented and as white as snow. I offered one twenty-five dollars for her dress, but met with an unqualified refusal. We purchased some moccasins etc., of them and rolled on much gratified to find some that realized the idea I had formed of what an Indian was in a state of nature—how this conceit was taken out of me will be seen later on.

Our trail lay over a high ridge of Bluffs. Road good and grass fair. This afternoon we had another thunder-storm, and during its continuance saw one of the grandest sights in nature, a water-spout on the plains. It commenced some distance to the left of us and at first was nothing but a small pillar or cloud reaching from the clouds to the earth. This pillar began travelling towards the right gradually growing larger and revolving swifter until it had passed a long distance off and appeared at least one mile in circumference when it burst with a tremendous explosion, louder than the discharge of a whole park of artillery then the thunder rolled and the lightening blazed in one sheet of living fire. The rain descended in torrents and hail-stones as large as eggs—aye! and larger pelted us and our poor animals most pitilessly. Fortunately we had taken the precaution ere the storm reached its fury to take our animals out and fasten them securely to the wheels, else had we surely lost some of them, as it was they were wild with terror and snorted and tore the earth at a furious rate. After the storm, which was as short in duration as it was severe in violence, we hitched up and rolled on about 5 o'clock, and reached the top of a very high bluff, from whence the most magnificent view burst upon us. Hundreds of feet below us lay ridge after ridge of bold bluffs in every conceivable variety of shapes, their sides and tops and the valleys between covered with verdure while far in the distance could be seen "Ash Hollow" filled with trees and covered with a rank growth of wild vines. Farther off we saw the waters of the "North Fork" rolling along with its swift and turbid current.

The pencil of "Cole" or the pen of "Irving" alone could do it justice.

*Its beauty and wild grandure will never fade from my memory nei-
ther do I think 'twill from either of my comrades.*

*We passed down the precipitous sides of the bluff into the ravines.
Travelling about one hour brought us near the mouth of the "Hollow", when we camped at seven o'clock. We found an oxtrain and
Mr. Emery camped a short distance ahead of us up the banks of the
river. The three waggons in company with us camped a few miles
back this caused some little feeling among some of the members of
our once more "Lone Waggon". All hands however turned to and
about 9 o'clock we had supper agreeing to stand each of us a two
hour guard.*

*Tom had the first watch, I on the mid from twelve 'till two. The
night during my guard was very fine—the first in 10 days—the stars
shone clear and bright and the atmosphere just cold enough to
make me wrap my blanket close around me and keep a brisk walk
around our "little" camp. My thoughts soon took the usual direction
and I thought of home, sweet home! and of my darling wife and little ones, and breathed a silent prayer to that Benificent Being who
has said: "In the silent watches of the night I will be near thee", for
their protection and welfare.*

*My reveries were frequently interrupted by the howling of the grey
wolves that would come up so close that I could see the glass of
their eyeballs and hear their short quick snuffing as they scented
the remains of our supper. Several times I was tempted to give one
of the sneaking rascals the contents of my rifle, but the certainty of
rousing out the whole camp prevented the enjoyment of this bit of
pleasure. Looking at my watch I found that I was one-quarter of an
hour over my guard, so roused Ned Townsend and turned in to
take "forty winks" and be roused out again.*

Distance today 26 miles.

Legendary Ash Hollow lies there still in western Nebraska, much
as Cartwright described it. A traveler these days can sense something of the emigrants' pleasure in the place by climbing up Wind-
lass Hill in the evening, feeling the air warmer on his face where
the setting sun has touched high ground later than the valley,
to look down where ropes and tackle tortuously lowered prairie
schooners. Deep ruts still lead to the beautiful hollow below,

and in the violet and lavender hills and purple ravines coyotes still bark and howl.

There is one present-day campground at Ash Hollow, a spacious one. Visions of little kids playing Cartwright's game on the very sites of his wagon circles, particularly this favorite one, had beckoned all the way from Pittsburgh. There was none. In fact, not one pickup sandlot game was to be found anywhere along the route from Illinois to Wyoming.

MC GREW, NEBRASKA. Here, beyond the great stone monoliths of Courthouse and Jail Rocks, a little cow pasture of a baseball field is distinguished by having equidistant views of even more famous Chimney Rock and Castle Rock, which figure in almost all accounts of covered wagons and which must be the most mystic trailmarks since Moses' pillar of cloud by day and pillar of fire by night. Chimney Rock, that portentous finger of rock pointing to the sky, is visible through the crude net backstop on a direct line through home plate and the pitcher's rubber. One has to hope that the McGrew team, whose name two little Sioux girls playing nearby do not know, is called the Dangerous Dans—and that it is suitably inspired by the view.

May 20, 1849

. . . *Up at 4 o'clock and off for better grass as soon as we could "catch up". Passed the ox-train of Emery at 4-½. No one visible but the guard, who asked "where on earth" were we going at that time in the morning. Told him we were "peep o'day boys", and rolled on, travelling along the North bank of the North Fork over a very heavy sandy road, occassionally marshy. The banks are lined with bluffs of most fantastic shapes—emigrants have named them "Castle Bluffs"—their general aspect one of utter sterility and desolation. We called a halt at 6 o'clock at a place where we found good grass. Cooked breakfast and while in the enjoyment of it, were joined by Mr. Emery. After our meal we "catched up" and rolled on. Trail still continuing over the same style of road and the country the whole day presents the same features. Came to camp at 5 o'clock, P.M. Camp fair. Distance 80 miles.*

May 21, 1849

. . . *Rolled this morning at 5-½ A.M. Our route lay over a heavy sandy and marshy bottom and so continued through the day. The general aspect of the country the same as yesterday. Saw some bluffs on the opposite side of the river of most curious shapes that looked as if Art must have assisted in their formation, so exactly do they resemble churches, castles and etc. Crossed a very bad "slough" and came to camp at 5 o'clock. Weather clear and warm, first time in two weeks. Distance 18 miles.*

May 22, 1849
. . . 5-½ o'clock saw "the restless" once more in motion. The weather clear and pleasant. The trail lies over a heavy sandy soil and at times through marshy ground, making the travel exceedingly hard for our mules. We nooned at 11 o'clock on the banks of the river, directly on a line—in appearance—with a singular bluff called "the Court House", resembling in shape the Capitol in Washington. In the afternoon the trail continued over the same kind of road. About 3 o'clock we had a thunderstorm, so violent as to make it necessary to unhitch and secure our "stock" to the wheels. This was done during the violence of the storm and we were wet to the skin, this however is a matter of daily occurance and gives us but little concern. After the storm had subsided we again hitched up and rolled on till we made our camp at 5 o'clock and on a wet marshy spot, cold and exceedingly disagreeable. "Chimney Rock", which has been in sight all day, about 8 miles ahead of us. The "Court House" presenting its finest front about 12 miles to our left. Weather at present—clear and pleasant. On guard from 9 'till 12 with Mr. Thomas. Distance— 15 miles.

May 23, 1849
. . . The weather is still bad, the rain pouring in torrents, cold and clammy. A fine hot breakfast of coffee, baked beans and pork about 8 o'clock cheered the depressed spirits of our party, and 9 o'clock bringing a slight cessation in the storm, we "catched up" and "rolled" at 9½. The trail still lies along the sandy and marshy bottom of the North Fork. Soon after starting it commenced that "infernal drizzle" and so continued until we came to camp about 5 miles from "Chimney Rock". A short distance from our camp are four singular looking bluffs, one very much resembling the Capitol, another a pyramid and the two others Turkish mosques. Chimney Rock is visable at a distance of thirty miles. [Cartwright means when approaching it, as he was then camped five miles from it. He was seeing Court House Rock, Big House Rock, Gable Rock, Coyote Rock, Chimney Rock and others, dramatic landmarks which

ever after symbolized the great landfaring of the pioneers. Chimney Rock in particular impressed all who saw it as an omen of destiny, a finger pointing to the stars, a natural steeple in the wilderness.]

May 24, 1849

. . . Still the same rain and cold. Took breakfast in our waggon, curled and twisted up into all sorts of shapes, we enjoyed the thing hugely. The weather being so very bad we concluded to stop for the day. About 9 o'clock the camp was startled by the appearance of a "one-horse shay" and such a shay—description fails me. I cannot do the subject justice so let it pass merely stating, as a sort of flyer, that "twas one of 'ems". This arrangement was driven by a young French trapper. He informed us that at a distance of 16 miles were "Scotch Bluffs" or "Cedar Springs" and that we should find a store and blacksmiths. Although it was still raining quite hard we concluded to "catch up" and reach there today. During today's travel we passed several singular looking bluffs. During the afternoon the wind shifted and it snowed "fast and thick". About 5 o'clock it broke away and we arrived at the Springs at 6 o'clock.

William Kelly of London met the same trapper a day later and described him as "clad in bucksin suit, with a fine rifle on his shoulder." Kelly also talked at length with him, and "he informed us he was the son of an old French trapper from the Hudson Bay settlement, brought out by his father when quite a boy . . ." and that "he married the daughter of an Indian chief, in whose society he forgot every feeling or desire to visit the crowded thoroughfares of the world."

Cartwright must have passed the Kelly party at Chimney Rock, but at some remove, for neither diary mentions another train. Somewhat surprisingly, the Kelly group discovered a fine black sand near the Rock which they assumed to be gold-bearing. In fear that their trip would end right there if others in their train heard the news, they told no one of what they found.

Much impressed by Ash Hollow, Kelly called it "a lovely wooded dell, so watered and sheltered . . . as if a hot house. The modest wild rose opened its velvety bosom. . . . Cool streams, filtered through the adjoining hills, prattled about. . . ."

Cedar Springs

The view here is one of the finest we have had on the route. Immense bluffs most fantastically and curiously shaped into representations of every conceivable hint and style of architecture surround the little plain whereon we are encamped. Through the center of this plain runs a deep and wild ravine, its precipitous sides lined with gnarled and stunted cedar. At the bottom runs a clear stream of cool, delicious water.

Here we found a log hut, its occupant Mr. Robidoux and a young man who had been trapping for him the previous season. We built our campfire a short distance from his hut and after eating a hearty supper, Frank and myself accepted an invitation from Robidoux to spend the night under his roof. We passed the hours 'till one o'clock spinning yarns of all sizes and colors, and at that hour turned in on the hard floor, but sleep refused to visit our eyes that night. Although accustomed to sleep on the earth in all sorts of weather I could not go the stoney couch of that night so after tossing about for a couple of hours, turned out and walked around the camp "till daylight did appear", having made up my mind to accept no more invitations, but stick to the greensward; distance today 20 miles. Camp 1st. rate for all things.

May 25, 1849
Messrs. Boylston and Emery having agreed to disagree, Boylston made up his mind to separate from him and pack to Fort Laramie, and I stopped behind with him to assist, as packing is a perfect science and both men and mules have to broken into it, so we did not fix things exactly right, though assisted and instructed by Robidoux.

However all things appearing right, we started to overhaul the train and in the vanity of our knowledge thought we would surprise them by striking across country, so coming into camp ahead of the train, which had several hours start of us. Accordingly we took the bearings of the road and boldly struck off. Things went on excellently well for about ten miles, when just as we were congratulating ourselves and agreeing as to the superiority of packs over wagons, Billy Button's pack took a turn and came under his belly. My eyes! There was a go and not the only go either, for the unfortunate Billy's lariat was fast to my pommel and as he started off my saddle turned and out I came. Away went Billy and his pack and my animal with his saddle, and away went Cale on his fast Mulligan who soon got the upper hand of him and in a twinkling he lay on the prairie. I made haste up to him and found him none the worse for his hoist. We could not help laughing at the ridiculous figure we cut and agreed that we had been rather premature about the superiority of the pack. By the time we had recovered our some-what scattered senses we found that our position was rather an unknown one. Our animals were by this time out of sight and where they would fetch up we could not tell. Worse than this they had all our fire-arms leaving us ten miles from any place, in a strange wild country abounding in all sorts of varmints and blood-thirsty Indi-ans.

However it would not do to waste time so we followed on in the trail of our runaways and after an hour's walk found ourselves on the broad waggon trail. Following this an hour and a half brought us back to our starting place. Here we found that our animals had been stopped and that Robidoux, suspecting something more seri-ous had occured, was on the point of starting in search of us.

He laughed heartily at our mishap and invited us to stop a while and refresh ourselves. To this, as we were considerably fatigued by our long chase, we joyfully consented. He set before us some coffee and jerked buffalo-meat of which we partook right heartily. After having once more "fixed" we prepared to start but could not leave until we had taken a "stirrup cup" of what Mr. Robidoux was pleased to call "A-No. 1 Brandy". I took a bumper "neat", but of all the drinks, that was a damndest. I can compare it to nothing but "liquid hell-fire". I writhed and twisted in agony. My contortion of visage must have been fearful. Rushing to a bucket of water I caught up a tin cup full and tossed it down my throat, but this only appeared to agrivate it. I could hear my stomach hiss as the water came in contact with the fiery fluid. God, what a ten minutes of agony I endured after that bumper of "No. 1". It was two hours be-fore I was fairly relieved from its influence. It was 11 o'clock when we started for the train. Our trail lay across the bluffs until we came in sight of "Horse Creek", when we came out on a broad plain of sand exhibiting a vast scene of barren desolation.

Numbers of grey wolves were to be seen prowling about and flocks of buzzards would fly across our trail with their harsh ominous croak. We crossed the creek, which was deep and rapid, with some difficulty, and as 'twas getting dark and we could see nothing of the train, we pushed on with renewed speed. We arrived at camp at 7 o'clock and after a hearty supper, related one day's adventures and were heartily laughed at. Camp poor. About one mile from the bank of the river. Some of the boys, in hunting for driftwood with torches, set fire to the long dry grass on the margin of the "Platte" and in a moment it spread like wildfire. We could see it all night as it followed the course of the stream, and do not know if 'tis yet extinguished. Killed an owl and snake both coming from the same hole. Distance today 22 miles.

The legendary Antoine Robidoux had been the man who set in motion the first emigrant wagon train to the Pacific by telling John Bidwell glamorous tales of California. How the United States role in California, the Mexican War, the gold rush and the entire settlement of the West would have altered without his storytelling cannot now be guessed. The first fur trader in Taos, perhaps as early as 1822, Robidoux was, according to an army officer traveling west about the same time as Cartwright, "a thin man, handsome, refined, with an intelligent face." Sadly, he went blind in 1852.

GERING, NEBRASKA. Here, across the Platte River from the town of Scottsbluff, kid-leaguers of wholly unmajor-league reticence and aptitude wave at passing pop flies on four immaculate diamonds. Behind the park looms historic Scotts Bluff. The small fry are oblivious of it, but it was here that Cartwright first met Robidoux.

TORRINGTON, WYOMING. The first unmistakable sign of baseball in Wyoming is the sight of a man and two boys flailing at a row of shrubbery on West C Street, bending over and peering intently at the ground. "Which side did it go on?" they query plaintively. It is that classic American vignette, The Lost Ball.

Here in Torrington are the first unorganized games—even games of catch—since Illinois. There are too many to be coincidence: picnickers, little girls playing between supper and bedtime, a group of young men in Pioneer Park playing until after dark, proud of their ability to stop the unseen ball by following its sound.

May 26, 1849
Weather clear and fine; turned out all hands at 4 o'clock— breakfasted, "caught up" and "rolled" at 5½ o'clock. Trail lay over a fine rolling prairie. Grass good. No game. Came to noon at 11 o'clock in a delightful spot on the banks of a stream. A trader rode

into camp who gave the distance to Laramie as 11 miles. Trail this afternoon over a fine level plain. About 6 o'clock we came to a ferry on the banks of the "Laramie". Here we found a number of traders belonging to the Fort, and after a hard two hours work, in which our party performed ⅞ of the labour, we at length, found ourselves camped on the opposite side, a few hundred yards from the Fort.

Fort Laramie

Fort Laramie is a trading post of the American Fur Co. & P. Chateau I. Co. and was under the charge of Mr. Husband, a Scotchman and a meaner Scotchman never left the "Land o' cake". The Fort is beautifully situated on the banks of the Laramie river with plenty of wood in the vicinity and good pasturage for stock. There is no game of any consequence within considerable distance of the Fort. Its principal trade is with the "Sioux". This is the first post for trading on the trail and I must say that I was not very favorably impressed either with the Fort itself or its occupants. A poor miserable set they appeared indeed, however these are not the real mountain men. In the distance we can see the tall peak of Laramie, the highest point of the "Black Hills", with its top covered with snow. Here we were told that Captain Paul, in advance of us, had lost some men and mules in a skirmish with the "Crows". We were cautioned to keep a good guard and keep our eyes open. We have found however that these fellows are very fond of exaggerating the dangers of the journey. On guard tonight from 12 to 3½ o'clock. Night clear and stars. Distance 25 miles.

Cartwright usually thought the best of people. Oddly William Kelly had an entirely opposite, favorable view of Husband.

"I found Mr. Husband, the manager, or governor as he is styled, a most obliging, intelligent and communicative person," Kelly wrote, when he encountered the Scot a day later. When his party changed to mule-train locomotion too, a concerned Husband "discouraged the project as one of very great danger, and earnestly remonstrated, telling me that the Crows . . . were a fierce, cruel and powerful tribe. . . ." Nevertheless a train using mules, under Captain Paul, was the very first to reach California in 1849. They led the long, long line of caravans consistently, reaching almost every point on the Trail first.

May 27, 1849

. . . This morning found us up bright and early. Weather clear and warm. After breakfast we commenced unloading our waggon for the purpose of lightening our load. This was done by throwing out all extra woodwork about it; throwing away all our extra lead, iron, provision, clothing, etc. After this was done and our waggon once more put in order we considered that we had lessened the weight once more at least 500 pounds. As we are just entering upon a very hilly country this will relieve our animals greatly. Mr. Emery also prepared for these hills by cutting 3 feet off his waggon and throwing out all "extras". The rest of those in our company would not throw away anything for which they had good cause to be sorry afterwards. Carrying much that was useless 1000 miles further over bad country only to abandon it at last, after breaking down their stock. Dined today on boiled pork and greens with mush and milk for a dessert. The milk we procured from one of the men at the Fort in exchange for several "large drinks of Peach". At 2½ P.M. we "catched up" and rolled on our way. The trail lay over a rolling prairie part of the time, the rest of the way through sandy valleys. About 7½ o'clock we came to camp in a valley a short distance from "Warm Springs" and a little off the trail. Grass poor. Today we took Caleb Boylston into our mess. Plenty of gophers and lizards seen today. Nothing like game to be seen. Distance 12 miles.

FORT LARAMIE, WYOMING. "Sure, they used to play baseball at Fort Laramie way back," a Park Service ranger said. "They played right out here on the parade ground, in front of Old Bedlam, the unmarried officers' quarters. There was organized ball here at least as early as the 1880's, when Colonel Burt was commanding officer. He learned his baseball at Yale, and he was the first officer ever to associate with enlisted men playing games."

The ranger unearths a remarkable picture of an early Fort Laramie team, rare evidence of a little-known facet of frontier life. He also digs out a biography of Burt and we discover that that worthy had been captain of the Yale team in the 1850's, just about late enough for Cartwright's game to have caught on at New Haven. An excerpt from Burt's biography reads, "In later more tranquil years, at the usual variety of military stations, he [Burt] had much time for his own pursuits. The Indians merely required paternal surveillance, and there was only an occasional white man's riot to quell.

He entertained celebrities, displayed his fossil and Indian collections, invented a better shelter tent, became the best rifle shot in the Army, composed a successful melodrama for stage-happy Buffalo Bill Cody and organized baseball teams at every post."

"Baseball was the most favorite pastime," says another ranger, "next to drinking cheap whiskey. We still have kids playing out here sometimes, right where a visitor could get socked on the head. We have to run 'em down to the flat."

GLENROCK, WYOMING. It is 19-7 in the sixth inning, an oil-well pump is grasshoppering beyond the right-field fence, and the four-foot batsman is named Dean. This has to be a Wyoming Little League game. A quarter-horse mare and her spindly-legged colt stand outside the park, the entrance to which runs under a wooden railroad trestle, and within a center fielder's throw of the diamond is a monument to the wagon trains that camped on this very ground within the memory of present residents. Alexander Cartwright camped here, too.

CASPER, WYOMING. In Babe Ruth Stadium there is a new Service League pitcher because the starter has committed the indiscretion of wild-pitching with the bases loaded. "After one-half inning of play," the announcer intones, "for Big Horn Life we have eight runs on three hits." The Big Horn Life manager is not satisfied. "C'mon, get the lead out," he shouts.

A little towheaded, blue-eyed, freckled girl about six years old, one of at least four look-alike brothers and sisters, happily initiates a conversation with a stranger. "That's my cousin Donny out there," she confides. "Donny Reynolds. He wears a red hat. I have a cousin Kenny in Little League, too. Donny is the one near the man in blue." That is reasonable, since Donny is coming to bat. Unfortunately, he flies out, but by that time his cousins are too busy playing in the sand behind first base to notice anyway.

JEFFREY CITY, WYOMING. In this uranium shanty and trailer town, population 800, the Game of the Week is on. At one of the city's two nameless cafés—boasting, honest truth, a paint-by-numbers nude over the bar—tiny portable color TV vies with jukebox country and Western. Amidst the collection of Western hats watching the game sits a Hemingway type in frayed demi-derby and rusty-red mustache and beard. The Tigers fall far behind the White Sox, and attention languishes.

The Black Hills

May 28, 1849

We started this morning at 6¼ o'clock. Weather foggy and chilly. Stopped a moment at "Warm Spring" and found the water of a tepid warmth and rather unpleasant to the taste. Saw near here the remains of several waggons of a company that must have passed last year. Our route lay over high bluffs, many of them covered with stunted pine and cedar. Road good. About nine o'clock the fog lifted and the sun came out clear and warm. About ten o'clock we entered a sandy valley through which runs one of the numerous off-shoots of the "Platte". This I believe Fremont calls "Bitter Creek". We crossed it 3 times and came to a nooning on its banks at 10½ A.M. at a most beautiful spot. Grass good. After 2 hours halt we rolled on. The trail ran over a sandy barren country for some distance then again became very hilly—we are now entering that spur of the Rockies called "The Black Hills." We ascended the bluff by a very steep hill. Some of the teams had to be doubled. We found this by far the hardest pulling we have yet had. No sooner at the top than down we had to go again on the other side, into a broad ravine through which we travelled 2½ miles and came to a camp at "Heber Spring" on a fine creek—the "Horse Shoe"—of good water. Camp excellent. Grass good. Water and wood plenty. "Heber Spring" clear and beautiful. Distance 30 miles.

May 29, 1849

Started at 7 o'clock this morning. Weather cold. Trail lay over high ridges of hills. The view from the tops of these ridges was splendid. Stretching away in the distance a range of 200 miles can be seen presenting hills of every form and color. The most prominent being the "Black Hills" with "Laramie Peak", a dark heavy looking bluff, its sides covered with pines and cedars and its top with everlasting snow. We came to our nooning about 1 o'clock on the banks of "La Bonte Creek". Camp pretty fair. Nooned 2 hours and then rolled on. "Forever rolling on"—. About 2 hours after starting we over-hauled some ox-teams and agreed to keep company with them for a few days. Shortly after we came to camp on "La Prele Creek". Camp excellent for grass, wood and water. Round and about us are singular bluffs and red clay called by "mountain Men" "Red Buttes". It rained quite hard when we came to camp and continued for about an hour afterwards to pour down in floods making it rather uncomfortable. However it cleared off beautifully at last and having got plenty of milk from Mr. Stewart, the head of the ox-train, we regaled ourselves on mush and milk consuming enormous quantities. Turned in at 10 o'clock after a pleasant chat with old man Stewart, his wife and daughters. Distance 21 miles.

This, again, was the train chronicled by William Johnston. On this very day, Johnston noted that "Captain Ransom's company" passed. Later, in Salt Lake City, he said, "News reached us that two men belonging to Capt. Ransom's company had been drowned in crossing Weber River." The coincidence that these should be so near the exact dates of Cartwright's passage and that a Ransom was his teammate on the Knickerbockers seem too great to be mere chance.

"A few companies only are in advance of us, and these have left a considerable stock of groceries and clothing here," Johnston wrote, surveying the Cartwright leavings at Fort Laramie.

May 30, 1849
Weather cloudy and cold. We "catched up" and "rolled" from camp at 7 o'clock. The ox-train right after us. The trail lay over a very hilly country and the roads in many places were heavy in consequence of the recent rains.

Mormons

About 2 miles from camp we met 2 waggons with Mormons from Salt Lake bound to Council Bluff for trading purposes. A woman in the company was quite sick so we gave them some brandy as well as what other little things we could think of for her comfort. They had "gold dust" put up in packages of $1.00 which they said was dug in California and passed as currency among them at the Lake. One of the Mormons was the ugliest human I ever saw as well as the most inquisitive. He asked us a hundred questions as to our homes, politics, business at home, and what we were going to California for and concluded by advising us to take in Salt Lake in our route. We bade them good-bye and continued on our winding way. Crossed several creeks and at 1 o'clock nooned on the banks of one of them. Our route this afternoon lay for a time over the hills, when we descended into a more level country. Saw a number of antelope, the first seen in several days. Came to camp at 7 o'clock on "Big

Timber Creek". One of the finest camps in all respects since leaving the line. On guard from 1½ 'till 3 o'clock. Night fine. Moon full and stars all out. Distance 21 miles.

May 31, 1849
. . . Rolled this morning at 7 o'clock. Crossed "Big Timber Creek". Weather clear and cold. Trail lay over rather hilly country until we descended to the "Platte" bottom. Roads good. Came to nooning about 1 o'clock at "Deer Creek". A splendid camp for everything this afternoon roads good over the "Platte" bottom. Came to camp on the "Platte". Weather clear and fine. Camp good. Distance 25 miles.

June 1, 1849
Rolled this morning at 6¼ o'clock. Trail lay over a rough country covered with creeks, gullys and ravines. 8½ o'clock brought us to the "Upper Platte Ferry" where we found two Mormons. They had rigged up a forge, converted their waggons into a house and located for the season. It takes a Mormon to accommodate himself to circumstances. Here we had our mules shod and having a little spare time, we "washed up". Exchanged some bacon for dried venison of which Tom made a Pot Pie and of which I was deprived, together with a milk punch, by a slight illness. Think however I shall make it up tomorrow. Here I stumbled upon the Tomb Stone of a young man drowned in crossing the river in 1847. The river here runs at this season of the year with great rapidity carrying with it immense bodies of sand, so that if one gets overboard with clothes on, the weight of the sand soon causes him to sink. The Mormons say several are drowned here annually—hope 'twill not be our turn. The ox-train came up while we were at dinner at 2 o'clock. We crossed our waggons by the Ferry. The animals we swam over, after a great deal of trouble Tom leading off on the back of one we got them in the water. As soon as they got out of their depth they commenced a general scramble in the midst of which Tom was unhorsed. He kept his hold of the mane however and in a few minutes the whole drove came to land and then such a scamper—it was a good hour before we got them all in again, when we "hitched up" and were off once more. We found Captain Lafferty's company on this side consisting of 7 mule trains. We may travel with them for a day or two. Two miles roll over the Platte Bottom brought us to a steep and heavy sand hill. With considerable fatigue we at length reached its top and descended on the opposite side to the bottom

again, over which our trail lay and over hills and sandy gullys 'till we came to camp on the Platte about 6 miles from the crossing. Weather fine and clear. Distance 11 miles.

Lafferty had been in the company of Jarrott and Berrien. "Captain Lafferty . . . brought in several fine Buffalo fish . . . which he shot in a small lake," Berrien said. Johnston later noted catching up to Lafferty's train at Bear River and leaving it behind at Echo Creek.

Crow Indians

June 2, 1849

We "catched up" and "rolled" at 6¼. Weather clear and fine. Tom, Mr. Emery and myself started ahead of the train to hunt. We took our way over the bluffs and after 3 hours hard travel, seeing numerous antelope, elk etc. going over the hills, gulches and ravines, we concluded to strike out for the trail as 'twas impossible to get a shot at anything. The game being of the wildest kind. The trail lies over a hilly country volcanic in character. Passed several lakes of mineral water and came to noon at 11 o'clock on a creek of warm unpleasant tasting water. Trail this afternoon over the same style of country. Crossed several spring creeks highly impregnated with mineral. About 2 o'clock we came upon a party of "Crow" Indians numbering 18 men and 2 women. They were seated in a buffalo-skin tepee on one side of the trail. Several of us who were ahead of the train rode up and dismounting accepted their invitation to smoke. They smoked dried sage and I found it so pleasant that I smoked the pipe out. We conversed with them by signs until the train came when after exchanging a pocket kerchief for a necklace of beads made by the Indians from the clay deposit of "Soda Springs"—afterwards presented by me to Captain Fraser of the Cutter "Lawrence"—and presenting them with some bisquit, we rolled on. These "Crows" were the finest specimens of mankind I ever beheld; tall, welformed and very muscular. They were on a hunting party and were in apparent dread of meeting any of the "lords of this particular soil", the "Sioux", or as they called them—by signs— "Cut throats". The "Crows" rank with the "Commanche" for bravery and do not hesitate when sufficiently strong to attack parties in open day. We came to camp on a stream running from "Willow Spring". Great signs of game about. Saw numerous buffalo in the distance. Shot a prairie dog. Must say I was disappointed on exami-

*nation of them as he was very like a rat. Lafferty train camped
right back of us. About 8 o'clock the ox-train passed our camp and
rolled a short distance ahead. About 11 o'clock we were aroused
from our slumbers by the reports of fire-arms and the whoop of Indians. A number of shots were fired from Lafferty's camp, but as
there was no one that we could see to shoot at, we held our fire and
finding after a short time the fight was over, turned in again and
were not disturbed 'till morning. Distance 24 miles.*

June 3, 1849
*Weather clear and fine. Catched up and rolled this morning at 6
o'clock. About one mile from camp we came to the fountainhead of
"Willow Springs" where we found the ox-train of Mr. Emery encamped. A few hundred yards ahead we found Captain Winter's
train of 11 mule waggons. We rolled past the ox-train, Winter leading off.*

Although Cartwright had no complaint to make of Captain Winter, the diarist Johnston wrote angrily at Ogden Creek, "In the afternoon we passed the company of the amiable Winter, who at
Green River cruelly denied us information as to his mode of crossing that stream. . . ." Such would have been aberrant, almost un-
thinkable behavior on the Trail.

*For a distance of 15 miles our trail lay over a fine natural turnpike
when we came to a creek about 11 o'clock and nooned and had a
delightful and refreshing bath in its cool clear water. At 12½
o'clock rolled on. Trail over a heavy sandy road. We are now
walled in by high rocky hills evidently spurs of the Rocky Mountains. Today we crossed two creeks, one of which had evidence of
coal upon its banks and passed over a great deal of low swampy
ground containing many huge lakes covered with a crust of carbon-
ate of soda or saleratus. About 4 miles from here we struck the
"Sweetwater" and soon after were at the foot of "Independence
Rock".*

Independence Rock

*This is a most singular and grand formation situated a few yards
from the bank of the river entirely isolated from all other rocks or
hills, it presents its bald front and sides to the view of the traveller,*

covered in many places with the names of those who had gone before him on this venturous journey. Some of the dates were upwards of 10 years back. Among many others we noticed Sir William Stewart and Sublette, his guide, dated 1843. We crossed the "Sweetwater" about 1 mile from the "Rock" and camped upon its opposite bank. We have surfeited for some days past upon buffalo and antelope. Distance 26 miles. Camp good.

June 4, 1849
. . . Rolled this morning at 6 o'clock. Weather clear and fine, sun shining very hot. Trail over rolling hills. Road sandy and good. Four miles from camp we came to "Devils Gate", a most remarkable fissure in the rock through which the "Sweetwater" finds its way. Its perpendicular walls are some hundred feet in height and the water dashes through with great swiftness and turbulance. The prevailing vegetation of the country for a long time past has been "Artemesia", or wild sage, which when crushed by the waggon wheels emits a rank and most unpleasant odor. It serves as a harbor for myriads of crickets. Our greatest annoyance is from the "black, or buffalo-gnats" which throng the air in myriads and blow in the face with a feeling somewhat like light sand which produces at first a prickling sensation that in a few minutes turns to a most intolerable burn. They leave the face covered with red blotches. We came to our nooning at 12 o'clock. Lafferty's train having come up we "catched up" and were off. The trail lay over sandy hills crossing several gulleys and creeks.

The "Sweetwater" mountains on our right are masses of rock bare of vegetation. Those on our left are more fertile being covered with grass, cedar and pines. The summits of these mountains are covered with snow. We have had a high wind today blowing clouds of sand in our faces. The sun shining with great fierceness at the same time makes travelling rather disagreeable. Camped at 5 o'clock on the "Sweetwater". Grass, water and fuel good. On guard from 9 'till 12. Distance 22 miles.

June 5, 1849
. . . Started this morning at 5½ o'clock. Weather delightful. Trail still along the "Sweetwater". About one mile from camp passed Winter's company who had passed us last night only by travelling two hours longer, showing the great superiority of our mules.

Three miles from camp we passed two remarkable dome-shaped mountains. About 4 miles from camp we crossed the "Sweetwater" again. There is some fine timber at this crossing. Here we leave the river and do not reach it again for 6 miles travelling over a fair road. 9½ o'clock brought us once more to the river. Here we should have forded but taking the trail of Captain Paul a few miles brought us to a very heavy sandy road through which we struggled a few miles further and came to camp—noon—at 11½ o'clock in a dry sandy waste, without water or vegetation. Considerable feeling in camp about the halt. After 1½ hours rest we rolled on.

The journal stops here. Either Cartwright's grandson developed writer's cramp and tired of transcribing the log, or else Cartwright himself became tired and preoccupied. He would have had good reason, for the hardest portion of the trip was beginning: the crossing of Great South Pass, the traverse of the arid country beyond, the difficult climb over the Wasatch Range to the Salt Lake Valley, the frightening desert of the Great Basin, and the arduous struggle over the Sierra.

It seems almost certain that Johnston spoke of Cartwright when he said on June 18, "An emigrant train engaged in crossing Bear River at the time we reached it lost a mule which became entangled in its harness."

Persevered they all—Cartwright, Johnston, Kelly, Berrien—through "the valley of the shadow of death, the Humboldt." They endured blasting sand, mirages, thirst, and winds "vomited from a stygian furnace." Bruce Cartwright, Jr., estimated their travel thus, and it seems quite accurate:

June 5–9, 1849	A very hard journey to South Pass, the Continental Divide, where they camped beyond at "Pacific Springs"
" 10	Along "Sublette's Cut-off to the "Little Sandy"
" 11–12	Crossed 44 miles of desert and reached "Green River," where they exchanged Overton for John Shaff
" 13	Crossed Grand River and proceeded to "Fontenelle Creek"
" 14	Along "Sublette's Cut-off" to spring
" 15	Across Ham's Fork
" 16	Reached Bear River
" 17	Rested in camp

"	18–19	Crossed Smith's Fork to Thomas's Fork
"	20	Over mountains to Bear River
"	21–22	Along Bear River to Soda Springs
"	23	Over Pass between Great Salt Lake and Snake River basins
"	24	Along Pontneuf River
"	25	Arrived at Fort Hall
"	26–27	From Fort Hall across Bannock River to camp near the American Falls of the Snake River
"	28	Passed the American Falls
"	29	Reached Raft River (now Yale, Idaho)
"	30	Up Raft River
July	1	Reached head of Raft River and "City of Rocks"
"	2	Along Goose Creek
"	3	Down Hot Springs Valley
"	4	Over the Divide by "Poison Wells"
"	5	Reached Humboldt tributary
"	6	To Humboldt Wells
"	7–8	Along Humboldt River
"	9	Over mountain east of present Elko, Nevada
"	10	Along Humboldt River
"	11	Around Fremont's Canon to Gravelly Ford
"	12–13	Crossing plains north of "Battle Mountain"
"	14	Crossing sloughs, Iron Spring Range
"	15	Crossed tule swamp near present Winnemucca
"	16	Crossing desert
"	17	Arrived at "Cold Springs" Eugene Mountains
"	18	Crossed "Larsen's Meadows"
"	19	Rested in camp
"	20	To Sink of the Humboldt River
"	21	Same as above
"	22	Crossed Humboldt Slough
"	23	Crossed desert to "Ragtown" on the "Carson River"
"	24–26	Rested in Camp on the Carson River
"	27–31	Proceeding slowly along Carson River
August	1–4	Proceeded south of Lake Tahoe and arrived in "Green Valley," California

In much of Nevada, of course, baseballs are even scarcer than trees. But Cartwright's pastime could be found even in these last long miles.

CARLIN, NEVADA. Four tykes from a trailer camp, one a Basque boy, arrive at hot, treeless, grassless City Park trailing gloves and bat. A Southern Pacific Diesel idles beyond outfield fence signs advertising an iron mine, and a long-unlimed block C marks the dusty foothills above the desert-quenching Humboldt River. More even than in most kids' games the object is less baseball than bickering. The catcher misses the pitcher with almost every throw, and each time the chucker screeches, "Awright, Ronnie, you go chase it." The pitcher has his own control problem. When the yard-high batsman refuses to offer at any of a bad assortment, the Basque first baseman loses patience. "If you don't swing," he threatens, "we're gonna hafta fast-pitch you."

RENO. The Reno Silver Sox look up, interested, when a skinny, bespectacled sportswriter walks in. "You another new player?" asks one Silver Sock. When the visitor says he is just looking for Duke Lindeman, he is directed to a cubbyhole under the stands by one Sock who betrays elder-statesman status by knowing the general manager's name. A locker-room sign lettered in red says, DO NOT ASSAULT UMPIRES.

"We had thirty-one guys in or out in a couple of days because the Cleveland Indians had thirty signees in college," GM Lindeman explains, between answering the phone ("Yes, ma'am, game time is seven") and making change for moppet concessionaires. He excavates statistics from the tiny concrete-block office he shares with a mimeo machine, boxes of bats, pipes, and steel lockers. They show that the Sox have been leading the California League in hitting, that Shortstop Jack Heidemann (.342) is still third individually and that Catcher Rick Underwood is up there at .333. "Heidemann is the kind everyone looks for," Lindeman says. "I'd defy any major-leaguer to make all three of the plays he made the other day."

In Moana Park, where outfield signs advertise, with fine impartiality, all three Republican candidates for Senator, Heidemann does look good against a Visalia team that had arrived in a bus marked Orange Belt Stages. He goes behind second on one ball, grabs it, and in the same easy motion flips the ball with his gloved hand to the second baseman. Center fielder Ed Southard makes a rouser of a diving catch of a wind-blown liner. Third baseman Mike Parks, three days out of high school, a cocky young man who says he plans "to make the Bigs," drives in two runs with his first pro hit.

"But this is the good part," Lindeman says. "It's something else when they come to you asking if they have a future. What can you tell them? They're limited? It's a business. Pretty brutal. You get attached to these kids. They're a nice bunch."

These are not the joke bush-leaguers of yore, staggering around under fly balls and relaying throws to the hot-dog vendor. The sparse crowd still vanishes almost immediately after the game and the lights still go out quickly to save electricity, but now wives—a pretty collection, as ball players' wives always are—wait outside the dressing room with babies in their arms. They look too young to be wives, just as their husbands always look too young to be—some of them—two years away from the Bigs.

LODI, CALIFORNIA. The name of the man who discovered gold at Sutter's Mill in 1848 was James Marshall. By one of those graceful coincidences whose meaninglessness is exceeded only by their extreme improbability, James Marshall was also the name of the manager of the professional baseball club nearest Sutter's Mill.

This Jim Marshall, then rookie skipper of the Lodi Crushers, is an amiable ex-Cub outfielder whose Nixon nose and sky-blue eyes are continually wrinkled by an easy grin. "I just can't tell you enough about minor-league baseball," he says. "The inspiration and desire of the American boy to succeed hasn't lessened at all. When I returned from the Orient [Marshall played three years with the Chunichi Dragons] I wondered if players here would work as hard as Oriental boys do. But my boys have shown me a lack of nothing.

"Sometimes they do wonder, I think, if anybody upstairs really cares. I constantly let them know that Mr. Wrigley and Mr. Holland do care." Does the manager, Mr. Marshall, care? There are subtle clues. A notice on the dressing-room wall reads, "SHAVE ONLY AFTER BALL GAME [signed] Manager." Manager protests the handling of the game that night with so much spirit that the umpire not only throws him out and calls him a nasty name, but also summons the police and forfeits the game 9-0.

Marshall's Japanese orientation fit right into the Lodi mode. In an area rich in Japanese-Americans, the Crushers had a Japanese owner, program ads for Japan Air Lines and Pan Am in Tokyo, a large box reserved for the Nisei Society, a Japanese pitcher, and a Japan Night.

The Crushers just plain had color. One good pitcher was a Cherokee Indian named Lloyd Kingfisher. Previously they had million-aire twenty-year-old pitcher Lee Meyers and another pitcher named Fast, who was slow but went to the parent Cubs anyway because he had an excellent sinkerball.

Even the name has to be the best since the Mud Hens. "No, they're not ore Crushers," Marshall corrected. "They're grape Crushers. No, they don't report for work in bare feet. They had a contest to pick that name. Some of the other suggestions were Idols [Lodi backward], Lodi Stars and The Stompers."

After the game, the grape Crushers adjourned to a café. The topic was the usual one for ball players. "Don't call her so often," one player was saying to a teammate. "Pretty soon she'll get used to the idea."

Someone told about the umpire whose kid still puts his thumb in his mouth. "He'll outgrow it," the umpire's wife says. "He'd better," the ump retorts, "if he wants to be a pitcher."

"There really aren't any problems to being married to a pro ball player," the wife of Modesto pitcher Mack Sinnott said over a hamburger. "Except moving."

"And maybe like tonight," Sinnott admitted. "We were too late to take the team bus, so we drove from Oakland. So what happens? Our car won't shift into third. We drive into Lodi in first and second. I keep fiddling with it—and finally get it into reverse. Naturally, it stays in reverse. We've been driving around the back streets, backwards. Finally I backed into a service station and got it in second. We will now drive back to Oakland in second gear."

CHAPTER TEN

ON AUGUST 4, 1849, ALEXANDER CARTWRIGHT AT LAST ARRIVED IN what he called "Green Valley" in California. (This may have been Grass Valley or Pleasant Valley.) Weary but still characteristically optimistic, he followed the American River to Sacramento.

Sacramento, a canvas city, a calico town built in a wonderful grove of high trees. Bales, boxes, and barrels innumerable crowded the streets, a navy of ships crowded the riverbanks, and men, mules and oxen stirred dusty activity everywhere. Yet, with its tents under its great oaks, Sacramento looked for all the world like a huge camp meeting. What would have been the revival's tabernacle tent was an enormous gambling hall, but the illusion did not break down completely.

"One is at once struck entering this city with the perfect confidence existing and the security of property," said Peter Decker, who passed Cartwright a few days before his own arrival in Sacramento. "There are many liquor establishments and much liquor drunk & yet no quarreling whatever. This may be the result of two causes: one, that nearly everyone feels satisfied with what he is doing, and another the summary manner in which punishment is inflicted."

From Sacramento Cartwright proceeded by steamboat directly to

San Francisco, where he met his brother. In a biographical account of Honolulu merchants printed in a San Francisco newspaper in 1892, a year before Alick's death, Cartwright reminisced about his arrival and the risible reason for his rapid departure.

Cartwright remembered, "When we reached the 'Embarcadero' the first wooden building was being erected for Barton, Lee & Co. on the site of the city of Sacramento. Captain Seely and I turned our attention to mining but after looking over the field we wisely decided that other openings offered greater inducements to men of our class. [In San Francisco] I met my younger brother Alfred De-Forest Cartwright who had preceded me to California by way of Cape Horn. My first business venture was the purchasing with my brother of the interest of J. Ross Browne in a mining enterprise which was being inaugurated by the party that came to San Francisco in the ship *Pacific*."

(John Ross Browne, an American secret service agent and popular by-liner in *Harper's* magazine, who was a friend of Mark Twain and wrote in much the same style, made a highly interesting business acquaintance.)

"This venture was soon given up," Cartwright says enigmatically. "Shortly after my arrival in California I was attacked by dysentry and was advised by my friend Charles Robinson, who had previously lived in Honolulu, to go to the Hawaiian Islands, of which he gave a glowing account. I decided to follow his advice, intending to proceed to China as soon as I had regained my health and from there secure a passage to New York."

In a letter to his wife, Rebecca, Alfred threw more light on Alick's doings. He told Rebecca happily:

Alick arrived here on the 10 instant [August 10, 1849] in good health after a very long and trying journey. They lost some of their mules and broke their waggons, and were obliged to abandon most of their truck, so that Alick says they "had left what they had upon their backs, and a cup and a spoon apiece." Now where do you think he has gone to? Why, to the Sandwich Islands. He left on the 15th with a friend whom he met here and who is going into business at those islands, through whose representations he was induced to think that he could do better than by remaining here. He will probably make arrangements there to come back here with a load of fruit and vegetables, which would prove a very profitable speculation.

Although totally eclipsed in Cartwright family tradition by his brother's westward trek, Alfred's voyage to San Francisco had been eventful enough, featuring a near mutiny. Fortunately, a Dr. Jacob Stillman from New York (he was on the staff of Bellevue Hospital, then a model medical facility) kept a journal of the trip. It shows why Alick chose the overland trail, however hard, over the sea route.

The *Pacific*'s brutal beast of a shipmaster, a Captain Tibbets, provoked insurrection "by refusing to provide wholesome food and medical aid to passengers." Stillman, Browne, Cartwright, and the others—including no less than future Central Pacific railroad magnate Mark Hopkins—insisted, on arrival in Rio de Janeiro, that Tibbets be deposed as captain. That the passengers had good reason to mutiny is demonstrated by the letters and diary of the usually mild Stillman. "Six of [the passengers aboard an accompanying ship, the *Brooklyn*] have died of scurvy," he wrote, "and many of them present a shocking appearance. Such would have been our fate, had it not been for the love of justice shown by our Consul at Rio de Janeiro, unless we had killed the Captain and thrown him overboard before we passed Cape Horn, which would have been the only alternative."

Reduced to a state of starvation before they were three weeks from New York, threatened by the captain's cruel and violent treatment, the passengers feared for their lives. As a last resort before outright mutiny, they held the *Pacific* at Rio and managed to get the captain arraigned before the American consul, where he was examined by six physicians and pronounced insane. Tibbets, however, claimed officially that the passengers were "disorderly, mutinous and ungovernable," that they were engaged in a conspiracy and that they were perjuring themselves. The American and British consuls and most of Rio's major merchants agreed with the passengers and the captain was deposed in disgrace.

On August 5, 194 days out of New York, the *Pacific* arrived at San Francisco. Stillman camped where both Cartwrights did, in "Happy Valley," a utopian place half a mile south of town.

"There are millions of dollars' worth of goods lying about the hills in the open air without a guard," he marveled, echoing the reaction of others, "yet no one thinks of losing anything by theft. There is no law regarded but the natural law of justice; and I never saw a more orderly state of society, where the genial influence of

woman is not felt. I have not heard of a theft or crime of any sort
. . . since I have been here. Firearms are thrown aside as useless
and are given away on the road."

Stillman was seeing a recurring phenomenon in American history, a phenomenon which remains seldom reported by revision-
ist historians—the continual cultural disparity between Christian-
ized Anglo-Saxons and the untamed Anglo-Saxons of the hills and
piney backwoods. Here the tough, tenacious, ambitious but less civilized whites of Greater Appalachia had not yet arrived in great
numbers.

Less encouragingly, he agreed with Cartwright, "Many who went
to the mines returned unsuccessful, and report that the exertion in
getting gold is too great. Some are leaving the country for the
Sandwich Islands and beyond."

Preserved in the Archives of Hawaii is a list of passengers on the
Peruvian brig *Pacifico,* which shows Robinson ("profession, Clerk")
and Cartwright ("profession, Merchant") aboard. The master was
Charles B. Swain, a good Nantucket name and a relative of Cartwright. Although this is certainly the right Cartwright, his age is
mistakenly given as twenty-four, adding a further filip to bizarre coincidence.

Strangely, there was another Alexander Joy Cartwright, Jr. He
lived on Nantucket until about this time (and perhaps afterward)
and *was* twenty-four. The twin son of another Alexander Cartwright and Phebe Joy, he was descended from Sampson Cartwright, an entirely different son of old Edward who first settled on
Nantucket in 1676. Further, there seems good reason to believe that
this Alexander Joy Cartwright also went to California in the gold
rush with the majority of Nantucket's young men. Had baseball's
Cartwright remained in California, he might well have met his
fifth-cousin namesake.

Odder yet, there was an Alexander Cartwright Joy, Jr., the son of
the Alexander Cartwright Joy who lived on Nantucket at the same
time Alexander Joy Cartwright, Sr., did. We have proof that Alexander Cartwright Joy, Jr., *did* come west in the gold rush. The poor
little chap's father died the same year he was born, 1836. His uncle
married the young widow and took the whole family to California.
Alexander Cartwright Joy, Jr., settled in Coultersville, a now quaint
and quiet little village near the southern end of the Mother Lode in
the Sierra Nevada, and had six children, all of whom were still alive

and living in Coultersville at the beginning of the twentieth century. One of them was named Alexander Cartwright Joy III, and at this very moment, somewhere in California, there may be an Alexander Cartwright Joy IV. Or an Alexander Cartwright Joy V, playing in a Little League and believing that General Doubleday Abner invented baseball.

OAKLAND, CALIFORNIA. This is the last resting place of the former Philadelphia Athletics, who were organized when Cartwright was still a young man.

Initially the setting seems most heartlessly twentieth century. The grass-banked circle of Oakland Stadium looks like the Yale Bowl updated. Tickets are bought at what are apparently telephone booths, and the grim, dingy concrete ramps are the underground-garage setting for a gangland murder. But the scene inside—except for those softball uniforms favored by Charlie Finley—is pure National Pastime. Good-humored vendors in boaters and striped shirts yell, "Hey! *Colossal* hot dogs!" The crowd is genteel, not the backroom beer drinkers of most Eastern parks.

With two on in the fifth, there is a murmur of apprehension. "That's Big Frank Howard," a father tells his son. Somehow, Big Frank looks too large for the playing field but too mild for his largeness. Almost before the pitcher lets go of his first pitch Howard is swinging. The ball blurs off his bat, headed in a straight line for the top of the center-field bleachers. He makes it look so easy even the Athletic fans applaud.

Oakland chances and interest fade. A kid stomps on a cup to make it pop. "Hey, fella," an adult yells, "you got that firearm registered?" Yet how quickly the amateurish A's are to become the world champions of 1972.

SAN FRANCISCO. Here, where his brother Alfred DeForest Cartwright lived for many years after briefly operating a store in Hawaii, Alexander Cartwright arrived on August 10, 1849, after five months on the trail. He found that another Knickerbocker, Frank Turk, had been duly elected second alcalde for four days.

The Cartwrights and Frank Turk presumably were responsible for the phenomenally early appearance of baseball in the United States' westernmost city, thousands of miles removed from the centers of population. The game was played there years before the Civil War, and the first formal club was founded in 1859. The names of those pioneer players are mostly known: James Ashley,

M.S. Austerkauth, C. Boyes, John Durkee, John Fisher, John Hall, J. Hasson, J.F. Miller, F. Norcrosse and another Norcrosse, his brother. Durkee, Fisher, Hall, and Miller may have participated in early ball in the New York area.

The Eagles, the first lasting club, began November 4, 1859. The first game formally played by what the team called "the New York rules" was between the Eagles and the Red Rovers on February 22, 1860, at Centre's Bridge. After nine innings, the score was tied at 33-33. Then the Red Rovers refused to go into extra innings, claiming that the Eagle pitcher was not pitching underhand in legal fashion. The game ended in a pioneer rhubarb, the Red Rovers forfeiting.

An old-time California player, Fred Lange, recollected in the 1930's that San Francisco baseball got a recharge of energy when William and James Shepard arrived from New York via the Oregon Trail in 1861. "These two brothers had played with the Knickerbockers of New York before leaving home, at Elysian Park," Lange correctly remembered. "This team was the first in the East to be organized. They had also played with Harry and George Wright. . . ." The Shepards, who had indeed played with the Knickerbockers and others who remembered Cartwright, were among the men who kept the history of baseball straighter 'way out in San Francisco than elsewhere. Had the "centennial" commission of 1939 been listening, they could have learned something from the far Westerners. Referring a bit scornfully to the $100,000 spent on promoting the 1839 date, Lange said in 1938, "My theory is that baseball was started in 1845. . . . Before that date it was known as rounders. . . ."

The first enclosed ball park on the Pacific coast was located at 25th and Folsom in San Francisco. The Eagles and the Wide Awakes of Oakland opened it on November 26, 1868, the Eagles winning 37-23. San Francisco was an original member of both the California League, begun in 1901, and the Pacific Coast League. For half a century the San Francisco Seals were a major success in the minor leagues. The Bay area produced such major-league stars as Joe Cronin, Babe Pinelli, Lefty O'Doul, Frank Crosetti, Tony Lazzeri, the Waner brothers, Harry Heilmann, Lefty Gomez, Billy Martin, Charley Silvera, Larry Jansen, and Bobby Brown. Not to mention Dom, Vince, and Joe DiMaggio.

Joe DiMaggio, Sr., coincidentally, lived briefly in New York not far from the original Knickerbocker field after coming to the United

States at the turn of the century. But his sons were born in Martinez, across the Bay from San Francisco, and they learned their baseball on Russian Hill, above Fisherman's Wharf, in the city itself. Their field was the asphalt and tar North Beach playground, their bases were bits of concrete, and home plate was a flattened tin can. A sawed-off oar from Papa Joe's fishing boat served as the bat.

Joe remembered, ever after, collecting baseball players' pictures that came in boxes of Zenith candied popcorn. He remembered the endless hours that his sister Frances would spend pitching a rubber ball to him in the concrete-covered alley behind their house. The saddest memory of his boyhood, he recalled, still with some wistfulness, was being too poor to buy a ticket when Babe Ruth came to town for an exhibition game.

Sooner than he could fantasize, however, the North Beach street player left concrete and the poverty inherent in being one of an Italian family of nine children, becoming, in some ways, more of a folk hero than Ruth himself. DiMaggio's short road and quick ride to adulation led entirely through the streets of San Francisco, from a semi-pro team named the Jolly Knights to the Mission Red A's to the Seals. Although the road led on to Yankee Stadium and a blond girl named Marilyn Monroe and a kind of resurrection by Simon and Garfunkel's "Mrs. Robinson," Joltin' Joe was a legend before he ever left the minor leagues.

Now, of course, baseball in San Francisco means the Giants, not the Seals. It would be pleasant to report, as some writers have, that the Giants—transplanted from New York in 1957—originated from the old New York Mutuals. Had they really descended from that team, which was begun in the early 1850's as one of the first modern baseball clubs, the Giants (not the Athletics) would be the team most directly going back to Cartwright's time. But in hard reality, the Mutuals folded soon after entering the National League in 1876. The present Giants are actually the old Haymakers of Troy, pirated away from that upstate New York city in 1882.

CHAPTER ELEVEN

ALEXANDER JOY CARTWRIGHT, JR., FIRST SAW THE PALMS AND PARADIS-ical beaches of Oahu on August 28, 1849. He was enchanted, and he was also sick. He got off the ship and forgot forever his plan to see China. Cartwright never again left the Islands, for a reason absolutely bizarre in a descendant of Nantucketers. Traveling by ship, he had discovered, made him deathly seasick!

Although the only Cartwright or Joy in two centuries to inherit the distaste for the ocean that nearly kept the first Mrs. Joy from coming to America in the 1630's, Alick did share their taste for seaborne commerce. Within two years of his arrival, he had established his own firm as a whaling agent and commission merchant. His work prospered, and he was soon able to send for his family and to build a fine bungalow of the latticed, airy Hawaiian kind. The author has stumbled upon a historic engraving of Honolulu in 1852 which shows Mr. Cartwright's bungalow in detail, situated so as to command a dreamlike prospect of the harbor.

At the important whaling port of Lahaina, Cartwright also formed a partnership with a Richard Bowlin to run a general merchandise business which included a hotel with a billiard room and bowling alleys. He operated stores at Kahului and Kula too. Bowling along with all other business at Bowlin & Cartwright's hotel fell off when petroleum "rock oil" replaced sperm oil for lighting and whaling men less often sought amusement in Lahaina. But Alick's Honolulu business burgeoned to include ship chandlering, banking, handling of trust estates, insurance, and real estate. It grew into the prestigious Cartwright and Company, Ltd., which survives to this day. Cartwright also helped found famed Bishop & Company, forerunner of today's Bishop First National Bank. It began in a corner of his office and shared his safe.

Cartwright became one of Hawaii's leading citizens and an intimate friend of the royal family, being particularly close to King Kamehameha. The native Hawaiians loved the jolly, mirthful American, and many named sons after him. Alexander served as a diplomat for five Hawaiian rulers, from Kamehameha to Queen Liliuokalani, and handled the personal financial affairs of the monarchy. In 1972, Cartwright and Company, Ltd., still handles the former royal properties, because before her death Queen Emma designated her good friend Cartwright—and his "heirs and assigns forever"—executors of her estate.

Old interests re-emerged, for Cartwright founded the Honolulu Fire Department (which he served as chief from 1850 to 1859) and the Seamen's Institute. Not to mention Queen's Hospital, the Honolulu Library, Masonic Lodge 21, the Waterhouse Trust Company, the Honolulu streetcar and bus company, and the Commercial and Pacific clubs, among other Hawaii institutions. He also became a major stockholder of the Waimanalo Sugar Plantation.

An extraordinary eden Hawaii was then, never duplicated by any place before or since, and Cartwright sampled its every joy. Cartwright loved the Islands, and the Islanders loved him. When his son Alexander III once bought a piece of property which Cartwright thought had great potential, the kindly man paid his son a fair price for it and gave it to a widow as an estate. When Cartwright organized a campaign to send money to victims of the great Chicago Fire, Hawaiians responded generously.

But busy, useful and content as he was, Cartwright never forgot baseball. As early as 1852 he and his youngest son were walking in a field known as Makiki Park. There he stopped, on impulse, and measured out by foot the dimensions of Hawaii's first baseball field. Rebitten by the bug, he organized teams and taught the game all over the islands. Thus baseball was played widely in ocean-isolated, territorial Hawaii before it was introduced in half the area of the continental United States! To see the goodhearted Cartwright drawing diagrams in chalk on some grammar-school blackboard, or teaching the game to native children, was commonplace. And he continued to play himself. A son said in 1909:

> My father played himself and was a "crank" up to the time of his death, never missing a game. His first and second right-hand fingers had been broken in playing [and never mended quite properly, from being constantly battered].
>
> I remember well a little black book about five by three and one half inches with the word Knickerbocker in gold letters on the cover, which gave the rules of the game, bylaws etc. of the original club of that name and of which he was the founder. I also remember a ball he brought across the plains. It was about four inches in diameter and very light. No human being could have thrown it over eighty yards. It was not a lively ball either. This was one of the first balls they ever played with.

Cartwright was bitterly disappointed when the Chicago White Stockings, on their world tour of 1888, failed to land at Honolulu to play a game of baseball. Ironically, if they had landed and played, the future Chicago Cubs—who probably did not even know of Cartwright's existence on the Islands—would have found themselves greeted by their game's forgotten founder. Perhaps his role would have been thoroughly rediscovered. Perhaps not. Cartwright was a very modest man.

It was only his grandson who insisted that Alick be honored. And only then, in 1939, did Babe Ruth come to pay a now also forgotten visit to Nuuanu Cemetery, where he laid flower leis on Cartwright's grave. Then Honolulu changed the name of Makiki Park to Cartwright Park and celebrated Cartwright Day. Then a plaque was placed at City Hall, a street was renamed, and a Cartwright Series was inaugurated by the Hawaii Baseball League.

But Hawaii itself had never really forgotten Alick and his game. Even now baseball, remains a preoccupation to an extent surprising in balmy islands offering unlimited varieties of recreation. The Hawaii Islanders, though usually low in Pacific Coast League standings, have often led minor-league attendance. And nowhere in the world can one find more colorful and racially heterogeneous baseball than in the state where vendors hawk sashimi, saimin, crack-seed, laulau and poi along with their peanuts, popcorn, and crack-erjack.

Forgotten though he may have been on the mainland, Cartwright was scarcely ever underestimated in the Islands, as may be judged from this Honolulu newspaper clipping, brittle with age. The un-signed writer said:

> His name should be revered by posterity for all time, and be em-blazoned on the tablets of fame somewhere near that of George Washington, the Father of his Country. Mr. Cartwright was the Father of the National Pastime.
>
> Oldtimers here say that when the feebleness of age prevented him from participating actively, he occupied the seat of honor at all the matches and was always an enthusiastic rooter.

After also mentioning that the original ball still existed, the old article continued with what it claims are residents' recollections of things Cartwright had told them, some of which seem to have been lifted from other sources. The article quotes Cartwright:

> It dawned upon the pitchers after a while that they could de-ceive the batters by certain twirls of the ball. . . . In 1848 they changed the method of putting a man out on the bases to the pres-ent rule—"Catch him out at first, touch him out at second, third and home." At this juncture the runners took to sliding bases to avoid being touched out. The batters learned that better results could be obtained by making frequent short hits than constantly slugging for a home run [a short-lived lesson, apparently].

The 1850's ball was so lively that one dropped from a housetop would rebound to the roof. "The first baseball manufacturers were shoemakers. They sewed on the covers in quarter sections shaped like the petals of a tulip. The seams were always splitting and bunching. The size and weight of the ball together with the rough and uneven surface, caught without gloves, battered the players' hands all out of shape, and the game was denounced by the New York *Herald* as barbarous."

Even from Hawaii, Cartwright kept contact with the old Knick-erbockers. One particularly interesting surviving letter was written to a former captain of the club:

Wells Fargo & Co.
Honolulu, April 6th 1865

Charles S. Debost, Esq.
318 Broadway, N.Y.
United States of America

Dear Charlie.

. . . What pleasant memories arise as I read your dear, good letter. Dear old Fraley Neibuhr, and Charles Birney, Henry Anthony, Walter Avery, Tucker, Davis, Duncan Curry, Eugene Plunkett, Dr. Adams, Onderdonk, and that genial gentleman Colonel Lee and his son Ben, not forgetting you old Charlie with your ground and lofty tumbling and that particular knack you had of striking the Ball. Dear old Knickerbockers, I hope the Club is still kept up, and that I shall someday meet again with them on the pleasant fields of Hoboken. Charlie, I have in my possession the original ball with which we used to play on Murray Hill. Many is the pleasant chase I have had after it on Mountain and Prairie, and many an equally pleasant one on the sunny plains of "Hawaii nei. . . ." Sometimes I have thought of sending it home to be played for by the Clubs, but I cannot bear to part with it, it is so linked in with cherished home memories. . . .

Once on a time I heard that a lithograph of the old members of the 'Knickerbockers' was to be published. Was it ever done, or if not is it not possible still to have it done? It would be interesting as a memorial of the first Base Ball club of N.Y., truly the first, for the old New York Club never had a regular organization. I will give $100—or $200 toward its publication. . . .

Though by no means rich, I am independent and occupy an excellent position in society. I have every reason to be satisfied and grateful, *and I am.* I have a few spare thousands in Uncle Abraham's bosum (6% Bonds, Gold), my health is excellent and always has been, my children are as good as most, and my wife is too good for me. . . .

The men Cartwright names are all old Knickerbockers. Had he sent them the original baseball as he thought of doing, it might now be in existence, perhaps as a trophy given to the winner of the World Series.

Seven years earlier, for another example, he asked after other old baseball friends in letters, ending one with the question "How flourish the Knickerbockers?"

The Knickerbockers were no longer flourishing so well, for 1858 was the year the first national association of baseball clubs was organized, and the Knicks were defeated in their attempt to gain control of it. Most clubs' sole requirement of members was that they wield a potent bat or glove; they cared little about their standing as gentlemen. Talk spread that some clubs even paid certain of their players. As a gentlemen's club of amateurs who believed baseball should be played primarily for fun and good fellowship, the Knickerbockers could not compete with such teams, nor did they wish to. It was only eleven years later that defected Knickerbocker Harry Wright openly turned the Cincinnati Red Stockings into a professional team. The Reds' shortstop was his brother George Wright, who may have been a Knickerbocker in the club's later days and who, as noted earlier, certainly at least had played against the Knickerbockers and knew them well.

Insulated from such commercialization in remote Hawaii, Cartwright might also have taken comfort from the fact that the explosive growth of amateur baseball exceeded even that of the professional game. In the late 1850's, every Yankee colony set down by New Englanders as they pushed westward, every white-steepled and elm-shaded village from Cape Ann, Massachusetts, to Iowa, caught the baseball bug like measles. The Civil War only further propagated the game. Many Southern boys learned baseball in Union prison camps, and those Northerners who had not yet contracted it were exposed to the virus. A very good lithograph shows a game, with a huge audience, being played at a notorious Confederate prison. Legend says that more than once a cease-fire was called on front lines to allow a contest between Union and Confederate troops.

Baseball rapidly spread west. In 1866 *Peverelly's Book of American Pastimes* (which at that date still correctly credited the Knickerbockers as "the nucleus of the now great American game of Base Ball, so popular in all parts of the United States, than which there is none more manly or health-giving") already mentioned a Frontier Club at Fort Leavenworth, Kansas.

The very height of fashionable modernity, baseball was new and exciting. How exciting can be judged from this contemporary description:

It is a game which is peculiarly suited to the American temperament and disposition; the nine innings are played in the brief space of two and a half hours, or less. From the moment the first striker takes his position and poises his bat, it has an excitement and *vim* about it, until the last hand is put out in the ninth inning. There is no delay or suspense about it, from beginning to end; and even if one feels disposed to leave the ground, temporarily, he will generally waive his desire . . . from fear of missing some good point or clever effort of the trial.

Mark Twain once said that "Baseball is the very symbol, the outward and visible expression of the drive and push and rush and struggle of the raging, tearing, booming nineteenth century."

More fulsomely, the Chicago *American* editorialized in 1906, "We owe a great deal to Base Ball. . . . It is one of the reasons why American soldiers are the best in the world—quick-witted, swift to act, ready of judgment, capable of going into action without officers. . . . It is one of the reasons why as a nation we impress visitors as quick, alert, confident and trained for independent action. . . . Therefore, PLAY BASE BALL."

Baseball had grown big enough to be an object of jealous pride. The ludicrous but effective piracy of its origins—we can now see just how ludicrous in the light of previous chapters—occurred at exactly this time. It was in 1906 that a fake genealogy was invented by Albert Spalding, attributing the game to Doubleday. The only person who really protested the attribution at the time was the sportswriter Henry Chadwick, who, through all the years of baseball's weedlike growth, maintained a constant if somewhat peripheral role, and served as a link to the game's beginnings. Chadwick, who had seen his first game at the Elysian Fields in 1848 and who had written the first press report of baseball, became the first editor of Spalding's annual *Base Ball Guide* in 1879, a position he retained until 1908. Although he seems not to have known the early Knickerbockers very well, he—as much as anyone—kept alive some mention of their historical importance. He also kept saying that town ball, the original unimproved American "baseball," was the direct descendant of rounders.

In 1903, the failing and underpaid eighty-year-old Chadwick publicly confronted his boss with this information for the last time, making it the subject of his annual preface to Spalding's own guide. "Just as the New York game," he repeated bluntly, "was an improved townball, so was townball an improved form of the two-centuries-old English game of rounders." Spalding was not greatly pleased. Unfortunately, Chadwick showed no ability whatsoever to construct a logical proof of his bare statement. The pontifical, persuasive, personable Spalding, a man "with the manner of a Church of England bishop" by his own friends' account, argued rings around his editor. Despite the fact that his reasoning was circular, circumstantial and suppositional, pompous, jovial Albert Spalding made a superficially plausible case when he wrote a rebuttal in the 1905 guide.

Spalding later had to belittle Cartwright's role because Cartwright rather clearly had improved rounders to create baseball. But if Spalding simply invented Doubleday as the founder of baseball, he could then picture Doubleday as inventing baseball out of whole cloth as a purely American game.

Spalding admitted himself that when he and the Boston and Philadelphia Athletic baseball clubs visited England in 1874, the usual English reaction was "Why, it's our old game of rounders that we used to play with the gals when we were b'ys." Spalding himself had actually played a match of rounders with American big-league teams against a champion English team in 1889 at Liverpool but still he refused to admit a connection.

In his bias against rounders, Spalding had been strongly influenced by an active player, pitcher John Montgomery Ward, of New York and Boston fame, who had composed a surprisingly well-organized, but explicitly prejudiced, pamphlet in 1888. Ward wrote:

> In 1856, within a dozen years of the systematization of the game, the number of clubs in the metropolitan district and the enthusiasm attending their matches began to attract particular attention. There were then, as now, persons who believed that everything good and beautiful in the world must be of English origin, and those at once felt the need of [an English] pedigree for the new game.

Ward proceeded to accuse, with unnecessary asperity, a certain unnamed English-born baseball writer—obviously meaning Chadwick—of abusing the high respect in which he was held to promote rounders as baseball's daddy.

But Ward contradicted his own contention by admitting that baseball in certain features resembled rounders, and implying that Two Old Cat came from stoolball or cricket. He admitted that One Old Cat doesn't even have a base, but then said, "From One

Old Cat to baseball is a short step." He got facts ridiculously wrong: "The first English writer to speak of rounders is 'Stonehenge' in 1856." And he utterly destroyed himself by saying, "Townball was so nearly like rounders that one must have been the prototype for the other." It was in the 1905 editorial that Spalding proposed the Mills committee and hand-picked its members. The committee was purely an inside job. James Sullivan, president of Spalding's American Sports Publishing Company, did most of the actual work. Reach and George Wright, like Spalding, were old National League players and managers turned manufacturers with an interest in not antagonizing the baseball-equipment-buying public. Although ostensibly in competition with Spalding, their companies actually were secretly partially owned by Spalding.

George Wright's failure to give Cartwright and the Knickerbockers due credit was especially shortsighted because, as mentioned, his brother Harry had been a member of the Knickerbockers in the 1850's. But Wright, originally a high-toned cricket player, had always considered himself a little above baseball. By 1904 he had abandoned it completely. He had become much more interested in golf, laying out the first course in Boston, one of the first in the United States. He had publicly declared that tennis was a better sport than baseball. Two of his sons were national champions. He was an elegant, worldly traveler, absorbed in music and theater, and a crony of golf-playing millionaires at Palm Beach.

But Wright had been one of the best of the early players. In fact, at $1,400 he had been the highest-paid member of the Red Stockings—and hence the highest-paid player in professional baseball. And, besides founding the sporting-goods company of Wright & Ditson—like Reach, still in existence in 1972—he had headed the Boston club in the Union Association, ranking as one of the outstanding managers in the 1880's.

Among many other aversions, Abraham Mills, the chairman of the committee, hated Wright's Union Association. He called it an organization of deadbeats and played-out bums. When Augustus Busch, the brewer, backed the St. Louis club in the Union Association in 1883, Mills sneered that the new circuit was floated on beer. Another source of Mills's and Spalding's unhappiness was that the Union Association teams played with Wright & Ditson instead of Spalding baseballs. But by 1904 the Union Association had disappeared, and Wright, venerated as a grand old man of baseball, could hardly have been left off the commission. Perhaps Wright was never even consulted by Mills. Perhaps he simply declined to participate.

The rest of the committee were all past presidents of either the National League or individual clubs. Two, Arthur Gorman of Maryland and Morgan Bulkeley of Connecticut, were U.S. Senators as well. Undoubtedly they had a lively appreciation of the beneficial publicity to be obtained by serving on the commission and the negative value of deciding the National Game originated in England. Most of the best players and most rabid fans of the period, as well as a great many voters, were Irish Catholic Celts who hated England and, several times again after 1812, had the United States on the brink of war with the mother country.

But Spalding discovered someone who could support his shaky hypothesis. Abner Graves, a mining engineer who fortuitously materialized from the blue sky of demi-frontier Denver, possessed only one dubious claim to authoritativeness: the fact that at one time he had lived in Cooperstown. Mills's posthumous beatification of his old war comrade and Graves's enshrinement of his home town were poor pickings, but they were all the evidence the Mills commission had.

Just how flimsy Graves's statement was becomes doubly clear on rereading:

> The American game of baseball was invented by Abner Double-day of Cooperstown, N.Y., either the spring prior to or following the 'Log Cabin and Hard Cider' campaign of General William H. Harrison for the presidency. The pupils of Otsego Academy and of Green's Select School were then playing the old game of Town Ball in the following manner:
>
> A "tosser" stood close to the "home goal" and tossing the ball straight upward about six feet for the batsmen to strike at on its fall, the latter using a four-inch flatboard bat. All others wanting to play were scattered about the field, far and near, to catch the ball when hit. The lucky catcher took his innings at bat. When a batsman struck the ball he ran for a goal fifty feet distant and returned. If the ball was not caught, or if he was not "plunked" by a thrown ball, while running, he retained his innings. . . .
>
> Doubleday then improved Town Ball, to limit the number of players, as many were hurt in collisions. From twenty to fifty boys took part in the game I have described. He also designed the game to be played by definite sides or teams. Doubleday called the

game "Base Ball" for there were four bases to it. Three were places where the runner could rest free from being put out, provided he kept his feet on the flat stone base. . . . There were eleven players on a side.

Well, shucks. Anyone paying any attention at all can see that the Cooperstown urchins weren't playing anything nearly as sophisticated as town ball. What they were playing might charitably be called the very crudest form of rounders, or a crude two-base *cat*. If Doubleday invented anything at all, from Graves's account he invented town ball. But of course as we have seen, town ball had been played by more advanced rules than the Cooperstown variety in Boston and Philadelphia in the 1830's, and elsewhere in the 1820's, or even well back into the 1700's.

One *can* get rather excited about the Cooperstown game, but for a completely opposite reason. Rather than producing a signal advance, Cooperstown may have preserved a startling fossilization. If the "tosser" stood as close to the batter as Graves indicates, its game very closely resembles Guts Muths' "German Game" and the ancient *om el mahag* and Scandinavian longball! The length of the run to the second base—50 to 100 feet—also parallels the ancient game. It is indeed possible that early American settlers preserved a sixteenth-century game by transporting it to a distant continent, just as Americans preserved Elizabethan accents, words, and cultural patterns.

Now Alexander Cartwright, to whom in earlier editions of Spalding's official baseball guide Spalding and his friends had previously given some credit, threatened the Doubleday fiction, so the Mills report concluded with the heretofore unsuspected news that the plan "showing the ball field laid out substantially as it is today was brought to Cartwright's field one afternoon" by a mysterious "Mr. Wadsworth." Mr. Wadsworth, whose Christian name, occupation, residence, and pedigree remained secreted in Mills's bosom, was never heard of before or until long after that fateful afternoon. Upon some sign from heaven, presumably, he journeyed on the stagecoach and milk train from Cooperstown to New York to present the Knickerbockers with Abner Doubleday's diagram. After 1906 in Spalding's official baseball guide, Cartwright's role was minimized.

A Louis Wadsworth did play with the Knickerbockers—beginning in 1854! He resigned in 1856, a member for barely two years.

Mills himself admitted, in the very first sentence of his "report," that it had been his own belief that "our National Game of Baseball originated with the Knickerbocker Club, organized in New York in 1845" and also admitted that the "evidence" favoring Doubleday was "circumstantial." What changed his mind, he said, was "the interesting and pertinent testimony, for which we are indebted to Mr. A. G. Spalding." Spalding later denied that he had ever told the commission anything about Graves and claimed that the first he had ever heard about Doubleday, Cooperstown, and 1839 was from the Mills report. Ingenuously, Mills noted with pride that General Doubleday and he were such good friends that he, Mills, had been chosen "to have charge of his obsequies, and to command the military escort which served as his guard of honor when his body lay in state." If Doubleday was a friend of his, how come Mills had to find out from Graves, fourteen years after Doubleday's death, that the general had invented baseball?

Particularly peculiar, Mills never mentioned Graves's name, referring to him only as "a reputable gentleman." He did not even quote Graves's remark directly, stating it instead as a mere conjecture on his own part:

> In the days when Abner Doubleday attended school in Cooperstown, it was a common thing for two dozen or more school boys to join in a game of ball. *Doubtless, as in my later experience* [my italics], collisions between players attempting to catch the batted ball were frequent, and injury due to this cause . . . often occurred. *I can well understand* how the orderly mind of the embryo West Pointer *would devise* such a scheme for limiting the contestants on each side and allotting them field positions, each with a certain amount of territory, also substituting the [tag out] for the old one of plugging [the runner] with the ball.

This was pure fantasy. Graves said nothing about field positions or the diagram imagined by Mr. Mills. And he said precisely the opposite about "plugging": "Anyone getting the ball was entitled to throw it at a runner between the bases and put him out by hitting him with it." Mills did concede that the "reputable gentleman's" statement said Doubleday had provided for eleven men on a side, "but this is a minor detail."

The whole "report" is only eight paragraphs long. Under pressure from Spalding to have the dilatory committee produce some kind of report by the end of the year 1907, Mills, after returning from a

long trip to Europe, simply dashed off what amounts to a mere letter. It was dated December 30, 1907, only one day before the dead-
line but more than three years after the commission was set up.

The 1939 Centennial Committee that seized upon this remarkable document as the basis for national commemoration numbered
Ford Frick, Will Harridge, Kenesaw Landis, Connie Mack, and
Clark Griffith among its members, not all of whom are remembered
primarily for their perspicacity and sagacity. It does seem surprising, however, that they would venture their weighty names upon so
shakily supported an undertaking. Even Spalding seemed embarrassed by the Mills report. "It would be an act of disloyalty to say
one more word about the subject, except to defend the report," he
wrote in 1911. Defensively, he redoubled his attack on rounders
and, for the first time, attacked the Knickerbockers.

"Not wishing to be drawn into too close fellowship with the rab-
ble," he characterized them, "and perhaps dreading the humiliation
of defeat at the hands of plebeian upstarts, the Knickerbockers held
aloof, practicing occasionally—between banquets—usually among
their own exclusive membership, satisfied with the moldy laurels
won before live competition had appeared. . . . How were the
Knickerbockers to meet the influences for evil which they thought
would surely assail their darling if it came in touch with coarse and
vulgar people who lived over on Long Island?"

Having thus established his credentials as a true democrat, Spalding triumphantly rested his case with an old quotation from the
Memphis *Appeal* which was supposed to show how antiquely, in-
digenously American baseball was. In actual truth, the description
destroys Spalding's case; besides being a splendid depiction of old
town ball, its description gives us one of the best proofs available
that town ball was, precisely and exactly, rounders. The game is
clearly derived from rounders and the description even includes an
explicit mention of "hitting one for the rounder!"

> . . . the mind can travel back to the days before Base Ball, or at
> least to the days before Base Ball was so well known and before it
> had become so scientific. . . . The bat, which was no round stick,
> such as is now used, but a stout paddle, with a blade two inches
> thick and four inches wide, with a convenient handle dressed onto
> it, was the chosen arbiter. One of the leaders spat on one side of
> the bat, which was honestly called "the paddle," and asked the
> leader of the opposition forces, "Wet or dry?" The paddle was then

sent whirling up into the air, and when it came down, whichever side won went to the bat, while the others scattered over the field. The ball . . . was usually made on the spot by some boy offering up his woolen socks as an oblation, and these were raveled and wound around a bullet, a handful of strips cut from a rubber over-shoe, a piece of cork or almost anything, or nothing, when anything was not available. . . . The diamond was not arbitrarily marked off as now. Sometimes there were four bases, and sometimes six or seven. They were not equidistant, but were marked by any fortuitous rock or shrub or depression in the ground where the steers were wont to bellow and paw up the earth. . . . The paddle-man's object was to hit the ball, and if he struck at it—which he need not do unless he chose—and missed it, the catcher, standing well back, tried to catch it (on the first bounce). If he succeeded the paddleman was "dead" and another took his place. There was no effort to pounce upon a runner and touch him with the ball. Anyone having the ball could throw it at him, and if it hit him, he was "dead"—almost literally sometimes. No matter how many players were on a side, each and every one had to be put out. And if the last one made three successive home runs, he "brought in his side," and the outfielders, pitcher and catcher had to do their work all over again.

How far Cartwright and the Knickerbockers removed baseball from this country idyllry, and how fast!

As Charles Peverelly said of their new game, "An American assemblage cannot be kept in one locality for the period of two or three hours, without being offered something above the ordinary run of excitement and attraction. They are too mercurial and impulsive a race not to get drowsy and dissatisfied with anything which permits their natural ardor to droop even for a brief space of time."

CHAPTER TWELVE

William Edward Cartwright, the sole surviving adult male descendant of Alexander Cartwright, now lives in Missoula, Montana, in a home overlooking a relatively untrammeled reach of the Rockies with a German-born wife, Anne, charmingly earnest in her hospitality; a daughter, Anna; and sixteen-year-old Alexander Joy Cartwright IV.

Bill Cartwright is a big, bluff, amiable man with a constant supply of good cigars in a sports-shirt pocket. He takes pride in showing his treasures, remarkable heirlooms that speak of his family's unusual past. He has a massive old black walnut buffet that came around the Horn in 1851 with Alexander's family, a minutely detailed ship model that Alick had in his New York office, and a six-generation-old pre-Revolutionary Revere mug that belonged to his great-grandfather's great-grandfather. But most of the pieces are gifts from the Hawaiian queen, Emma, to her most trusted adviser. These include her own baptismal font, a candelabrum given to her as a wedding present by Napoleon III, a delicately carved ivory chess set, and polished bowls made of coconut and coral.

"Great-grandfather was also Peruvian consul in Hawaii, and my father was an envoy to Samoa," Cartwright mentioned. There is an unpublished account of Cartwright's adventures in Samoa. "They made him a chieftain in Samoa. The title is hereditary, but you have to go there to get it. Somehow, I haven't made the trip.

"Captain A. J. Cartwright, Sr., Alexander's father, was a merchantman in the grain trade to Portugal who was captured in the War of 1812. His ancestors were sea captains from Nantucket, as you know. I've been interested enough to do some research before that and shook all kinds of strange people out of the family tree: Lady Godiva, Mark Antony—not Cleopatra, unfortunately—and a famous pirate who became the first owner of Coney Island. It's all in *Burke's Peerage*."

Bill Cartwright has donated most of his more recent ancestor's papers to the Honolulu Archives, but he does retain some portraits of Alick, notably one showing him as he was when he left New York. But no one, he says, has the original Knickerbocker ball.

"My father saw it once," Cartwright remembers, "but when Grandmother died the family lived in a hotel for a time, and the ball was definitely lost."

Young Alexander Joy Cartwright IV, although he likes to play baseball (he is a Giant fan, and Juan Marichal is his favorite player), has other interests too. "I just thought I'd *try* butterfly collecting, and the first day I caught fourteen," he explained, his eyes lighting up as he began a tour of a bedroom walled with mounted specimens. "This blue one is a *Morpho polyphemus*, and this is an *Ornithoptera*—that means birdwing, because it looks like that for protection. Did you know most butterflies have something in their bodies that tastes yickity, and birds know it by instinct? I'd like to be a lepidopterist when I get older."

When Alick's lecture was finished, Bill remembered more items of interest. "We have a nugget of gold Great-grandfather picked up in California," he said, displaying an astonishingly large lump of metal. "Right off the ground."

The visitor exclaimed over the nugget and remarked what a fine thing it was to hand on to future generations. "Yes," Cartwright said. "I just hope Alick doesn't hock it to buy more butterflies.

"Oddly," he continued, "my grandfather never cared for baseball at all—only horses and women—and I've never played on a team myself. I was more a football player.

"The San Francisco Seals—Lefty O'Doul was their manager then —visited Hawaii in 1949, and when they heard about me they invited me to see them at the Maui Grand Hotel. 'Are you really the great-grandson of the man who laid out the diamond and all?'

somebody asked. 'Yes,' I said. 'Have you ever played ball yourself?' somebody else asked. 'Yes,' I said. 'What position?' 'Oh, fullback and quarterback.' Lefty O'Doul just roared. 'Get him out of here!' he said."

So all the San Francisco Seals threw Alexander Cartwright's great-grandson bodily out of the room.

William Cartwright also remembered, later, that one of Alexander Jr.'s sons, his own grand-uncle, had married a Hawaiian princess and that Alick's Van Wie grandfather, the father of his mother Eliza, had been a bosom friend of Martin Van Buren, a not entirely dignified President. "In their younger days, Van Wie and Van Buren got pinched once or twice for a little more conviviality than the upstate New York Dutchmen liked," Cartwright chuckled.

Indirectly, through his clue that the Cartwrights came from Nantucket, Bill came to the discovery of more people interestingly linked to his family. It developed that there are still Cartwrights living on Nantucket Island—brothers Clyde and Archibald and Archibald's son Benjamin.

I first called Clyde Cartwright on a sunny, blowing late-October Sunday, a perfect coastal New England autumn day. The dry warmth of his seaside Yankee accent sent a salt breeze through a stuffy New York office.

"Shuah, we're related to Alexander Joy Cahtwright," Clyde said enthusiastically. "I got my big brass sextant from him, and I think the big spyglass is too. Cahtwright went to Hawaii and in the gold rush. My grandfather was Benjamin, and his father was Alexander. My brother had a genealogy book somewhere. We'll try to find it for you. Why don't you come up to the house some evening?"

Archibald did have a considerable collection of material. His island reserve diluted with shy friendliness, he spread his family's history over the kitchen table of his modest, neat home. At once disappointingly and intriguingly, his great-grandfather Alexander turned out to be the *other* Alexander Cartwright.

However, all the Nantucket Cartwrights believe that his son, the other Alexander Joy Cartwright, Jr., did also go to California in the gold rush in one of the nineteen ships that left the island for El Dorado. Only two returned, but the Cartwrights know for certain that this Alexander Jr., their grand-uncle, returned to whaling and shipping and to Nantucket. He and his brothers all became captains.

The ocean is and was no tame element. The Alexander Cartwright who reinvented baseball also lost many a relative. His grandfather, Benjamin Cartwright, died in the West Indies in 1803. His uncle, Obed, died at sea near Long Island in 1811. His first cousin, Benjamin III, died at sea while Alick was playing ball in New York. Had his father remained on Nantucket, Alick too would presumably have followed the vocation of the sea. Possibly he too would have died.

With Bill Cartwright's help, the visitor found the only other surviving descendant of Alexander Cartwright, Jr., granddaughter Mary Check Taylor. A sweet and pungent lady in her seventies living in San Francisco south of Golden Gate Park, Mrs. Taylor suggested that this scarcity of kin may be another reason Cartwright's contribution was so long unknown: "Two daughters died, one of scarlet fever, and one son was poisoned."

Mrs. Taylor had a surprise—an old notebook containing an account of Cartwright's journey to California. William believes this to be the extract from Alexander's diary copied by his son, Alexander III; Mary believes it to be some part or version of the original. In either event, it contains some additional material, including a list of animals seen—"Prairie Hens, plenty; Plover, millions; Brown Wolves, plenty . . ." and also Indians ("We have passed through and had intercourse with the following Tribes of Indians: Shawnee, Caws or Kansas, Delaware, Pottawattomies, Pawnees, Sioux, Crows"). "I think this if the original journal," Mrs. Taylor says, "because the start of the trip to Hawaii is in the back." And, indeed, one short paragraph seems to begin a new log, and then break off.

Mary is the daughter of Alick's son Alexander III, the one who loved baseball. "Bruce didn't do anything but wear four-inch collars and gardenias in his buttonhole and his nose in the air," she says, "but my father played baseball constantly. They played without gloves, you know, and his fingers were all out of shape.

"We used to go to baseball games every Sunday. He took me before I could talk. I played baseball myself, any old position. I still follow the Giants and get mad at them. I used to cut school in the most polite way to watch the Seals. I had bands on my teeth, and I would go to the principal and tell him they hurt. We used to root for Truck Eagan, who was built like a truck and ran like one.

"Although Father was called Little Alick, he was six feet four and very heavy on his feet himself. He gave up playing when, one day, he planted himself on a base and his best friend ran into him, bounced off and broke his leg. Father said never again, and hung up his glove.

"Grandfather named me, but he died when I was six months old. Mother said he looked like Santa Claus, had a very keen sense of humor and just loved life. Father remembered his talking about how he scrawled out the first rules in a notebook balanced on his knee and how he fiddled around with baseball a little while in San Francisco."

When Mrs. Taylor had told all she knew of her grandfather and the visitor had finished the 7-Up she had provided, the visit—and the long search for Alexander Cartwright and his invention— seemed at an end. Mrs. Taylor accompanied her guest to the door.

"Oh, there is one other thing," she said. "My father remembered having cut up a baseball when he was a child to see what was in it. He got the only licking of his life for it. Years afterward, he often thought that that might have been the Knickerbocker ball, the original baseball."

INDEX